This book is dedicated to the Ancestors.
Those who came before us, those who come after us,
and blood that links us all together.

UNDER WORLD

SHAMANISM
MYTH
MAGICK

CHRIS ALLAUN

Cover art/design Amanda Manesis www.amaradulcis.com

Other works by Chris Allaun

Deeper into the Underworld: Death, Ancestors & Magical Rites

Upperworld: Shamanism and Magick of the Celestial Realms

Contents

Preface to the Revised Edition

Underworld was published five years ago and many things have changed since then. I've changed a lot since then. *Underworld* was my first book to be published and as I look back on these five years I see that I was blessed by the gods to be able to share my work and experiences with the world. This book opened up many doors for me. I have been able to meet so many people, both in person and online, who resonated with the energies of the worlds that are "below" us. Before *Underworld* came out in 2016 there were no books available that dealt exclusively with the subterranean shamanic realm. You could find a few pages here and there in shamanic books but never a whole book dedicated to this fascinating place. I spoke with so many people who were inspired by this book and incorporated the teachings and techniques into their own spiritual practice.

The world has changed so much in the last five years. Currently, as I write this we are still in the COVID pandemic. Many people have died and millions have become sick with the virus. With so much death in the world right now I thought that now is the time to create a Revised Edition of *Underworld.* The world needs Spirit Walkers and Healers to heal the wounds that have been inflicted not just on the earth but on our fellow humans as well. We need to journey into the Underworld and face our demons in order to find wholeness and balance. This is the time.

I have developed my writing style a great deal in the last five years. I have published five books so far and how I write and relay information and magick has evolved. For the better I hope. As I revised this book I did my best to maintain the style of writing that captured the imaginations of so many people. At the same time, I modernized some of the writing as well as kept the idea of appropriation in mind. I have Cherokee blood in my veins but I study under Lakota teachers. Here in Chicago there are several Lakota spiritual groups in the surrounding area who I have had the blessings to work with and share in community. That being said, I rewrote some things such as "Totem" which is an Ojibway word and replaced it with the term "Spirit Animal". I don't practice Ojibway so I thought it best to change the world to something a little more universal.

People have asked me over the years why I chose to add Native American stories to my books. The answer is two fold. Native American teachings are a part of my spirituality and they are sacred stories that teach us how to better human beings. Secondly, many Native American reservations are suffering. There is so much poverty, suicide, and health problems on the reservations and no one seems to care. Or maybe my readers don't know. My goal is to share the beauty of some of the Native American culture so people will begin to see the value of these wonderful people and the healing they give the earth. Maybe then people will start to donate to the reservations or charities who help the people of the reservations.

My talented friend John Hijatt took the manuscript and did some wonderful editing with it. There were many things that were missed last time around that I wanted to fix. When an author writes a book we might read it 1000 times. Our brains tend to miss things such as grammar and sentence structure. This is why it was a goddess-send to have John take another look at the book for me and correct mistakes that were made the first time around. Thank you so much John!

If this is your first time entering the Underworld you will be going on a fantastic adventure into the depths of the Universe and even your subconscious mind. If you read the first edition of *Underworld* then you are in for a treat with this revision. Close your eyes. Take a deep breath and find yourself in the world of the ancestors, demons, and adventure....

Chris Allaun
Autumn Equinox 2021

Introduction

The Underworld is a place of magick and power. Most of us, when we are learning magick and spiritual wisdom seek the four elements, the world around us, and the stars above. All of these things do, indeed, hold power. But what of the world below? There is a vast world beneath us that many fear. Shamans, witches, and magicians know that the Underworld has many secrets. The Underworld, to many, is dark and a place of monsters and the sinful dead. It can certainly be that, but there is much more to be revealed.

Some of us are taught that the Underworld is a place of devils and tortured souls. A place to stay away from at all costs. Yes, there are such places, such as the Greco-Roman Tartarus that keeps the Titans chained up in the depths, but these are only a small portion of the Underworld. The Underworld is also a place of healing, rejuvenation, and ancient wisdom. In the Nordic Myths we have the Well of Mimir. Mimir is a god who's severed head was placed in a well, giving out prophecies and oracles to all who would dare enter. There is also the land of the ancestors. This is a place where our loved ones dwell after death. In some myths, they are protected by the Nordic goddess, Hel (Hela), in others, by Hades and Persephone.

The Underworld is also a place to find spirits to heal the sick and protect our community. There are spirits who teach us how to cure disease and rid ourselves of the dark spirits who try to harm us. The Underworld is linked to our subconscious mind. Facing the mysteries of the depths can help us understand our innermost fears and the shadows of our own mind. It is taught that the energies of the Underworld are frightening only when we allow fear, hate, and regret to keep us from awakening to our spiritual path. When we journey into places we fear, we are able to face our "personal monsters". We have all heard the saying, "where there is fear there is power". This is part of the ordeal each of us must face. In Egyptian mythology, the sun god Ra, must take his nightly journey into the Underworld. Each night he faces the monster Apophis, who tries to destroy the sun barge and kill Ra. Each night, Ra defeats the monster and is able to give the Egyptian people the healing light of the sun once more.

I have worked with the Underworld for many years. I have seen some of the most dark and odd places and yet I have also seen some of the most beautiful things. To me, the Underworld is the healing place for our ancestors. The Realm of the Dead is peaceful, beautiful, and serene. It is here that our loved ones are protected and cared for by many great healing spirits and deities. Our ancestors have many things to teach us. They can also help us with things related to family and genetic diseases that stem from blocked energy. One of the most rewarding parts of my spiritual practice is communing with the ancestors.

But what of those dark places? What of the monsters that hide within the caves and caverns? There are certainly spirits that do not wish us well. The deep caverns of the Underworld are the resting place of the Titans, the chthonic gods who cause destruction and chaos to our world. It is also the place where, Fenrir, the giant wolf is chained so that he cannot bring the end of days. There are also chthonic spirits who some call demons who seek destruction. Yet, I have found these spirits to be more chaotic than "evil". When we face our demons we release the chaotic energy back into the depths, freeing the magick inside of us.

In my travels to the Underworld, I have discovered that it is a place of great healing and power. Both the dark and the light have great things to teach. You may be wondering why it is important to face the dark? The dark times in our lives are when we grow the most. When we face adversity and challenges, we must decide if we stay complacent and suffer, or do we face the challenge and allow ourselves to become more than we are now. The mystery is, of course, who is it that we become? Do we embrace the darkness? Or do we stay in ignorant bliss in the light?

I have a story told to me by one of my teachers:

Before there was fire everyone was cold. There was no sacred bonfire. There were no sacred torches to light the way. During the night all was dark and so very cold. The animals had a great meeting to figure out what to do. They said, "Who will find heat and light for us? Who will help us?"

The little mouse said, "There is a volcano that goes way deep in the earth. I will go there and get fire." So, the little mouse ran to the mouth of the volcano. He peered in and saw fire and great spirits that made thunderous noise. "The underneath is too frightening. I cannot go down there. I will surely die!"

After the mouse came back empty handed, the animal council asked again. "Who will find heat and light for us?"

The adder said, "I will go into the volcano for us!" So, the adder slithered to the mouth of the volcano. As he peered down, he saw the brightness of the lava and said, "The light is too bright and too hot. I will surely die if I go there."

The adder came back empty handed, and the animal council asked again. "Who will find heat and light for us?"

Finally, the crow said, "I have a magical bag and I can fly. I will go into the volcano and get heat and light for us." So, the crow took his magical bag and flew to the mouth of the volcano. He saw the fire and the great thunderous spirits. He also saw the brightness of the lava. He had much fear but without hesitation he took flight! He flew down into the depths of the volcano. He flew down into the earth and there he found a hot coal and put it into his bag. He flew as fast as he could past the fires and the thunderous spirits. He brought one coal to the animal council. They rejoiced in his bravery. The placed the coal on the little wooden pile and this is how the first sacred fire was made

Shamanism, Myth, and Magick

The people of the tribe sat around the sacred campfire. The light and the heat from the flames was magical—the source of life. The tribe's Shaman, dressed in skins and bones, was about to tell the story of the dead. The people were hushed. No one dared speak. The shaman's words were magical: a spell for all those who listened. He began his tale about the young hero who left the peacefulness of the tribe to seek adventure. The shaman explained how the young man found himself deep beneath the Earth, surrounded by the dead. But the hero found the courage to journey forth in the subterranean lands. For days and days, the hero explored the strange lands. He saw many strange things. He saw creatures who were ancient and kept their magical secrets very close. He saw many strange things: lovely maidens who revealed themselves as old hags, landscapes that would shift into nothingness and then back again, and dark beings that crept about in the deep. But he also saw great places of beauty and healing. The Shaman went on to tell of the great demons that tried to kill the hero, but the hero prevailed. Eventually he confronted the darkest part of the depths. It was through this darkness that the hero found the true healing of his spirit and the wisdom needed for the survival of his tribe. "What was this wisdom?" the shaman asked with a dark laugh. "Journey into the Underworld and find out for yourself."

When the ancient people lived in tribes, they told stories around the fires to explain the world around them. These stories became myths, and these later became the foundation of religion. Myths are stories told to explain the forces of creation, life, death and what happens in the afterlife. When we look closely, we find that they are much more than simply stories told to people to explain natural phenomena, such as the rising sun, the moon overhead, or a terrible storm. Myths were designed in accordance with the energy of the spirits, or even the god or goddess they referred to. Myths were also told as a guide to the social structure of the tribe, village, or city. They tell the listener what was expected of them during their lifetime and after death. The hero's journey was common to all ancient cultures and civilizations. These stories showed what happened when he or she journeyed out of the safety of the village. Sometimes bad luck would fall, unfortunate occurrences that would lead the hero on a path of transformation.

Myths were crafted in such a way that they also spoke to the hopes, fears, and struggles of the everyday person. Because human beings have the same needs, we also have the same hopes, fears, and desires. If we compare myths from around the world, we can see many of the same themes repeating. Psychologist Carl Jung calls these "archetypes." A few examples of archetypes include "The Shaman", "The Villain", or "The Maiden." Let us take the example of The Shaman. The Shaman archetype includes all shamans that ever were and all shamans that ever will be. In many societies shamans were needed to journey into the spirit worlds to gain wisdom and power for the benefit of the tribe. Myths contained archetypes because the listener related to them. As the story was being told, it was possible for the listeners to see themselves as the shaman going on the adventure.

Myths have "spiritual truth" in them. Spiritual truth is not the same as dogma or stories that are to be taken literally. Shamans and other people who worked with the spirits used their psychic vision to observe the universe and their surroundings. Shamans teach through stories and myth. In tribal cultures, there are no books of spiritual laws or commandments to teach right and wrong. The lessons were taught in the tales of the shaman. It was up to each individual to take the stories and draw their own conclusion. When we are young and inexperienced, we understand the "surface" lesson of the myths. Later, as we grow spiritually, we discover a deeper meaning with the stories. We begin to relate to the hero's journey. When I was a child, I loved the stories of King Arthur and the Knights of the Round Table. I loved reading books and watching movies about Arthur and the wizard Merlin. It was not until I studied Paganism and spirituality that I began to understand the complexities and spiritual meanings of the King Arthur stories. To learn how King Arthur was magically connected to the land and how Avalon was a sacred place of the dead was rewarding and has had a lasting impression on me.

When we look closely at the myths of the Underworld, we can use them to create our own magick. Myths were more than just stories to the ancient peoples. It became part of their culture and spiritual practice. The story was often told in a ceremony that was designed to leave a powerful imprint on the seeker. In this way, the myths became a living part of spirituality. If we take the example of the Elysian Mysteries, the myth of the Rape and Descent of Persephone is woven into Greek spirituality. The priest would take the seeker down into the "Underworld" that was a temple dedicated to Hades and Persephone. It was there the myth was played out so that it would have a great impact on the seeker.

In many shamanic cultures, the shaman journeyed into the three shamanic worlds to find wisdom about the spiritual nature of the

Universe. It was here that they met spirits, monsters, and gods. Some of these spirits and gods are fond of humans and would not mind sitting down for a spell to speak of the creation of the Universe or even more mundane topics with mortals. Today, unless we are fortunate enough to be part of a tribe of indigenous people, we do not have spirit walkers and shamans readily available to make these journeys for us, and it is up to us to do this work on our own. In my personal experience with spirits in the Underworld they love to tell you just enough for you to be interested in the journey; but they do not give away all the secrets. You must discover them for yourself, just as you must discover the deeper meanings of the myths for themselves. And to be honest, some of these secrets are immediately useful for you on your path, but others are so mysterious that you may not understand the meaning for days, weeks, or even years.

There are many myths and stories about the Underworld. I have found throughout my research and experience that the Underworld has a similar function in almost every part of the world. Here are some themes that are common from culture to culture in the Underworld myths:

- Underworld as the home of the Dead
- Trials and "Hells"
- Underworld as the home of Monsters
- Underworld as the place of oracles and guides
- Underworld as a place of nourishment, rejuvenation, and healing
- Death and Resurrection

It is also interesting to note that the Underworld terrain almost always looks like the terrain of the storyteller. The Underworld is a mythic reflection of the world we live in now. If there are mountains where the storyteller lives, such as in ancient Greece, then the Underworld has mountains. If there are wetlands, then that is the terrain of the Underworld. We will go over these themes in detail later.

Myths can act as a map to the Underworld. The Norse myths gave directions to which Underworld realm a traveler needed to go. They also go on to say what one can expect to find once they arrive. For example, the lore tells us of the river Slid and it's guardians Modgudh and Garm. As we investigate the Egyptian Book of the Dead, more properly called The Book of Going Forth by Day, there are directions, spells, and information for the dead to maneuver the Underworld to get to the House of the Gods in order to complete a quest for spiritual "resurrection." It is likely that ancient shamans were trained how to leave their bodies. This is now referred to as "astral projection" or "shamanic journeying". It was recommended that they "practice" the Underworld journey often because part of their healing was to perform soul retrievals for the community. This entailed journeying down into the Underworld to find an aspect of a person's soul or consciousness so that they could return it to the person for them to find health and wellness. Sometimes, when someone died, their spirit may have been confused or did not realize they had transitioned into death. The shaman would escort the spirit into the Underworld and the land of the dead as a psychopomp.

Learning about the myths and journeying in the Underworld is a special kind of magick. It was never thought of as a place to be feared, but as a reservoir of power to be used for healing. Most often the rites and rituals of the Underworld were kept secret. The priests and shamans of the ancient world believed that the common person would not be able to understand the mysteries of the Underworld. These sacred mysteries were kept hidden until a seeker who appeared ready for the dark journey made– themself known to them. Only then could true transformation take place. The priests believed that those who were not ready for the mysteries would surely profane them. This is why the Eleusinian Mysteries, a tradition in ancient Greece which celebrated the mysteries of life and death, were kept secret. Those who broke the secrecy were punished with death.

To take the Underworld journey is to become a more spiritual and evolved being. One of the most common ways to do this is to take what Joseph Campbell called the "The Hero's Journey." By taking a journey or adventure into unfamiliar lands, the soul and spirit of the hero becomes transformed into something greater. In myth, the hero would often go on a quest in search of some great thing. The thing could be anything from a treasure to a concept or power. Along the way, the hero would have many adventures, battles, and near-death misses. The hero would also meet fantastic creatures and lovely beings. At the end of the adventure, the hero would understand, through experience, the order of the cosmos and more importantly, who he REALLY is. This self-discovery could not happen if the hero did not take this adventure. It could only be accomplished because of the odd and fantastic things that occurred. This is the very task that you will be undertaking.

On a personal level, learning, mapping, and navigating the Underworld helps us learn about our own subconscious in all of its complexities. On a macrocosmic level, we are traveling through the soul of the Universe. Exploring the Underworld realms allows us to go on a journey of self-discovery. We will be challenged and tested. We are tested in the Underworld, not to show the gods and spirits how good or powerful we are, but rather to prove to ourselves what we are made of. The Underworld journey will show us our strengths and at the same time show us our greatest fears. We are not meant to "pass" every test and gain rewards. There will be many times when we fail. We may try to perform a task over and over again and fail each time. But it is through these mistakes that our soul will learn, grow, and transform into something that is greater than it was before we started the quest. The travels that we have ahead of us are not meant to be simply landmarks that we can say we "have been there"—they are places of great power. It is the kind of power that allows us to spiritually evolve. There is a magical quest ahead of us. There will be many trials, many triumphs, and many strange and mysterious discoveries. Through all of this, we will learn more about the Universe and the deeper meaning of our own spirit.

1
Underworld

The concept of the Underworld may be unfamiliar to some people who have not had shamanistic training or experience. Let us discover what the Underworld is and how it relates to us here in the physical plane. In several cosmologies, the world we live in is the here and now; this is our foundation or the Midworld. The world of the gods and other beings is the heavens or Upperworld. But there is a world that is "under" our own. It is a world that few understand and even fewer have visited. People who come from a Judeo-Christian background call this world Hell. The idea of Hell got its origin from one of the Nordic Underworlds called Hel or Helheim. This is a pagan Nordic world of the Ancestors. In Christian belief any world that was of pagan origin had to be a world of the Devil. A brief overview of pagan myth and legend tells us that the Nordic Underworld has its rough terrain, but it is not a place of despair and torment. Instead, the Underworld is a necessary part of the cosmos and the spiritual nature of the Universe. Without it, there would be no order to the Universe. The Nordic Underworld has many inhabitants; some of whom are the Ancestors. Helheim is the home of the Ancestors that is governed by the Goddess of Death, Hela or Hel. It is her duty to keep the Ancestors safe and she does not allow her inhabitants to leave except under special circumstances. Without Helheim, the dead would roam freely upon the Midworld and cause destruction and havoc. In some cosmologies, allowing the dead to walk the land of the living may bring disease or death. This is perhaps because the dead may have had the energies of death around them that may affect the living.

In many myths, the Underworld is the place where the spirits of the dead dwell when their lives in this world have ended. It is most often described as a place of peace and rejuvenation where the spirits of the dead are kept happy and safe. In other myths, the Underworld has many other terrains that are both mysterious and frightening. But in both belief systems there is great power. There are stories of gods and heroes who adventure down into the lower depths of the universe, who seek treasures, healing, power, and even the return of the dead to the land of the living. But, as in all aspects of creation, there is an order that must be maintained, otherwise chaos would wreak havoc throughout the three worlds. In the vastness of the Underworld, powerful spirits dwell—guardians and gods who protect the powers under our world. There are spirits that guard places of wisdom. It is also believed in some cosmologies that the Fates live here and to spy upon their work is to know one's fate. There are also very ancient deities that harbor the powers of mass destruction. There are tales of great magick and powerful allies who reside in the Underworld. These powers and entities can help us on our evolutionary path; or, if used unwisely, could lead to the very destruction of the known universe.

The Underworld is expressed in symbols and metaphor. In pagan cosmology, the Universe is often portrayed as held together by a Great Tree. In Nordic myth, this Great Tree is called Yggdrassil. Imagine a gigantic tree with a trunk so large you cannot see the end; branches so tall they go into the deep reaches of space; roots that go down into the furthest reaches of the Earth. Some believe that this tree exists in the astral realm, which I will talk about shortly. The trunk represents all that is in the Midworld or the physical existence that we live in. This includes all living humans, animals, nature, and the cycles of our Earth. The great branches represent the Upperworld. This includes the gods, angels, planetary intelligences, star peoples, and spirit guides. The great roots represent the Underworld itself. This is a place of the Ancestors, gods of death, and many other beings that we will learn about as we go further in our discoveries.

The Psychological Underworld and the Mind

Ever since the idea of shamanism was introduced to modern society, people have asked the question, "Are the three worlds real or a part of the imagination?" I think this is a very valid question. Are we really journeying for healing or are we simply deluding ourselves? To answer this question, we should look at the indigenous cultures that put shamanic techniques into practice. There are many instances where the person has been healed with soul retrievals and other shamanistic practices. How does this work? Is it a placebo effect or is it actual spirits coming to heal the person in question? I believe both answers are true. One way to view this is to understand that the human mind acts as a vehicle for traveling into other worlds of reality. Another way is to think of the mind as a mirror of what is happening in the three worlds, much like a television monitor projecting to your living room what is happening far away. Skeptics may ask, "If it is only the imagination, does shamanism still have the capacity to heal me?" Yes. It does. It does because if we try to understand our mind psychologically, we will find that our mind has the wonderful ability to heal itself, the body, emotions, and our spirit. Some psychotherapists are using shamanic techniques to help heal their clients. In her book *Shamanism and Spirituality in Therapeutic Practice*, Christa Mackinnon uses shamanic journeying to aide her clients in healing. In her book she states that shamans, "work towards integrating the different aspects of the mind with each other and with the body, as well as the mind/body with the soul and spirit, and furthermore the individual with the wider community and the community with 'the whole and the spirit'."

To heal and make transformations within ourselves, there must be communication between the subconscious and the conscious mind. Our subconscious thinks in emotions, symbols, and imagery. It is also the seat of repressed memories, desires, fears, and our shadow self. The Shadow Self holds our emotions and memories that we have repressed within our subconscious. It is also the primal, animal self that we may feel has no place in our modern "civilized" society. It does not think in the logical state that our conscious mind does. This is one of the reasons that dreams are often wondrous and strange. Imagery and symbols, such as those found in the Underworld, have a powerful effect on the subconscious. By using imagery and symbols, the subconscious begins to open itself up more and delivers information to our conscious mind. When we journey to the Underworld, we can say that we are visiting some aspects of our subconscious mind. There, we may meet strange beasts, friends and family long dead, and men and women of great power and wisdom. They are all symbols. We may also discover archetypes. In her book, *Journeying: Where Shamanism and Psychology Meet*, Dr. Jeannette M. Gagan says, "…the spirit world encountered in journeying is none other than the landscape of this collective unconscious illuminated by the release of archetypical energy long bound to its internal matrix."

As we journey into the parts of the Underworld that are dark and mysterious, we will most likely come across the Shadow Self. The Shadow Self is the part of the consciousness that holds our repressed fears, secret desires, and prejudices. The Shadow Self is only interested in self-preservation. It has no need for spiritual evolution because this would destroy it. The Shadow Self gets its energy from fear and negative reinforcement, including negative thoughts and feelings we have about ourselves. This is one of the reasons we use the term "personal demons." This phrase is fairly accurate. The Shadow Self is responsible for our uncontrolled anger, deep depression, and the abuse of others. It only serves to harm us in the long run. In the Underworld, we come across our Shadow Self in a number of forms and symbols. Remember, our subconscious speaks to us with symbols and archetypes, so this is how our Shadow Self will manifest. Most often, the archetypes that will appear are monsters, vampires, trolls, and demons. The most common way to deal with these symbols is to destroy them, but it will serve you better if you confront them head on and find out who they are and what they want. Most likely, they will reveal themselves as fears and negative emotions you must deal with. By transforming these shadow archetypes, you can potentially release a lot of the energy that may be blocking your self-healing and transformation.

The subconscious can reveal your own personal monsters, but it can also reveal personal healing and transformation. The Underworld is not just a sewage pot filled with monsters and devils, it is a place of wonder and a place of the Ancestors. There are many beings and spirits there that can aid in your personal healing. They can also take you to places that have the power to heal. The Underworld is filled with many myths and stories about wise women with magick potions and sacred wells and other places that have transformative powers. So how does this relate to the subconscious mind? We all have heard that the mind can aid in our own healing and wellbeing. How do we access this healing at will? We do it by journeying into our mind and finding healing through symbols and archetypes. Indigenous cultures as well as modern holistic healers understand that the deep subconscious holds powerful healing. By journeying to the healing places in the mind's Underworld, we can give our subconscious "permission" to open its healing powers to us.

The question still remains: is the Underworld journey real or is it just in our imagination? Again, it is both. There is an age-old axiom that states, "As above, so below. As within, so without." This is my theory of how it works: your mind is your catalyst to enter the Underworld. It is the vehicle in which you travel. A strong and healthy mind leads to more productive journeys to the Underworld. You must begin to think of it as peeling the layers of an onion. The deeper you are able to journey into your subconscious mind and transform your personal issues, the deeper you will be able to journey into the Underworld and discover new things about the universe and yourself. Also remember that some of the entities that you come across will have strong psychic abilities and will be able to read deep into your subconscious. They may even be able to use your Shadow Self against you. This is one of the many reasons why it is so important to constantly learn about your fears and insecurities. Only through learning about these less than pleasant aspects of ourselves can one transform and evolve. If you are caught off-guard, then your deepest fears can be used against you. Seek to be better than you are. Be brave and go through those things you fear the most. Once you have faced yourself and begun the healing process of the deep mind, you will truly become a powerful, spiritual person. So, what if there is no Underworld and it is all in your head? As longs as you find healing and are transformed, then it does not matter. Healing is healing, no matter if it is found in a magical place far away, or a symbol that reveals your true inner self within your mind. As long as it works…do it!

Creation of the Underworld

Different mythologies explain the creation of the Underworld in many different ways. Several myths claim that the Underworld was created as a sort of cosmic "storage unit" for the Universe. They tell of gods who do not want the dead near their dwellings, as with Greco-Roman cosmology which places the dead far beneath the world in a subterranean world called Hades. Other myths say that the gods of the Underworld who controlled death and the comings and goings of the dead, loved the dead so much that they could not bear to be apart from the spirits. Therefore, the gods and the dead must forever dwell together down below. Many myths often also say that evil monsters, unwanted gods, demons, and strange and unusual creatures live in the Underworld because they are not wanted anywhere else, and the Underworld is open to all who seek its refuge. Some examples of this are the Titans of Greek myth and demons of Judeo-Christian myth. There are also tales of the Underworld being an accident of creation and that the creator gods never intended for it to exist. If we take a look at the Kabbalistic Underworld called the Qliphoth, we will find that it was created when the higher planes, called Sephiroth, were being formed. The Qliphoth is the culmination of the "shells" that were cast off from the creation of the universe.

When you learn more about the Underworld and work with those energies you will discover that the Underworld has a very holy and divine purpose. That is no accident. It is true that there are those Upperworld gods who do not go down to the Underworld and have a disdain for it. That is simply because their energies and powers do not resonate with those of the ancient worlds below and their powers are best suited for the Upper and Midworld. Usually, those gods send messengers down below. If we take a look at the King of the Gods in Greco-Roman lore, Zeus, we see that he will send Hermes, the messenger god, to the Underworld to speak with the Underworld god, Hades. I believe that the Underworld carries a lot of magical power and wisdom. It holds the memories of the past and the visions of the future. By working with these energies one can obtain much personal transformation and growth.

Why go to the Underworld?

We go to the Underworld for several reasons. One of the most common is for personal transformation. The Underworld has places of great wisdom. One such place is the Well of Mimir. Mimir is a Nordic god of wisdom and is often sought out for this purpose. The wise Mimir can tell you many truths and oracles, but sometimes the cost may be great. For Odin, the Norse All-Father, the price was one of his own eyes. Another reason to journey to the Underworld is for prophecy and oracle work. The Underworld is fluid in the sense that it is not as physical and rigid as the Midworld and its laws of time and space are very different from our own. This gives the spirits and entities the advantage of seeing things from the past, present, and future much more clearly than Earth-bound humans. The Underworld is also a place of healing and renewal. There are many fountains, springs, and lakes that flow from below the Earth into our physical world. These waterways are sources of great healing. Therefore, the Underworld contains much healing power. One such myth that represents this power is the quest for the Grail. Healing, in most traditions, means to bring someone or someplace back into wholeness. The Underworld is a place of transformation and evolution; therefore, the Lower World has the power to bring much healing to us. One of my favorite reasons for traveling to the Underworld is to connect with the Ancestors. The Ancestors are our direct link to family and our divine purpose in this life. They can help us do many things on the spiritual levels. The Ancestors are our family, and they have a great interest in us that many of the gods and spirits do not. It is amazing how much your personal gnosis and magick grows once you have reconnected with the Ancestors.

We may also travel the Underworld to prepare for our own death. To most people, this seems like a strange and morbid idea. To the ancients, preparing for the moments that led up to and followed the death process was especially important. The Egyptian Book of the Dead and the Tibetan Book of the Dead were created for this reason. Not only were these books written to help the newly dead find their way through the Underworld, but they were also written to help each person mold their consciousness in such a way that they were literally practicing for their death. If you think about it, it makes more sense to practice going through the Underworld so that you may battle demons, meet your Ancestors, and join with the gods. The theory was that if you fail this task, you could become lost or trapped in the Underworld. I think of it like rehearsing for a play or a show. The more you practice, the better prepared you will be.

Odin's Sacrifice (Norse)

All-Father gazed into the cosmos. He saw all of Creation. He saw Yggdrasil, The World Tree. The splendor of the universe spun around its axis point. Odin, who constructed the earth with his brothers out of the corpse of the giant Ymir, looked upon his work in wonder. It took on a life of its own. He knew the cosmos was perfect the way it was. There were many mysteries—many things to discover. Everything was given the power to create life on its own. The cosmos gave off nine magnificent lights. Even the dark worlds had their own magnificent light. These lights were a mystery yet to be discovered.

Later, Odin felt the bliss of the Great Tree, Yggdrasil. He could feel the pulse of life streaming from the Universe into his body. The pulses began to grow more powerful. They penetrated his body with such energy and beauty that he became overwhelmed with ecstasy. He could hear the chorus of songs coming from deep within Yggdrasil. Such beauty. Such bliss. He stretched out his arms and fell. Further and further, he fell into the tree. No horse carried him. No chariot drove him. No spirits accompanied him. He fell into the greatness of creation. He was a comet that fell into the blackness of the tree. Suddenly, he was pulled up short and stopped, so that he was swinging on the branches of creation. "What is keeping me here?" he thought. "Is it a rope? Or is it some other magnificent power that is holding me in this blissful place?"

His mighty spear was in his hand. He had carried it all the way down with. With a great thrust he stabbed it into his side. His bliss now carried the added ecstasy of pain. Sacrifice, he thought. I must give up my old self, my old way of being. Death is necessary to destroy the old self so that my inner being, that which is closest to the deepest insight of the universe, can be realized. His blood spilt above him like a fountain trying to reach the heavens. "No," Odin, thought, "I am hanging upside down. The blood is spilling down. Or perhaps it is spilling up. No matter. Where I am, I am." Odin seemed to float endlessly on the tree of creation. All things seemed to stop in place. If he looked in other directions, he could make out one of the nine worlds. "No, my mind is leaving me! There is nothing down here. Wait, is that life I see?" The mighty Ash rotated in such perfection around him. The energies coming to him from the tree were powerful. But they were not just energies. They were magnificent voices, singing the praises of the cosmos. Days passed; each one more agonizing and blissful than the last. It was not the bliss of pleasure, but rather the bliss of sacrifice. Pain and pleasure mingled into one. More days passed. Odin was one with the tree. He was cradled with beautiful voices streaming to him from the tree. For a moment he wondered who the voices belonged to, but his consciousness faded. Nine days in all was his sacrifice.

There was a glimmer above him. A magnificent power. A magnificent voice, no, many voices singing to him the praises of the universe. They sang songs of prosperity, love, death, and magick. Odin regained his consciousness. The voices streamed with such energy that they wrapped a brilliant light around him: a cradle of magick and power. He looked above his head to see the magnificent lights spinning round, singing the songs of magick, power, love, and death. Such sweet, beautiful glyphs; so simple and complex at the same time. He saw a drop of his own blood fall into the waters of the Underworld. The alchemy of blood and water took the form of another mystery, a Rune. The runes spun around him with the splendor of the universe. They entered Odin's body, entered his mind, and his spirit. Much power poured through his veins. This was Magick. Odin took the runes back to the nine worlds where they would always sing the spells of creation, destruction, and rebirth.

The above myth is my interpretation of Odin's sacrifice to the Runes. Odin journeyed down into the Underworld to obtain wisdom and power. This wisdom manifested as the Runes that the Nordics use for divination and magick. Myths were never meant to be stagnant or dogma. Myths can be seen in the spirit worlds as living and evolving stories that teach mankind in way that we can best understand in our current times. I will admit that this style of the myth appeals to my imagination.

Mapping the Underworld

The Underworld has many wonders and spectacles to see. It is vastly different from what we are used to here in the physical world. At times, when we think it looks familiar to our world, we quickly learn that things are not what they seem. Children's stories are full of wells that lead to magical places or a ferry boat that leads us into a distant land in the west. Stories of the Underworld tell tales about beautiful landscapes as well as the most mysterious places ever discovered. These stories have warnings embedded in them that we would do well to heed. In *Alice in Wonderland* by Lewis Carol, we see how Alice falls into a hole in the earth and is transported into the Underworld. Once there, she sees many wondrous things including smiling cats and a Queen of Hearts.

We must always remember that the Underworld is technically the Spirit world. The rules and laws there are different from our own, but they are still laws. In our world, the laws of physics are solid and firm. We know that the sun comes up in the morning in the East and goes down at night in the West. We know that mountains are solid, and the oceans are cold and wet. We know that winters are cold, and summers are hot. We know that life is both powerful and fragile. We know that there are twenty-four hours in a day. The Underworld is quite different. There are many illusions and things are not always what they seem. This is not a trick intended to confuse travelers or the dead. There is a purpose for everything. Illusions are put in place to keep out those who do not belong in certain parts of the Underworld. It keeps beginners from stumbling upon things that can really hurt them physically, mentally, spiritually, and emotionally. Sometimes the illusions that we discover come right from the minds of the traveler. The Tibetan Book of the Dead has many prayers to the newly dead, or the person preparing for death, that remind them of their purpose in the Underworld and that many of the fantastic creatures, gods, and monsters are a part of their own deep-rooted desires manifesting in the world of spirit. At other times, illusions are there to test the traveler. The deeper one journeys into the Underworld, the more complex the world is and the more dangerous are its inhabitants. If you can pass through the illusions as well as your own fears, then you will be admitted into the deeper realms.

Some examples of the illusions you may encounter are monsters that seem to attack from nowhere, fog that goes on forever, cliffs with no bridges or any other way to get across, or oceans with no boats. If you cannot seem to get through the illusion, it is best to believe that the spirits there know what is best; and sometimes it is best to "not wake the sleeping dragon!" Try to find another way. If you cannot, then graciously end your journey and try again a different day. The mysteries of the Underworld are meant to be discovered by those who can bring the wisdom back to the Midworld for the betterment of not only themselves, but all humanity. It is far better to have the intentions of self-transformation and helping your community evolve when going on such a journey than just doing it for sport.

Time and Space

Time does not run the same in the Underworld as it does here in the physical world. There is a sense of time, but it is drastically different from what we are used to. We are so accustomed to minutes, hours, days, and months that it has become routine for us. We can usually tell when a couple of minutes or hours have passed. We can look at the sun and evaluate the approximate time of day from its position. We even have something referred to as a "biological clock". Our bodies have become so used to our perceived time that we often automatically know when to wake up, eat, and go to sleep. As human beings, we are acclimated to the environment around us.

When we journey to the Underworld, time runs on its own terms. Time may run very quickly or sometimes very slowly. There are many myths and stories about people finding themselves in the three worlds and having marvelous adventures that last days and weeks only to return and discover that only a few minutes have passed. There are also the stories of people who have traveled to the Underworld for what they thought was a short time, and upon returning discover that so much time has passed that their friends and loved ones have been long dead. In the story of *Rip Van Winkle*, by Washington Irving, Rip fallows a Dutch man to a hollow hill where they get drunk on beer. When he awakes, he finds his wife and friends are gone and he has been away for 20 years. Part of the reason this happens is because we are so used to our "Earthly" time that our minds and bodies cannot help but try to place the same rules of time we are accustomed to onto the Underworld. The spirits know this and sometimes use it against us, especially trickster spirits and spirits who do not wish to be bothered.

There are many theories about how time works in the Underworld. One theory says that energy and events begin with the source of all things: God, the creator, or the Great Mystery. The energy from the source of creation in the Upperworld then passes through the Underworld, and then to us here in the Middleworld. If we use the Great Tree of Life as a symbol of the connection between the Three Worlds in the Universe this view makes a little more sense. I like to use the analogy of rainfall when explaining this concept. Imagine rain as a symbol of time/events and energy. Rain comes from the sky (Upperworld) then touches the ground going into the roots of the tree (Underworld) and the roots then pull up the rainwater into the trunk of the tree (Midworld). Another theory says that the Energy begins in the Upperworld (future) travels down to the Midworld (present) and then into the Underworld (past). So, which view is right? I think both are. It all depends on your point of view. There are many places in the

Underworld were you can perceive the passing of time and watch upcoming events pass before your eyes. To be able to do this, a few things need to happen. First, you must be able to find these locations. Second, you must appease the guardian spirits that guard these sacred places. Once you can find the places you must have "access" or have the ability to see in the astral (psychic vision) to be able to see the upcoming or past events.

When you are divining from this world with the tarot, runes, ogham, bones, or other such tools, you are accessing these secret realms in the Underworld. The difference is that you are using the divination tools as a medium for the information versus going into the other realm. It may seem less difficult to simply use a divination tool, but you are seeing events with the symbols via the tool rather than seeing things right from the source.

Sometimes, when there is an important event occurring or about to occur, it is better to go to the Underworld and see exactly what is coming. That way, what you perceive can be a lot clearer. Fate and destiny are not set in stone. By using the Underworld to foresee what is coming, we may be able to avoid oncoming negative events or perhaps give power to positive things coming our way.

Entrances into the Underworld

The Underworld seems to be a place that is far away in the world of stories, dream, and fantasy. But we do have the ability to access the Underworld. It is not as hard as you think. There are many entrances that will take us down into the depths of the Underworld. Before you begin your journey, you must first work to suspend any disbelief. What I mean by this is that you just must "go with it." Let yourself believe it is true, at least for now. Allow your mind to become more and more convinced of the reality of the Underworld as you journey and learn about this wonderful place. The second thing you must do is not have too much expectation. Allow the events to unfold before you. You may not see a lot at first, but have gratitude for what you do see and experience and know that you will discover more as you develop experience in journeying. You also must remember that physical entrances to the Underworld are only possible if you journey in spirit form or by astral travel. If you close your eyes and simply jump into a faery mound, do not be surprised if you get a big bump on your head! There are techniques and basic guidelines that need to be followed, especially by the beginner. I will lay these out for you shortly.

To enter the Underworld, you can do several things. You can do a meditative journey to where you send your astral body to a central point such as a Great Tree or stone. This is where I recommend beginners to go first. Using the imagery of a central Great Tree helps balance and orient you to the new sensations of the three worlds. It also usually leads you to more easily accessible realms. Why a tree? Well, the Great Tree is used by many neo-shamans and neo-pagans. It is something that a lot of us agree upon because of its rich history and lore in traveling into the other worlds. It is mentioned in the Nordic sagas as Yggdrasil, the Great Tree that Odin traveled up and down upon into the nine worlds from Asgard in the Upperworld. Some indigenous tribes use a large stone. The stone serves the same purpose as the tree. The middle of the stone represents this world, the top is the Upperworld, and the base is the Underworld. Try both and see which works better for you.

There is also the Celtic cosmology of Land, Sea, and Sky. This is not exactly the same as the four elements of Earth, Air, Fire, and Water. By the time of the Iron Age, most of the ancient Celts lived on the islands known today as Britain and Ireland. Their homeland is surrounded by water. They were very well trained in seafaring and the energies of the oceans. To them, the Land is the Midworld; it is the land of trees, mountains, and rock. The Sky is the land of the gods. The Sea is the land of the Ancestors and subterranean beings. This cosmology may work for you as well, but unlike the Great Tree cosmology it may not bring you to the center of the Universe. In that case it is better to find spirit allies who are willing and able to help you navigate your way from this starting point here in this world.

Once you are used to traveling into the Underworld you may use "hot spots" or Underworld entrances as told in the lore and myth, such as the well that takes the little girl to the realm of Frau Holle in *Grimm's Fairy Tales*. There are many stories and legends beyond ancient mythology that tell of holes in the Earth that lead to the Underworld, such as *Alice in Wonderland*. In some tales there are actual gates that lead down into the Underworld. In Greece and Rome there were Underworld temples that were built into the Earth that were said to be the actual entrance into Hades. In the story of "Mother Holle" from *Grimm's Fairy Tales*, a young girl falls into a well and finds herself in a new land. There she does chores for Mother Holle and is rewarded with Gold.

The Planes of Existence

To better understand how our Universe operates it is important to understand about the planes or worlds of existence. As we have learned, the universe can be categorized as having three major worlds: the Upper, Middle, and Underworld respectively. For the beginner, this is a wonderful place to start, but as you progress in your understanding and experiences of the three worlds, you will find that they overlap and may discover other worlds within those worlds. As an example, the Nordic cosmos has three major worlds, but each world is separated into three more worlds giving nine worlds in all. To further understand the nature of the universe, it is helpful to realize that the Midworld can exist in several modalities or realms of existence. These are the physical, etheric, astral, mental, and spiritual planes. In my experience, the Midworld is the only one to have all of them, including the physical plane. I have found that the Upper and Underworlds only have the astral, mental, and spiritual planes. However, it is interesting to note that the ancients believed the Upper and Underworlds to have an actual physical existence as well. For example, in Greece, the Upperworld of the gods can be found on Mount Olympus and the Underworld could be accessed through rocky underground caves and rivers. For our purposes in this book, we will work with the idea that the only world that has the physical and etheric plane is the Midworld.

Physical

This is the plane, or world, we are most familiar with. It is the physical manifestation of all the other worlds combined. It is what most people refer to as reality. It must be said that reality is a perception. Most Native Americans and Australian Aborigines believe that the spirit/dream world is just as, if not more, "real" than the Physical world. The Buddhists would say that the physical world was an illusion, or maya. The physical world is made up of solids, liquids, energy, and gases. From our human point of view, it is the most tangible. It follows the laws of physics. Its element is Earth.

Etheric

This plane is very closely related to the Physical world. It is an intermediary between the Physical world and the Astral world. Chakras, meridians, and auras of the body are closely related to the etheric world. However, these things can also manifest on the Astral, Mental, and Spiritual planes. One could also say that life force or chi is also etheric. This is the energy that gives the Physical plane (as well as our bodies life). It takes only a little psychic perception to be able to see the Etheric world. Usually, dim lights and an open mind will do the trick. To the person with sensitive touch, the Etheric world feels like "energized fog" or even like going through a spider web. Its element is also Earth.

Astral

This is the plane that is between the etheric and mental planes. It does not follow the same laws of the physical or etheric realms. It exists partly as an intermediary between the Spiritual and Physical/Etheric planes. All life and all things have an astral counterpart. This plane is called "astral" because astronomical phenomenon such as the sun, moon, planets, and stars have an influence on it. It is shaped by our hopes, desires, dreams, fears, and emotions. It is thought that before something manifests on the physical plane, it must first be imagined on the Astral plane. What we imagine briefly appears in the astral plane. When we add energy to our "thought forms," as it were, then they will manifest in the physical plane. This is also commonly thought of as the dream world. However, some believe that the dream world is a separate plane of existence all its own. Its element is Water

Mental

The Mental plane is more abstract than the previous or "lower" planes. It is the plane of logic and thought. It lies between the Astral and Spiritual worlds. When we imagine something or hear the running monologue in our heads, it is happening on the Mental plane. I think of the Mental plane of existence as being the source of all logic and mathematics in the Universe. Everything from atoms to the sum total of the Universe has a mathematical logic to it. Without this the Universe would only be a place of chaos without order. The Mental plane keeps things in a "logical" place of being. However, just because something seems chaotic it does not mean it does not have a divine logical purpose, as we shall see once we delve further into the mysteries of the Underworld. Its element is Air.

Spiritual

The Spiritual plane is the most abstract of all the planes and is often thought of as a plane of pure light. It is the highest of the planes and it is here that all of creation first begins. This is the first created plane of existence by the Source of All Things, The Creator, or sometimes called Great Mystery. There can be nothing in our modern interpretation of existence without the Spiritual plane. It is the place of the gods, angels, and higher spirits, but they can manifest on all planes! It is the plane that is most "refined". This is where our own spirit dwells. Its element is Fire.

Astral Projection and Shamanic Journeying

To travel into the Underworld, you will be using our astral body. The astral body is our energetic double and is sometimes called our body of light. The astral body can be easily controlled by the emotions and the mind. When you become proficient at leaving your body, which is called astral projection, you will have the ability to journey through time and space. You will be able to travel at the speed of thought to anywhere in the Universe.

I have studied a lot of books and been to workshops that teach astral projection. When I was a novice magician, I remember learning the formulas and magical conjurations that would allow me to leave the body in spirit. The magical spells seemed exceptionally long and the techniques for leaving the body were tedious and it took months of meditation and visualization exercises to even get one's feet wet. To most students, this was daunting and left people feeling more frustrated than empowered. After having received a formal magical training, followed up with a lot of experience traveling to the three shamanic worlds, I can tell you that you that astral projection is very simple; you just have to practice at it with some regularly and not get discouraged if you do not immediately get results. I will give you a couple of fun exercises to do that will get you started. The key here is to visualize as clearly as possible and FEEL the sensations of walking around, seeing, hearing, smelling, and touching. To do this, you simply use your imagination. Visualize. The other key to controlling your astral body is to use logic, imagination, desire, and will. Meaning, you must imagine yourself in the Otherworlds as clearly as possible using logic, then with the desire to travel, you simply will yourself to do so.

The first few times you may wonder if astral projection is just "all in your head." Well, to some extent it is, but it is supposed to be. Remember, the Astral and Spiritual realms are the places of imagination, dreams, and visions. We travel around in the Physical plane in our physical bodies, so we travel around in the Astral/Spiritual with our astral (imagined/visualized) bodies. I know some magicians who will argue with me that I am oversimplifying ancient magick. And I am. If at first it feels like it is "all in your head" go with it. Eventually, you will meet entities, spirits, and gods who will take you to wonderful places and tell you secret information that you simply cannot "make up." The trick here is to have fun and explore. See what you find. Read some of the mythology listed in Suggestions for Further Reading at the end of this chapter and try your best to understand the spiritual meaning behind the stories. Then go have a spiritual adventure.

So, what is all this talk about shamanic journeying? Basically, shamanic journeying and astral projection are the same thing. You are using your astral or energy body to leave your physical body to travel in the spiritual realms of the Universe. The term "astral projection" is more popular in ceremonial magical and New Age communities while "shamanic journeying" is a term more popular in neo-shamanism. At the end of the day, it really does not matter what term you use because the end result will be the same.

Astral Exercise 1

1. It may be helpful to play a shamanic drumming recording. If you have someone to drum for you, all the better. The drumming should be light but audible enough to hear comfortably. If you are using a drum or having someone drum for you, have them beat at a moderately quick pace. If for some reason you cannot get a recording of shamanic drumming, don't worry. It is not necessary to have a shamanic drum beat to astral project. If you do not like shamanic drumming feel free to use any type of music that puts you in a trance and makes you feel magical. I will often use synthesized songs that sound ethereal to accomplish this for myself.

2. Sit or lie in a comfortable position. Make sure your back is as straight as possible.

3. Close your eyes and take a few deep breaths.

4. Relax your body as best you can. Begin with your feet. Tell them to relax and release all tension. Then move up to your calves. Tell them to relax and release all tension. Go up to the thigh, glutes,

back, belly, chest, shoulders, arms, hands, neck, and head in turn, telling them all to relax and release all stress and tension.

5.   Imagine yourself getting up and walking around. Remember, this is done entirely with your imagination. Try not to move your physical body at all.

6.   Walk around the room you are in and look at the furniture, walls, shelves. Look at yourself. See yourself lying (or sitting) down.

7.   When you are ready, see yourself walk over to your physical body and sit or lie back into yourself. When you are close to your body this will most often happen automatically.

Astral Exercise 2

1.   Play your shamanic drumming recording or other music as per the previous exercise.

2.   Sit or lie in a comfortable position. Make sure your back is as straight as possible.

3.   Close your eyes and take a few deep breaths.

4.   Relax your body as best you can. Begin with your feet. Tell them to relax and release all tension. Then move up to your calves. Tell them to relax and release all tension. Go up to the thigh, glutes, back, belly, chest, shoulders, arms, hands, neck, and head in turn, telling them all to relax and release all stress and tension.

5.   Imagine yourself getting up and walking around. Remember, this is done entirely with your imagination. Try not to move your physical body at all.

6.   At this point, see a door or gateway in front of you. Know that the door leads to the World Tree.

7.   Step through the door and on the other side see the World Tree. The Word Tree is the largest tree you have ever seen. Its trunk

extends out further than the eye can see going both left and right. The branches go up into the heavens and you cannot see the top of the tree. You can see that the roots go deep into the Earth.

8. This is the Center of the Midworld, and it is your starting point. Until you are very proficient with traveling, you may want to start here.

9. You notice that there is a door in the trunk of the tree leading down, deep into the roots of the tree. Go through the door. You may see a staircase or simply a tunnel.

    Note: You may also simply see a hole in the ground leading down into the Earth, following the roots, leading down into tunnels.

10. Go down further and further into the roots through the tunnel or staircase. Know that you can travel down very fast and sometimes in just a blink of an eye.

11. Finally, when you arrive at the Underworld, take note of the first thing you see? Explore the immediate environments carefully. When you are ready, go back the way you came and back up the tunnels into the World Tree, then back to the Trunk of the Tree and into the Middle World.

Astral Exercise 3

1. Play your shamanic drumming recording or other music per the previous exercises.

2. Sit or lie in a comfortable position. Make sure your back is as straight as possible.

3. Close your eyes and take a few deep breaths.

4. Relax your body as best you can. Begin with your feet. Tell them to relax and release all tension. Then move up to your calves. Tell them to relax and release all tension. Go up to the thigh, glutes,

back, belly, chest, shoulders, arms, hands, neck, and head in turn, telling them all to relax and release all stress and tension.

5. Visualize a spiral of light, beginning at your feet, spiraling around you, going clockwise; it surrounds your entire body. The only thing you can see is the spiral of light. Know that this magical spiral of light is transporting you to the World Tree.

6. This is the Center of the Midworld, your starting point. Until you are very proficient with traveling, you always want to start here.

7. You notice that there is a door in the trunk of the tree leading down deep into the roots of the tree. Go through the door. You may see a staircase or simply a tunnel.

   Note: You may also simply see a hole in the ground leading down into the Earth, following the roots, leading down into tunnels.

8. Go down further and further into the roots through the tunnel or staircase. Know that you can travel down very fast and sometimes in just a blink of an eye.

9. Finally, when you arrive at the Underworld take note of the first thing you see. Explore your immediate environment carefully. When you are ready, go back the way you came and back up the tunnels into the World Tree then back to the Trunk of the Tree in the Midworld.

10. After awakening from your journey, record your experience in your magical journal and ground yourself back to the physical plane. You may do this by eating something light, drinking water, and/or doing "everyday" things around your home.

At this point in learning about astral travel and journeying through the Underworld, it is not about trying to see how far you go or finding exotic places right away. It is about taking the first steps in learning a new skill.

Just as with any skill, it takes practice. You must remember, the astral body is a direct manifestation of your mind, desires, memories, will, and your imagination. What this means is your astral body will look as you want it to and do what you want it to. Usually, the astral body looks like you do now but in more "idealized" form. Therefore, if you look at your astral body in a mirror, you may look younger, stronger, and healthier.

The astral realm itself takes on the appearance provided by your mind, or the group mind. As we have stated before, if there is a locked gate or a blocked entrance way, most likely your subconscious mind has put it there because either you are not ready to go forward in that direction, or you think you are not ready because of your own personal fears. When this happens, try to find out why you cannot go through, or come back later. Group mind phenomenon happens in the Astral/ Underworld when we discover ancient sites such as Hades or Hel and they appear exactly as the ancients described them. This is because of the many people who believe they look a certain way. This massive thought forms echoes through the astral and takes form. The more people who believe something to be true, the stronger it manifests. This is the reason why each type of Underworld in every culture around the world exists. This is also the reason why there is no "one truth".

Exercise:
Finding an Underworld Guide and Spirit Animal

In order to successfully journey into the Underworld, it is important to find your spirit animal and Underworld guide. You will be able to explore the Underworld faster and find treasures and allies much quicker than you would if you traveled alone. Also, the spirit animal can protect you from dangers that you are not ready to face. Your spirit animal can also protect you from spirit attacks in the Underworld. Spirit attacks upon a beginner are extremely rare, and I have often found that the "attackers" are really projections of the traveler's own fears. Put simply, the beginning student is "attacking" themselves in the Underworld because of their own fears. In essence, they believe the Underworld is a dangerous place, so they imagine danger at every corner. This is simply not the case. The Underworld does have some dangerous places, but the world of the Ancestors is a place of beauty and spiritual transformation. However, your spirit animal can help you fend off this astral thought form should it occur.

Finding Your Spirit Animal

For this exercise, you will travel to the Midworld to find your Spirit Animal.

1. Choose one of the astral exercises from the section on "How to Use Your Astral Body" above and travel to the World Tree.

2. Once there, make the following statement: "I wish to find my spirit animal". Open your heart chakra and reach out with your energies to your spirit animal. You may not know what kind of animal it is. That's ok. Reach out with your heart and they will respond back to you.

3. Begin walking in whichever direction feels appropriate to you. Keep the goal of finding your spirit animal in mind and try to intuit the direction you should go. The landscape will vary from person to person. You may find yourself traveling into a forest, mountains, valleys, or grass plains. Trust your instincts. For the time being, do not worry if you are "making it up." Visualize your surroundings to the best of your abilities.

4. Keep an eye out for any animals you see. You may see several. Some traditions say that you may see other animals, but you will see your spirit animal four times as your walk along your path. This is a good approach to take.

5. If you do not see any animals at first, keep walking. You should eventually begin to see more and more animals.

6. Once you see your spirit animal four times along your path, walk up to it. Ask it, "Are you my spirit animal? "

7. If the animal seems distant, unfamiliar, or unwilling to speak with you, then this may not be your Spirit Animal. If it is not your spirit animal, keep searching.

8. If the animal is your spirit animal then it will feel like a long-lost friend or relative. Your spirit animal may even feel like a part of you. This is because in reality, your totem IS a part of you.

9. Ask your spirit animal its name and record it in your magical diary or journal upon returning to your physical body.

Once you are fully conscious, visualize your spirit animal in front of you. You may choose to dance with them or simply imagine your spirit animal combining with your aura. To combine the spirit animal with your aura, visualize your animal in front of you. See them walking toward you and energetically combining itself with your aura. Know that you can call upon your spirit animal at any time in any world! I recommend getting an animal fetish - a little statue of clay or stone that represents your animal. If you have the fur, teeth, or a claw of the animal, then all the better. These things are not necessary but do help you connect to them in a deeper way

Finding your Underworld Guide

1. Choose one of the astral exercises and travel to the World Tree.

2. Once there, make the following statement: "I wish to find my Underworld Guide".

3. Call upon your totem spirit animal.

4. In the trunk of the World Tree, visualize a door that leads down into the Underworld. Follow this path down.

5. Follow this path down until you reach the Underworld. What do you see? What does the landscape look like?

6. Keep the intention to find your Underworld Guide in your mind. Begin to explore the Underworld. Ask your totem animal to show you the way.

7. Trust your intuition. Look for people along the way and ask them if they are your Underworld Guide. If not, ask them to point out the direction in which you can find your guide.

8. Once you find an entity who is a likely candidate to become your Underworld Guide, ask if they are willing to help you navigate the Underworld. If the answer is "no," the entity is not your guide, and you should keep looking. If the answer is "yes," ask for their name. Then ask your Guide if there is anything they would like in return. If the request is reasonable and you are able and willing to do it, then by all means do it. If not, graciously explain why you cannot meet the request.

9. Know that you can call upon your Underworld Guide each time you enter the Underworld.

10. Come back to the Midworld the way you came. Then open your eyes and journal about your experiences.

The Underworld is a wonderful place to find transformation of the spirit. It is through the myths that ancient cultures have learned to navigate and find their way through the strange terrain. The power of the Underworld has many great rewards for us and to the community we serve. As we learn how to use our astral bodies, we will begin to further our understanding of the world that holds a vast amount of wonder and beauty. Take some time and discover what the Underworld has in store for you. Journal your experiences and the beings you encounter. Write down what happened and the names of the spirits and gods that you meet. Each day you will develop and strengthen your relationships with the Underworld beings, ancestors, guides, and many other spirits who will help and guide you upon your spiritual path.

2
Navigating the Underworld

The Descent of Ishtar

Ishtar knew all things in Heaven and Earth, but she did not know the secrets of Death or the Underworld below. One day, she decided that she must also know the secrets of the Underworld, so she journeyed to the depths below. When she arrived at the gates of the Underworld, she noticed how gloomy and dusty the place was—like a world that the gods had forgotten. She demanded that the gatekeeper open the gates! She told him that if he did not, she would crash down the gates herself and release the dead so that they would rise to the Midworld and destroy the cosmic order of things. The gatekeeper bade her wait so that he might announce her arrival to Ereshkigal, The Queen of the Underworld, who was also her sister.

When Ereshkigal heard of her sister's arrival, she was very angry. She knew that Ishtar had arrived seeking more power, perhaps even her power! Ishtar was already one of the rulers of Heaven. Would she rule the Underworld, too? Ereshkigal told the gatekeeper not to give her sister special privileges. She would be treated as any other who entered the Realm of the Dead. The gatekeeper went back to Ishtar and allowed her to come through the first gate, but to do so she would have to remove her tiara. When she asked why she must remove her tiara, the gatekeeper relied, "These are the rules of the Queen of the Underworld."

Ishtar approached the second gate, but before she could enter the gatekeeper bade her remove her earrings. When asked why he replied, "These are the rules of the Queen of the Underworld."

Ishtar approached the third gate, but before she could enter, the gatekeeper asked her to remove her necklace. When asked why he replied, "These are the rules of the Queen of the Underworld."

Ishtar approached the fourth gate, but before she could enter, the gatekeeper asked her to remove her garment pin. When asked why he replied, "These are the rules of the Queen of the Underworld."

Ishtar approached the fifth gate, but before she could enter, the gatekeeper asked her to remove her girdle of birthstones from her wrist. When asked why, he replied, "These are the rules of the Queen of the Underworld."

Ishtar approached the sixth gate, but before she could enter, the gatekeeper asked her to remove her bracelets and anklets. When asked why, he replied, "These are the rules of the Queen of the Underworld."

Ishtar approached the seventh and last gate, but before she could enter, the gatekeeper asked her to remove her clothes. When asked why, he replied, "These are the rules of the Queen of the Underworld."

Now naked, Ishtar went deep into the Underworld and greeted her sister, Ereshkigal. Ereshkigal was furious at her sister's arrival. Ishtar was used to being Queen of Heaven and Earth and always sat in the place of Honor. Without courtesy, she sat upon Ereshkigal's throne. This infuriated Ereshkigal so much that she made her servants unleash sixty diseases at Ishtar, killing her. Ishtar, by decree of the cosmic order, was forced down into the depths of the Underworld to dwell among the spirits of the dead. When this occurred, the animals among the Midworld would not breed, men and women would not lust for each other and fall in love, and all love and pleasures stopped in Heaven and Earth.

In the heavens, the gods grieved when Ishtar did not return. The wise Ea created a messenger who was a male prostitute. His name was Asushunamir. He had the powers of both worlds and so he was sent to retrieve Ishtar from the Underworld. The powers of the seven gates could not stop him so he was able to pass right through with no effort. When he found Ereshkigal, she could not resist his charms. She was so pleased by him, she granted him anything in the Underworld he wanted. He demanded Ishtar. Ereshkigal knew that the gods had tricked her with a male whore! She granted his wish, but she cursed him to have a horrible life and to be a whore for men! She told her servants to travel into the realm of the dead to retrieve Ishtar. Ishtar was anointed with the waters of life and she went back through the seven gates.

At the first gate, her clothes were brought back to her.

At the second gate, her anklets and bracelets were returned to her.

At the third gate, her girdle of birthstones was returned to her.

At the fourth gate, her garment pin was returned to her.

At the fifth gate, her necklace was returned to her.

At the sixth gate, her earrings were returned to her.

At the seventh gate, her tiara was returned to her.

When Ishtar emerged into the Midworld, she expected to see her lover Tammuz in mourning, as was the custom at the death of a person's loved ones. But to exact further revenge, Ereshkigal had put a spell on Tammuz so that he would be lusting over female prostitutes when Ishtar found him. This was an outrage to Ishtar. Through Ishtar's journeys, she learned the mysteries of life, death, and resurrection.

Entering The Underworld

The Underworld is a vast and magical place. It has been told of in ancient myths, legends, and stories. It is the setting of epic drama and battles. There are more stories and tales of the Underworld than anyone could possibly write about in one volume. It has many different names and many different terrains and landscapes. In many cultures, however, the Underworld is akin to the world of dreams. It is, therefore, much easier to navigate one's way through the Underworld with stories and imagination than through the waking consciousness of logic. We use stories to teach of the three worlds and magick because stories have a deep connection with the artistic part of our brains and the subconscious. Through stories we can tap into the deeper part of the psyche that helps us discover our magical abilities. The Underworld is often described as a dark and terrible place and yet there are also stories that describe it as the most beautiful place one could ever see in the Universe. Regardless of whether it holds dark terrors or shining wonders, the Underworld is shrouded in mystery and magick.

Once you have entered the Underworld, you may find that it is a wonderful and exciting place. How wonderful and exciting is up to you. Before we go further into the Underworld, I would like to share with you my theories about how the Underworld works on the mind, the subconscious, and the imagination.

The Universe is made up of energy. Everything from light and radio waves to rocks and mountains are made up of energy. The energy of light moves at a much faster rate than the energy of physical matter. Knowing this, it is safe to say that the Upper and Lower worlds are made of energy as well. There is no "physical" matter in these worlds, but our minds still perceive the landscapes and environments we encounter there to be physical. This happens because when we visualize something in our mind, or experience something in a dream, our brain does not distinguish between "real" and "un-real." Scientists have recorded brain waves from subjects that see an actual picture and then visualize the same picture in their minds, and the brain waves read the same. What we picture in our minds or see in dreams is not any less real than what we see physically. In fact, I believe that this scientific evidence makes these things even more real. When we go through guided meditations or visualizations, our minds take the energy that we perceive and give it a picture so that our minds can understand what is happening around us. However, this does not mean that the landscapes we see and the entities or spirits we engage with are simply random patterns of energy. On the contrary, all beings and intelligences are made of energy. Our minds simply give it a form that we can understand so we can communicate with it in a better way. This is the reason that the spirits and gods that someone sees on these journeys often appear to be dressed in the clothing of the culture they came from. If you are from Egypt, the gods and spirits you see will look like the people you are most familiar with. So if this is the case, why do we still see the Greek gods in togas and the Nordic gods dressed as Vikings? Simply put, this is because this is how we think they are going to appear. I believe that if Persephone wants to appear wearing a Chanel gown, then she will!

Our imaginations may sometimes fill in the gaps that our mind is having a hard time perceiving. During your first couple of journeys into the Underworld, you may see what you expect to see. When this happens, give yourself permission to let your mind experience what it wants. Even though you may feel like you are making things up, keep moving forward. I believe this is a safety mechanism that your mind has so that you will not become overwhelmed with the new experiences. Over time, you will become more and more comfortable with your journeys and experiences, and you will begin to see more and more things that you did not see before. This may happen in the physical world as well. How many times have you walked down the same sidewalk or road day after day and looked up and saw something new and said to yourself, "Has that always been there?"

On a psychological note, for argument's sake, let's say that everything you experience on your journeys is simply your imagination and nothing more. Say it is nothing but the by-product of an overactive imagination. Even if this is the case, we must remember that we only use a small portion of our mind's functions and capabilities. If we can go into our own psyches to retrieve useful and profound insight and information, then what does it matter if imagination is involved? I choose to go forward with the thinking that the products of my imagination and dreams are real and that the things I experience in the Underworld are just as "real" as anything I experience going through my everyday consciousness. Scientists say that our dreams are linked to our imagination, but to indigenous tribes such as Native Americans, dreams are more real than our waking "reality". As we will soon discover in this book, dreams are our link to the spirit world of the gods and the dead. Perhaps are imaginations are linked to the spirit world as well. As we continue on, I will let you make your own discoveries in this.

As you go forward in your journeys, remember to react to everything you encounter as real, just as a dream is perceived to be real in your mind when you are in the midst of the experience. This will help you in the long run with your journeys and the information you receive from them. At this point, you may be wondering if the things that you encounter would be able to hurt you and cause you harm. The short answer to this question is YES! We must understand that not everything in the Underworld wants to hurt you, but just like living in the physical world, there are dangerous places and entities (corporeal and non-corporeal) that you should avoid. Later, I will give instructions on basic psychic self-defense. At this point, the best way to go forward is to be polite and gracious with all beings that you encounter. Most of the time, honorable behavior will keep you out of trouble. Most of the spirits I have encountered in the Underworld appreciate politeness. However, if you find that does not work and you feel threatened, simply end the journey, and purify your space with a smoke cleansing or a banishing to purify your working space. You may also call upon your gods and ancestors to protect your space energetically.

We must realize that death can have its beautiful experiences as well as its gruesome ones. Neither one is better than the other. They both have their divine purposes. However, the places of beauty are usually easier to navigate. While journeying, if you find yourself in a place that seems dark and dangerous, ask yourself a couple of questions:

1. Do I need to be here?
2. What is my purpose in navigating through this place?
3. Will I know what to do if I am in danger?
4. Do I know how to get back to where I came from?
5. Am I being respectful and courteous to all beings I meet here?

Remember to be polite and courteous to all beings you meet in any of the worlds. When we are journeying, we are strangers in someone's homeland. You do not have the right to journey everywhere. To be allowed to journey through the world is a privilege and the gods, ancestors, and nature spirits will take that privilege away from you should you abuse it. Be kind. Be honest. Have honor in your words and actions and you will do well in your travels.

Landscapes

The landscapes of the Underworld are as varied as the landscapes in this world, perhaps even more so. A lot of them can be related to our own landscapes but we must remember that the energies and powers of the Underworld have their own laws. What you may think will happen, most likely will not. In many myths and legends, there are stories about the landscapes changing at will. Sometimes this is because there is a glamour protecting an entity or a treasure of some sort. Other times, this is because the spirits who live in this area of the Underworld are testing you to see how you will react and how determined you are to continue on your journey. They may also test you to see how well you know the "laws" of the land. Other times, the spirits are tricksters and think it is great fun to confuse you in any way possible. The land of the Underworld is filled with prairies, valleys, mountains, and hills. The terrain can be smooth or rough. There are many mountains with spirits, trolls, dwarves, dragons, and many other spirits who dwell in them. Most of the stories speak of people who find these mountains to be filled with wondrous caverns that hold many wonderful treasures. But be warned! Any treasure in the Underworld is rarely freely given. There is usually some task or favor to be performed! Whenever a task or favor is asked of you, always make sure this is something you are able and willing to do. Never under any circumstances should you steal something or take anything that is not freely given. You will upset the owner or guardian of the treasure and you can be cursed or haunted by a wide variety of spirits. If you do not know if something is yours to have, then leave it.

Caves, Caverns, and Tunnels

When most people think of the Underworld, they think of a place that is filled with tunnels, caverns, and mysterious caves. Most of the Underworld is not like this at all, but there are places that match this description. Sometimes, the beginning journeyer will use an underground tunnel to get deep into the Underworld. Other times, tunnels will lead you from one of the Underworld "realms" to another. You do not always need to use tunnels, but for some people it helps them travel more easily. You may discover caves that hold hidden treasures, magical items, and spirits and beings that prefer dark places. I will give a word of caution: knowing that there are spirits that prefer dark places, be aware that some of them are friendly and some of them are not. If you are unsure about these places, approach with caution and humility. Do not go barging into unfamiliar places. You may upset the spirit that lives there. This is never something we wish to do. Always be polite and courteous. We sometimes forget that spirits in the Underworld expect the same courtesies and we do. We would never enter someone's home unannounced and expect them to be nice to us. Always treat sprits as you would anyone else or how you would expect to be treated.

Stars, Planets, and Galaxies

The Underworld is sometimes considered the Upperworld in reverse; it is in essence inverted. This is not the same as the reverse of something, such as good being the reverse of evil, but rather a mirror reflection of the Upperworld. Thus, the Underworld can be perceived as having a night sky with stars and moons. It also has what is sometimes referred to as the "Underworld Sun." Some say it is dimmer than the sun in the Midworld, others say it is just as bright. It is interesting to note that scientists believe that when our Solar system was forming, everything was developing out of the debris of a star gone supernova and part of the star energy was caught, forming Earth's gravity, and part of Earth's inner core. I find it fascinating that many myths have a little bit of truth in them.

Fire

In the depths of the Underworld, you may find the Land of Fire. Just as in the depths of the Earth in our physical world we have our fiery mantle and core, so does the Underworld have a realm of fire. Fire in the Underworld may have a frightening effect on those who come from a Judeo-Christian background, bringing up tales and myths of the fiery torment of Hell. In myth and practical experience with Underworld energies, however, I have found that fire establishes magical boundaries and is used for purification and transformation. In a practical sense, when working with the dead in the physical world, fire transforms the body into ash, allowing for the spirit to longer be attached to the physical body. In all three worlds, fire may also represent spirit in a rarefied form.

Water

Water is universally associated with the Underworld. Part of it may be the fact that when you peer into still water you can see your own reflection. Ancient people may have wondered, "Is that me? My ghost? Or is the part of me that is in another world?" This is why water has also been considered a portal or gateway into the Underworld. In many of the landscapes in the Underworld there are numerous rivers, streams, oceans, and lakes. Large bodies of water were always mysterious to the ancients and hold a lot of magical power. Water may also represent the translucent dream state and the subconscious mind. The journey by water is to journey deeper into the Underworld mysteries. The Celts have many myths of the Otherworld journey via water. The Voyage of Bran tells of how Bran sets sell into the West only to be caught in the mysteries in the Otherworld.

In the Underworld itself, water is usually associated with knowledge and magical power. To drink of the water is to gain much power, but it is wise to listen to your spirit animal and guides on such matters. There are rivers in the Underworld that may cause you to forget. You may have to begin your quest all over again and re-learn what you have learned. There are also rivers that are made of acid and may damage your astral body. There is much magick and power in the watery places of the Underworld. It is important to learn as much about them as possible before we journey into situations that may have consequences. Psychologically, water also represents the subconscious and the fear of the unknown.

The Well

Wells go deep into the Earth and contain nourishing water that life very much depends on to thrive. In myth, the Earth has great healing powers. With the combination of water from the Underworld and the healing powers of Earth, the well becomes a place of great power. Wells are also a powerful entrance into the Underworld. From the viewpoint of ancient people, the Underworld was "below" and the well went down into the depths of the Earth where the Underworld was said to be. There are many stories of people falling into wells and landing in a strange world below. In Grimm's "Mother Holle," a young girl falls into a well only to find herself in the Underworld. There she discovers the home of Mother Holle and is instructed to do chores for the old woman. Upon returning to the above world, she is rewarded with gold. After seeing this, her lazy, greedy sister jumps in the well hoping to find gold as well. The sister is lazy and does not perform her chores well. Instead of gold, she is rewarded by being covered in pitch.

In the Underworld, wells have even greater power and wisdom. To drink from these wells usually grants the seeker great magical powers and wisdom. However, there is almost always a guardian who protects the well from those who are either uninvited or not ready for the well's power. In Nordic mythology, the sacred well at one of the roots of the World Tree is called Mimir's Well. The well is guarded by the great god Mimir. He can offer you great wisdom. However, as stated before, there is a price. Odin, the All-Father, went to the Well of Mimir seeking wisdom. It would be granted for the price of one of Odin's eyes. Now, All-Father's eye forever remains in the well seeing the great wisdom it contains.

To understand the well and water more fully, it is helpful to understand the Goddess Mysteries of the Underworld too. In Neopagan mythology, the Goddess is often symbolized by the chalice. The chalice symbolizes the womb and the creation of life. The water inside the chalice/womb is the healing and rejuvenating power of the Goddess herself. To drink of the chalice is to literally drink of the powers of the Goddess. This is where we get the Pagan mysteries of the Holy Grail.

Be warned, to drink from the Underworld can be life-changing indeed. The water from the sacred well can grant blessing, healing, and wisdom, but at times, the guardian may claim the seeker for themselves or as a new resident to the Realm of the Dead. Before drinking from the Underworld, find out what consequences there are for those who dare to drink.

Rivers

Rivers in the Underworld have a variety of purposes. In Greco-Roman myth, there is a river of "Forgetfulness" and a river of "Memory." These rivers are to ease the transition of the dead to their new state of being. They also serve to detach the dead from their formal earthly life. If one were to cling to the Midworld, then they may not find peace in the Realm of the Dead. Rivers also have a protective quality. Because they are usually moving, they sometimes keep undesirable entities away. At times they can have a sinister effect. The deeper you go into the Underworld the more mysteries are contained there. There are protective rivers that are "deadly" that keep unwanted beings away. In the Mayan tradition there is a River of Blood and a River of Pus. In Norse myth, there is a river named Slidh that you must cross to get to the hall of the Death Goddess Hel. Rivers are either seen as energies that go to and from the Underworld or are there to test the traveler. Never step into a river. You never know what you will find.

Charon is the ferryman from the Greco-Roman tradition. Once a spirit of the dead finds themselves at the entrance of Hades, he ferries the spirit over the river to the other side. But he only does this if the spirit's body has been buried properly. This is usually done by burial with two coins, one on each eye; this represents money for the ferryman. Those who have not been buried properly are doomed to roam the outer reaches of the Underworld and the Midworld for a hundred years. Only then will they be ferried across. Charon is very stern. However, he has been known to make exceptions in extraordinary circumstances. In a similar fashion, Modgudh and Garm are the guardians of Hel's hall and only they decide who comes and goes in the land of the dead.

Oceans

Oceans surround the landscapes of the Underworld. They make boundaries around different "lands" and realms of existence. Oceans in the Underworld keep the beings of that realm exactly where they are. It is possible to sail on top of the oceans and swim beneath them, but just as our own oceans are vast and dangerous, these oceans are even more so. There are giant monsters and entities that rarely wish to be disturbed. There's a reason these oceans keep the residents of that land safe where they are. In the "Epic of Gilgamesh", Gilgamesh grieves for his dead friend, Enkidu. He set out on a quest to find the gods of death to restore his friend back to life. By the sea, a maiden named Siduri instructs Gilgamesh to travel the ocean of death to find the ones with the secrets of eternal life.

Oceans are also entrances into the Underworld itself. Many myths speak of the Underworld as being full of water and it takes a boat or ship to get all the way through. In the Celtic tradition, if one sailed west, one would find themself on the islands of the Otherworld and the lands of the dead. From a historical standpoint, seafaring was very dangerous, and many men died from shipwrecks to find themselves forever in the watery Underworld.

Illusions

When journeying into the Underworld, there are many illusions you may encounter. What this means is that what you perceive can be a trick, a mask, or a façade. The Underworld is full of spirits that look like demons but are really gods, or monsters that take the shape of harmless animals and other creatures. This can become very confusing and frustrating to a new journeyer, sometimes to the extent that the journeyer feels that the Underworld is nothing but a trick of the mind or just a figment of the imagination, or sometimes even a cruel joke of the universe. We must remember that the Underworld is a place of energy and does not follow the same rules as our physical Universe. So, yes, sometimes it is like a dream. But for this reason, the Underworld is all the more powerful. One reason that things are not what they always appear to be is that we are not ready for the teachings and the power of the Underworld. Another reason is that by receiving the information too early, you may not be ready to use its full power, or you may hurt yourself or others. There are beings in the Underworld that are very powerful, and you do not want to encounter them until you are ready. Usually, illusions and gates are put in place so that you encounter only the Otherworlds that you are ready for.

The best thing to do is continue journeying and try not to become frustrated when you encounter the strange illusions. Take comfort in the thought that when you are ready for things, they will be revealed to you. I can tell you from personal experience it is better that way. You do not want unwanted things following you back to your home. Not every entity can nor should be friended, but neither should they be banished. "There are more things in heaven and earth" to quote the immortal bard. In my journeys through the Underworld, I once ventured into territory I was unfamiliar with, and perhaps I traveled further than I should have. I sensed a strange entity nearby. I decided to leave and return to my physical body. Upon waking up the strange entity was in my living room as plain as day! I used my intuition and understood that it meant no harm to me. Because I traveled further than any book had described to me, I had no idea how to send the entity back to the Underworld where it belonged. The strange creature spoke no language that I could speak. It took me the better part of the night to get the entity back to its home. It was with the help of my gods and ancestors that I was able to do so. Luckily, the strange entity was harmless. I was lucky. But what if it was not? That is one of the best lessons I have ever learned about traveling further than needed!

Places of Oracles

There are several ways you can use the Underworld as an oracle. One of the ways is through a practice called Seidr. This is a Nordic shamanic practice of journeying to the Underworld to speak with the gods of the dead or the dead themselves. In this practice, one uses the trance technique of swaying and quaking to induce an altered state. Once this is done, the Seidmadr or Seidkona journeys down into the depths of Hel to visit the realm of the dead. With the permission of Hela, they gain access to a certain member of the dead who possess the power of prophecy. Being that events begin in the Upperworld then go down to the Underworld before manifesting on the Middleworld, the spirits have a firsthand view of what is to come to the Middleworld. The Seidr person could also visit Hela herself and ask for prophecy, although this is something that should not be undertaken by people who are not expertly trained in this art.

Another way to gain access to prophecy would be through the Well of Mimir. As we remember, the head of the wise Mimir is in a well that accesses the Underworld. Mimir has the power to foresee all things to come. It is a very dark and unnerving place and those who are clever and brave enough may ask Mimir his questions. Be warned, he will ask for a heavy price for the wisdom he offers. There are also the Three Norns who are said to know the past, present, and future. These are similar to the Three Fates in Greco-Roman myth but have some differences. The three Norns are named Urdr (That which was), Verdandi (That whish is), and Skuld (That which is becoming). They are three great beings who weave the intricate tapestry of Fate. In this tapestry, the magical thread contains everything that was, that is, and that will be for everything in the Universe, even the fate of the gods. The Norns are not as easy to get information about the future from as you might think, however, so be warned.

You may also observe the coming future of events firsthand. One you become proficient in journeying; you may find places where you may perceive the future. Sometimes you stumble upon these places; but often, gods and spirits will reveal these areas of oracles once you have proven your motives. You cannot fool the gods. If you are acting for the good of your own transformation and the good of your community, the spirits will help you. If not, they will either tell you to turn back or send you on a wild goose chase. There are many stories of Underworld entities setting the journeyer on the wrong track. It is best to remember, before seeking oracles in the Underworld, to give offerings to the spirits and gods that you wish to commune with. Even then, this is no guarantee that they will help you.

Realm of the Dead

One of the more commonly known places of the Underworld is the Realm of the Dead. It is here that those who have died and passed beyond the veil reside. It is not a place of suffering, but rather a place of peace, rest, and community. The Realm of the Dead in the Underworld is not a scary place and is not set aside from the Upperworld or realm of the Gods to punish or to keep the people there separate or segregated. The dead are in a different "land" or "world" from the gods and the living because they were simply possessed of a different energy. The energies of the gods vibrate on a much higher refined divine frequency than the living or the dead. Because of this "higher" vibration pattern of the energies, the gods are said to live in the Upperworld. The dead vibrate on a "lower" vibration, so they dwell in the Underworld. There is no judgment on whether the Underworld is better or worse than the higher worlds. In Greco-Roman mythology, Hades is the ruler of the dead, not out of punishment, but because the Underworld is large and contains many riches that lie beneath the earth. In a spiritual sense, Hades rules the dead because it is cosmically ordained by forces greater than he. Simply put, it was the "right" thing to do. They are simply different, nothing more, nothing less. Being a spirit of the dead does not make one any more or less holy than the gods themselves. In fact, some cultures place more sanctity and importance on the Ancestors than they do on the gods. In China, the Ancestors were worshiped above and before the gods. It was custom to give offerings of incense and prayers to the Ancestors. This was important because the Ancestors would provide good luck and financial fortune for the family. In his book *The Deities are Many*, Jordan Paper says:

"The fortunes of the family are dependent on the well-being of the dead members of the family, and the fortunes of the clan on its larger set of dead. Unless the dead are kept well, they will not have sufficient power to assist the family, and unless the dead are pleased, they may not care to help the family."

In Christianity, the belief is that when someone dies, their soul goes to Heaven so that they may spend eternity sitting next to their concept of God. Christianity is a monotheistic religion, and they believe that there is no other place in the Universe other than Heaven that can you find God. The only other alternative is Hell, a place that is believed to exist "under" all of God's creation. In Neo-paganism, we believe in many gods; so whatever world you choose to go to, there will be a god who rules that place. Many Pagans do not believe in a place of punishment. However, there are pagan philosophers, such as Plato (427-347 BCE), who believed in places where a soul would suffer torment for a period of time if it had been wicked in the Middleworld. This seems to serve the function of purifying the soul before it is ready to ascend to the Middle Realm and live a new life. In his book *The Republic*, Plato tells the "Myth of Er". In the myth, Er dies and sees two great chasms. One going to heaven and the other going into the earth. Those who did good deeds traveled into heaven, but those who did evil deeds when into the earth for penance and purification:

"For every wrong he has done to anyone a man must pay the penalty in turn, ten times for each, that is to say, once for every hundred years, this being reckoned as the span of man's life. He pays, therefore, tenfold retribution for each crime, and so for instance those who have been responsible for many deaths, by betraying state or army, or have cast others into slavery, or had a hand in any other crime must pay tenfold in suffering in each crime."

Similarly, in Tibetan Buddhism, people believe in the purification of souls after death. What this means is that the place of "hell" is more of a place where the illusions, misdoings, and self-deceptions are removed to make the soul ready for either reincarnation or to join the Realm of the Dead permanently. There are many versions of this place. While researching different cultures and spiritual philosophies you can see some similarities in the Land of the Dead from culture to culture. They all seem to have aspects of healing and renewal, as well as dark places of despair. In my research on the dark places of the Land of the Dead, it is rare that the gods place the Ancestors in such places. It is the fears and guilt of the dead that seems to impose self-judgment on each individual person. I believe these dark places were created so that the dead would have a place to purge and cleanse themselves of these dark energies.

Some people may be confused as to why there are so many different versions of the afterlife. If there are so many recordings in different mythologies about the Realm of the Ancestors, does that mean that only one is right and the rest are wrong? Does this mean that they are all wrong? In my experience, the answer to this question is that they are all correct! It is the collective consciousness, or in some cases the collective un-conscious that affects the Underworld realms of the Ancestors. Because many people throughout the ages believe something to be true, then the collective power of their minds have a direct effect on the Underworld. It has already been established that the universe or multi-verse is made of energy. Everything from the most "spiritual" essence to the most physical substance is made of energy. Energy is influenced by our minds. This is how we can do magick and energy work. Energy follows thought. In this way, the places where the dead dwell is influenced by that culture. Of course, there is the theory that says that the gods created these places, and we simply are a product of these creations. But this poses the question, did the gods create man or did man create the gods? I personally believe that it is both. I believe that we influence each other. Our environments also influence us. In our minds we create a place that is both beautiful and scary, depending upon what our culture and environment dictates. In quantum physics, scientists are theorizing about the existence of parallel universes. Most of their theories have come from experiments involving protons that are in one place, disappear (possibly to a different universe all together), and then instantly appear someplace else without a direct path. It is also interesting to note that physicists have discovered that photon particles change and alter simply because we are observing them or on some level we are thinking about that energy. There is also the theory that if black holes in space suck in all forms of light, then it must go somewhere because energy cannot be destroyed, only altered. So where does it go? A parallel universe? All of these are fascinating theories that may help us understand some of the complexities of the Underworld.

The realms of the dead are based on the environments that the residents are used to. If you come from a culture that lives in the desert and has sandstorms for days on end without rain, then most people from your culture will believe that the afterlife looks like this, and that is what the afterlife will be. The same is true for cultures from the mountains or rainforests. However, the lives of ancient people were usually very harsh. The priests of these harsh cultures envisioned an afterlife that was free from hardship and instead filled with blessings and luxuries. In the ancient past, religion and the hope of a better afterlife was big business. For many people, this hope for something better after death was all they had. In turn, this is one of the reasons Hell came into being. If the Christian priests could convince people that if they did not worship as they were instructed, then the promise of an easy and peaceful afterlife would be forfeit. Another reason that the concept of Hell as being a place torture and pain comes from the Greco-Romans in the ideal of Tartarus. Tartarus is a place in the Underworld where the Titans are imprisoned because of their destructive nature. It is also a place where some of the dead who caused great suffering to humanity were kept.

Because of mythology, we sometimes envision the places of the afterlife to look the same as they are described in the ancient stories. Remember that when these stories were told, they were very modern places at the time. They told of landscapes that were similar to what the people knew. They spoke of temples and dwelling places that were like their city structures, but which were more magnificent. The most important thing they spoke of was the reuniting with family and friends that had died before. This was a main selling point of the afterlife.

This poses another question: if this is true and each culture has their own version of the afterlife, do they exist in the same place or separately? This question I believe can be answered in the following manner. As we have been discovering, the Otherworlds, especially the Underworld, do not follow the same laws as the physical universe does. Our minds are used to compartmentalizing everything. This goes in this box and that goes in that box. The easiest way to describe it, based on my own experience, is like the layers of an onion. They all exist at the same place but in different levels of existence or dimensions. And yet, this is still only partially correct. Truthfully, I have not found the Underworld do be so easily sectioned off. Even with its many landscapes and places, understanding of the Underworld is not so easily "cut and dried." Energy always follows the path of least possible resistance. So, I believe that both answers are correct. They are in different places separately and yet are in the exact same place at the exact same time.

Beginning Your Underworld Journey

When you first begin journeying into the Underworld, you will encounter strange and wonderful things. When you become more adept at journeying, if you travel deep enough you will encounter things that are both healing and harmful. For now, you will not have to worry about dangerous entities too much. The spirits you will first encounter are those found closest to our world here in Middle Earth. They are those Underworld entities that usually have had dealings with humans in some way before. Any odd or frightening spirits you find during your first initial travels are not trying to harm you. They want to challenge your worthiness, especially when they can tell that you are a beginner. They know this by looking at your energy signature. During your first journeys you may be filled with a sense of wonder and fear. This is normal and the entities will be able to pick up on your emotions. This is another way they will be able to see that you are new to the Underworld. It is better in shamanic journeys to have a goal or intention when traveling through the Underworld. Some say it is mandatory. There are a couple of reasons for this. First, as with any journey, you want to have direction. You may not know exactly where you are going, but you know that there is a goal. The goal will help focus your mind so your subconscious will be better equipped to help direct you. This will also put out a call to any spirits that are willing to help and guide you on your journey. Many goals are quite simple ones, such as: "to meet my Ancestors," or "to map the Underworld," or "to find healing." All these things are good and purposeful, and, as simple as they are, can lead to profound insights and revelations. I personally travel to the Underworld to work with the Ancestors and seek healing for myself and others.

When you begin, you may only see deep caves and ancient forests with large flora. This is common; however, you are barely at the entrance of the Underworld. I have seen many workshops on the Underworld journey where beginners experience finding two-story tall sunflowers and giant bees. This is nothing unusual. You are definitely in the Underworld, but you have not gone that far. I have found that your hopes and fears influence your experiences, especially in the beginning. It is common to see exactly what you think you are going to see. This may make you ask yourself if you are imagining everything. Yes, you are. And no, you are not. You are doing the work correctly. To me, this is a sort of an astral "safety net". Your mind and spirit need to know that journeying to the Underworld is safe, so your mind interprets its experiences in a very non-threatening way. I think students would be scared off if on their first couple of experiences in the Underworld they found some ancient being with three heads and giant teeth! The funny thing is that most spirits that look menacing are powerful helpers. Even in the Underworld, we should never judge something by how it appears! Things that look frightening or strange are usually our own mental projections of our fears placed upon the energy of a being. If we do not understand something, or do not want to deal with a particular energy, our minds may interpret the entity as looking hostile and threatening. This is not to say that there are not hostile entities in the Underworld. There certainly are, but as I have said before, if we are cautious and treat everyone, we encounter in the Underworld with respect we will generally be all right. In the unlikely event that you do encounter something hostile in your first initial journeys there a few things you could do. First, you could simply leave and end your journey. Afterward, I would purify my working space with cleansing smoke. You could also try speaking with the entity. It is better to understand why the entity is hostile. All situations in the Underworld are opportunities for learning. I would not try to banish or send an energy attack at an entity at this point. Remember, you are in their home. You are the intruder. By entering the Underworld with an open mind and an open heart, you will gain many spirit helpers and have many wonderful adventures.

Where The Dead Live

In myths, the dead are taken to the Underworld to live in spirit. This is a place that is well protected from outsiders and keeps the dead safe within this eternal place of rest. The descriptions of the Land of the Dead vary from culture to culture. As I have said before, we see the Underworld and the land of the dead however we think it will look. In many cosmologies, it is taught that the Underworld is a reflection of the Midworld. So, it is only natural that the Land of the Dead reflects our daily lives here. For our Underworld journeys, the Land of the Dead has many mysteries and spiritual wisdom for us to discover. I encourage you to travel to your ancestral Land of the Dead as well as those of other cultures. For some of us, there is sadness hovering over these places. This sadness is ours and we must understand that this feeling is our own and not of the Ancestors. The Ancestors are in a place of healing and rejuvenation. We can sometimes feel sad that they are there because we miss them. Honor your feelings, but at the same time, try to understand that this is where they need to be. There is a cosmic order to things.

The Spirit Wife (Native American Zuni)

A young man's wife had died and he could not stop grieving for her. He sat by her grave, poured sacred corn pollen on the ground, and painted an eagle plume in red. The spirit of the wife came out of the grave and sat down beside him telling him that she was happy in the Land of the Dead. He did not want to be without her, and he was determined to follow her back. She finally agreed to let him follow her. She explained to him that he could see her spirit at night, but during the day she would be invisible and that to follow her, he must tie the red plume into her hair to see where she was going. He agreed.

During the day, the man could not see his wife, only the red plume floating in the air. He followed the plume by day and rested by night. At night, his spirit wife was beside him. For many days, he followed the plume, and he began to grow very tired. Still, he persisted after her. One day the plume walked over a great canyon, just floating into the air. "Wait!" the man said, but the red plume floated to the other side. So, the man climbed down the canyon's side and crossed it. He then began to climb the other side when he got stuck. He could not go forward or backwards. A little squirrel decided to help him and took a nut from his mouth. He stuck it into the side of the canyon and commanded the nut to grow. Out sprang a tree from the side of the canyon and the man was able to climb up to the other side where the red plume was waiting for him.

The man followed the plume to a large dark lake. The plume went down deep into the waters. This was the place of the dead. He despaired because he knew he could not follow the plume. He sat in his grief. An owl saw that the man was crying and decided to help him. The owl told the man to follow him to a cave in the nearby mountain and he would help him. Once, in the cave, the owl was met by his relatives. The owl took off his owl clothing revealing the spirit of a man. He made a magical medicine bag. The bag was sleep medicine. The owl spirit explained that the medicine would put him to sleep and send him to a faraway place and that when he awoke, he was to go to the anthill to await his wife. The owl spirit warned the man that he must have patience or grief would strike him again.

The owl spirit and his relatives flew down into the lake and into the Land of the Dead. There, they used sleep medicine to make the guardians fall asleep. They then retrieved the spirit of the wife. The man awoke and went to the anthill and found his wife in full flesh. But again, he was warned to be patient. They were told to journey back to the land of their birth. Only there, would the wife be fully alive. But he was warned that if he should touch her before they returned home, she could not stay with him. For four days they journeyed back home. On the forth night, before returning home, the wife fell asleep. The husband could not wait anymore! He reached down to touch her, and she instantly awoke! She faded away into spirit and returned to the Land of the Dead. An owl was in a nearby tree. "I told you to be patient!" he said. The owl explained that is was just as well, because if no one ever journeyed to the Land of the Dead, then the Earth would be too crowded.

Hades/Elysian Fields

Hades is the Land of the Dead in the Greco-Roman pantheon. Hades is named for the Underworld itself and the god Hades that rules there. Hades was originally called "The House of Hades" but was shortened to Hades. The Creator Gods of the Greco-Romans divided the Universe into three parts. The Upperworld ruled by Zeus/Jupiter, the Midworld ruled by Poseidon/Neptune, and The Underworld ruled by Hades/Pluto. In the eyes of the ancients, this division kept the Universe in cosmic balance. Hades had many different landscapes and levels. To get to Hades, a spirit of the dead had to cross the River Styx guided by a dark ferryman named Charon. Once you were taken to the entrance of Hades, your spirit was then met by the three-headed dog, Cerberus. The role of this giant creature was to keep the souls of the dead in and the living out. Once within the gates of Hades, one encountered the dark spirits that caused disease and death. Modern spiritualists would call these entities demons, but the ancient Greco-Romans did not view dark spirits in the same way as we do now. It was at the entrance that these dark spirits waited to be released so that they could cause sickness, harm, and death among the living. As we enter through this part of Hades, these dark spirits may be curious about us, but they will not harm you. If we maintain a healthy lifestyle, we will have a bright healthy aura, and entities cannot "latch" on to us. If we are in a place in our lives that we have bad habits and making poor health choices, then we may have a weekend aura that may cause lower spirits to cling on to us. If you are unsure whether you have a lower spirit clinging on to you, purify yourself with incense or a bath upon your return to the physical plane.

There is a river of Memory and a river of Forgetfulness in Hades. The purpose of these rivers is to make the blessed spirits of the dead forget their troubles and loved ones in the Midworld so that they can remain happy in the fields of the blessed. For those who did wrong in life, they would remember their crimes for all eternity.

There were many paths in Hades that held the sorrows of the dead. At the end of one path were the spirits of those who were killed because of love, either by suicide, scorned lovers, or simply dying of unrequited love. On another path, were the eternal battles of the fallen soldiers. There was also a path for those who committed crimes in life and were not punished. Above these souls, boulders always threatened to crush them so that they would forever be on edge and unhappy. It is easy to see that these torments may have been put here by the souls' own making. In the Underworld, our beliefs, conscious or not, are manifested. This is one of the reasons we see the Underworld the way we think it will look like. If our guilt is overwhelming at the time of death, we will carry this guilt with us, and it may manifest as torments. But this will only happen if you are convinced, upon death, that you need to be punished. To me, this is one of the aspects of karma. You pay for your "sins" because you believe you must. These paths of Hades were a self-imposed punishment of sadness, grief, anger, and guilt. This is also one of the reasons that religions speak of living a good and pure life. In this way you do not put shackles on yourself once you cross over to the Underworld.

There is a place of the blessed people called the Elysian Fields. Priests, poets, lovers, songwriters, and anyone the gods favored spent eternity here. In some myths, the Elysian Fields are in Hades, and in others, the fields are in the far side of the Earth at the edge of the ocean —much like in the Celtic traditions about the Isles of the Dead. The Elysian Fields is a place of happiness, warmth, and bliss, and it has a sun, moon, and stars of its on. When one enters this wonderful place, they can see people dancing and feasting, playing sports, or simply strolling through the magnificent fields. This is a place where one often hears songs and poems being read.

There is a dark place in Hades called Tartarus. When one sees the edge of the cliff that leads down to this horrible place, it is said that it is as deep as Heaven is high above. Tartarus can be somewhat related to the Christian Hell and perhaps this is one of the sources where the Christians originally got the idea. Tartarus is a prison in the Underworld. It is a place where the wretched beasts such as the 50-headed Hydra is kept. It is also where the Titan race of gods is kept bound with divine chains so that they will never again cause chaos and havoc in the Universe.

The rulers of Hades are Hades himself and Persephone, his Queen. It should be noted that in ancient times, one never gave offerings to Hades because the thought was that by doing so you would invite Death into your home. Instead, you would give offerings to the lovely Persephone. It was she who walked among living people for six months out of the year and understood them. Hades was considered too far removed from us and his heart was thought to be cold. However, the beautiful and kind Persephone could melt his heart with only a glance. To give her offerings and win her favor was to win the favor of Hades. It is often said down in Hades that Hades could not deny any request made by his wife.

When I go down into Hades, the first part is usually the same. I astral project myself to the River Styx where I am met by Charon the ferryman. For a token, I am taken across the river to the gates of Hades. Cerberus is used to my comings and goings, so he does not bark or growl at me. He barely notices me and allows through. I'm sure he has more important things to do than worry about a living Spirit Walker going into Hades. Once inside, the caverns are vast and deep. I quickly make my way to the Realm of the Ancestors. The place of the Ancestors, from my experience, is not a place of gloom, but a place of bright colors and everyone is happy for the most part. I often say that the Ancestors are "living" their lives, but in this place, they happen to be dead. The Ancestors here are, of course, Greco-Roman with the occasional outsider who chose upon death to live their afterlife in this magical place. I always ask for an audience with Hades and Persephone when I am there. There are many tales of Hades being dark and brooding, but I rarely see him that way. I see him as a kingly father figure who protects the dead and keeps the Chthonic Gods safely secure. I once asked Hades why he keeps the dead in the Underworld, and he replied with this:

"I do not keep the dead here as prisoner. I keep them safe. The dead are my children as the living are the children of Zeus. Most other gods are too busy or have no need of the dead, but I would never cast them off. They are my people, my children, my friends. I would do anything for them."

Tartarus is also a place I like to visit. Sometimes Hades will escort me. I believe this to be out of protection for me rather than a formality. It makes him sad in some way that his own ancestors are kept locked up in the depths of the Underworld, but he knows the Universe cannot survive with them. Not just yet.

Hel, The Nordic World of the Dead

In Nordic cosmology, there are nine realms or "worlds". The worlds are pictured as rotating around an enormous ash tree, called Yggdrasil. There is a lot of lore on where the nine worlds are, but I take some liberties in their placement based on my own experience with the energies of these fantastic worlds. In the branches of the cosmic tree are the three Upperworlds: Muspelheim (the primal realm of fire), Asgard (realm of the Aesir gods), and Vanaheim (home of the Vanir gods). Rotating around the trunk of the cosmic tree are the three Middleworlds: Ljosalfheim (home of the Light Elves), Midgard (the physical world), and Jotunheim (the home of the Giants). In the roots of the Great Tree are the three Underworlds: Svartalfheim (the realm of the Dwarfs and Dark Elves), Helheim (the home of the Dead), and Niflheim (the primal realm of ice). The world of the dead is called Helheim or sometimes just Hel. The Christians took the Nordic Underworld world of Hel to represent their fiery world of torment that they now call Hell. To the Norse, Hel was not a place of torment at all, but a place for the dead to rejuvenate and rest.

When someone dies, they are sent to the Underworld realm of Hel, unless they die in battle. If a warrior dies in battle, then they are either chosen by Freya, the goddess of love, or Odin, the All-Father, to live in his great hall of Valhalla, the hall of the slain. Most of the Nordic people were not warriors so many went to live with the Goddess of Death, Hel or Hela. Hela is said to be half beautiful maiden and half rotting corpse. The poems and writings never tell which half is which. Some say the left side of her face is rotting while the other half is beautiful. Some say that from her waist up she is a beautiful maiden, but if you were to look under her robes you would see the rotting flesh from her waist down. I see her neither of those ways. When I journey down to the realm of Hel, Hela always appears as a beautiful Goddess of Death. However, as I speak with her, her form flickers back and forth between maiden and rotting corpse. It can be quite disconcerting if you are not prepared for it. I think she thinks it is quite fun to see journeyers in her realm become startled by her rotting corpse form. Hela is a gracious goddess and takes great care of the dead who come to her. She is the Mother Goddess of the Underworld and has vowed that all the spirits of the dead who come to her will be taken care of.

The world of Hel can be dark and dank in places. There are certainly parts of Hel that are dark, and many unsavory creatures are lurking about. There is fog everywhere and the inexperienced traveler can become quickly lost and confused. But if you journey to the land of the Ancestors, you will see a quiet place of light and happiness. The dead are kept in a place of beauty and peace. I am not sure if Hela created this wonderful place or the Ancestors did. However it happened, contrary to some of the poems written about this place, in my experience it is a place where the Ancestors are happy.

Traveling down to Helheim is one of my favorite places in the Underworld. Like the myths and legends say, things are not what they seem. I first find myself at the great golden bridge that crosses a river to the great hall of Hela. The hall, to me, looks more like a fortress than a Nordic hall, but this could just be my perception. Once I cross the bridge, the gate opens to a dark a gloomy castle. But because I have had many conversations with Hel, I know the secret of getting into the realm of the Ancestors. There is a veil that the traveler must open. Much like opening the veil in a pagan ritual. Once the veil is open a castle of light, music, and merriment is revealed. I often see men and women feasting at a great table. Why should those in Valhalla have all the fun? The great castle glows with such a wonderful shimmering light that I am often struck with the beauty of it all. Deep in the center of the great castle, there is a great cavern that goes to the depths below. If you look down, you will see that the great castle spirals down deep to the vastness of the Underworld. At the bottom is a great well used for magick, healing, and scrying. When I am wandering through the land of the ancestors here, I often enjoy the beautiful countryside and see many houses and cottages that the ancestors have. I can feel the presence of Hela in the land, trees, and mountains here. Her grace is everywhere. I recall one time when I found some of the villagers doing a ritual in Hela's name. "Was there a special occasion?" I asked. One of the ladies chuckled and replied, "In this place we honor the power and protection of Hela always. She is our mother, and we love her."

The Celtic Otherworld/Underworld

One of the most mysterious and strange aspects of the Underworld appears in the myths and legends of the Celts. The Celts did not necessarily see the Underworld in the way modern Neo-Shamans do. How they see the Underworld more closely relates to how indigenous people see it. The Underworld is on, in, and around the physical world. They call it The Otherworld. The Celtic Otherworld is not as neatly organized, or rather, separated, like the Three Shamanic Worlds we are used to hearing about. The Celtic Otherworld contains the lands of the dead, nature spirits and the gods. It is more complicated, and at the same time, easier to understand than it sounds. This is the beauty and the Mystery of the Celtic Otherworld. At times, the realms of the Celtic nature spirits, gods, and the dead bleed into one another and you can see how all three interact. In Celtic myth and story, we often see that the hero or heroine frequently stumbles across the Otherworld by accident. Usually, they are not looking for anything in particular. The myths are filled with castles that appear and disappear, faery hills that lead into the land of the fey, and places of the dead that lead straight to their realm. We will focus primarily on the journeys of the dead and the powers of the Otherworld in how it relates to our topic of the Underworld.

Anwyyn

This is the Celtic Underworld according to the Welsh people. It is similar to the idea of the Celtic Otherworld; however, the primary difference is that it is "underground" or in a place called The Hollow Hill. The Hollow Hill is a grave mound or burial mound that houses the bodies of people of importance. It is called "Hollow" because it is a sacred place of burial. In myth, it is also the "hollow" because there is another world inside, or rather, an entrance to another world. The grave mound is a portal or gateway to the Land of the Dead. It is also thought to be a gateway to the Welsh land of faery. It must be clear that the Ancestors and the Faery Folk are not the same entities as some authors suggest. They are two completely different families of beings. The grave mound is a portal to the Otherworld and not the Otherworld itself. Think of it like a "spiritual train station" that can take you to other destinations. Although, in Celtic belief, if one dies than they may live in the world of faery if they wish, and of course, if they faery folk allow it. There are indeed magical people who have Faery Blood or who have developed a deep kinship with the Faeries. When this happens, they may be invited to dwell among the Faeries after death. One such story relates to the author and folklorist, Rev. Robert Kirk. Kirk was a minister and folklorist in the 17th century in England. He wrote many stories and tales of the Fey folk and nature spirits. He would often visit the Faery mounds at night. One night, his body was found dead on such a hill. It was believed that the Faeries rewarded Kirk by taking him to live in the Faery mounds forever.

Anwyyn is a place of magick, renewal, and mystery. It is a place where the dead can rest and find peace. It does have a mystery of its own and there are many tales of people crossing a Hollow Hill and "accidentally" finding themselves in the Welsh Underworld. Once there, they find many strange things such as magical creatures and vast amounts of treasure. When they return to the world of the living, their lives are changed forever. Like most descriptions of the Underworld from around the world, Anwyyn is a place that tests the character and Will of each individual so that they may pass further into the depths of mystery and spiritual evolution . This is done because if you do not find your Divine Will and face your fears, you cannot tread deeper into the mysteries of death and the dark gods and spirits. Once you pass the tests, you are granted a greater understanding of the Universe and are able to take these invaluable teachings back to the Midworld to heal yourself and others; and perhaps to bring a greater understanding of the difficult (but inevitable) phenomenon of death to people.

Anwyyn is ruled by the Lord of the Dead, Gwyn ap Nudd. He has been described sometimes as a horned or a cloaked man who comes up through the Hollow Hill during the Wild Hunt to hunt down the souls of the dead that will forever dwell deep within his realm. Those who have "the sight" have told tales of seeing the Hill open up to release the terrifying figure of a cloaked man and his ghostly train looking for souls. This does sound scary indeed! In reality, it is more like a Father gathering his children to take them home in order for them to become happy in the Otherworld. The living often find the dead and the Underworld frightening because we fear death and its mysteries. We will not understand these dreadful things fully until it is our time to be gathered up by the Cloaked One, to be taken down into the Hallow Hill Forever, but we might gain a glimpse of these mysteries by exploring the Underworld.

Traveling into the Hollow Hill, for me, is quite different than traveling to Hades or Hel. By my home in Chicago, there is a manmade large hill (I suppose all Hollow Hills are manmade) named Cricket Hill.

I use the hill to connect astrally to all hallowed hills. Once connected to all hills, I use the hill as a gateway into the Underworld realm of Gwyn Up Nudd. When I arrive in the Underworld I am surrounded by a large forest. The forest is thick, and I know there are small family villages of ancestors deep within. Once I journey through the terrain, I am in a beautiful countryside which is in the middle ages. I see castles and fortresses all through the land. I journey further to the castle of Gwyn Up Nudd. His castle is also an entrance to star gates. The Ancestors who live in this land are happy and enjoy the comings and goings of the faery folk that sometime come to this part of the Underworld. I do not have a formal relationship with Gwyn Up Nudd like other Underworld Deities, but I am still invited to see parts of his Underworld that many do not get to see. I believe this is because he recognizes me to be a seasoned Underworld traveler. Or perhaps I humor him in some way. Either way, he shows me the enchanting land where he keeps the dead safe and happy.

The Celtic Islands of the Otherworld

The Irish Celts looked to the west at the setting sun and saw that the sun sank under the sea and brought about the night. Sea travel had many dangers such as storms, starvation, and getting lost out on the great ocean. The sea, to the Irish Celts was the Under/Otherworld itself, the Great Mystery. The sea seemed to be the edge of the world; a place the dead would go for their final journey into the arms of the Otherworld. To journey into the realm of the sea was to journey far into the mysteries of death.

The Irish Celts viewed the Otherworld as having many islands in the west. The further one traveled into the Islands of the Otherworld, the deeper into the mysteries one would go. There are many tales of heroes traveling to the islands of the Otherworld in search of knowledge, power, and adventure. There are also tales of heroes finding themselves off-course from their destination to be led into the depth of the Otherworld islands. These tales told of strange places, creatures, and people who taught the hero many valuable lessons about life, death, and spirituality.

When working with the Otherworld Islands, you may explore these wonderful places to find powerful and magical things such as the secrets of magical abilities, the powers of the ancestors, and the forces of the Otherworld just as the ancient Celtic heroes did. You may also use the islands to practice your own personal transition to the afterlife if you follow a Celtic cosmology. I find that the Celtic Islands of the Otherworld can seem familiar to the Underworld realms of the Egyptians, Maya, and Tibetans. The islands can be linked to the subconscious mind and we may "practice" the art of dying or simply learn about ourselves in this fantastic journey.

One popular Celtic myth is the "The Voyage of Bran Son of Febal." In this Irish saga, Bran meets a woman who is from the Otherworld. She tells him tales of the wonders of the islands there, of the joys and beauties, and the beautiful women that await him and his traveling companions if they will but journey there. Bran takes the journey by sea but is met by a man who calls himself Manannan, Son of Lir. The reader knows this man to be the Irish God of the Under/Otherworld and the Lord of the Dead. He tells Bran and his crew about the journey ahead. Most of the tale was written in the 1100s so it has a very Christian slant, referring to Christ, Adam, and Eve. Manannan tells Bran of the mysteries of the island Otherworld and the prophecy of he and his men. Bran sails further and finds the island of women where his men stay for a time. But as we have discussed before, time in the Under/

Otherworld is not like time in the physical plane. It has its own rules if it has any rules at all. Bran eventually convinces his men to sail back to the land they came from. One of his crewmen, excited about returning home, leapt from the ship onto the land where he immediately turned into ash. Bran and his men had not known how long they were in the Otherworld. Once returning home, time caught up with them. Bran turned his ship around and sailed back into the Otherworld islands to forever become part of the mysteries.

There is another tale called "The Voyage of Maelduinn." This tale is similar to "The Voyage of Bran," however, this story goes deeper into the mysteries of the Island Otherworld. The poem offers more details about each of the islands and the experiences of Maelduinn and his crew. The crew discovers islands with strange and wondrous creatures. They find giant ants, birds, cannibal horses, the Ancestors, mists, and the island of women. Each of these islands takes Maelduinn and his crew deeper and deeper into the Otherworld. Some of the islands and creatures they encounter are life threatening. Other islands are there to challenge their will. Once they overcome an island, their spirits are better prepared to face the next challenge of the Otherworld.

As you can see, the islands may be linked to the deeper realms of the Underworld and the subconscious. An interesting thought may be that the Underworld is the subconscious of the Source of all things, or the Creator. If we look back to the analogy that God/dess created the Universe in Their image, then perhaps our subconscious is linked to the subconscious of the Universe. I personally believe that when we journey into the Underworld, we are doing so astrally and spiritually as well as traveling into the depths of our own minds. I like to think of this as a mirror of the Universe. In Buddhist belief, all aspects of the world and the Universe are simply reflections of our own minds and emotions. I believe this to be also true with the three worlds. With this theory, it is safe to say that by journeying through the islands of the Celtic Otherworld we are also discovering the deeper mysteries of ourselves and aspects of our deeper psyche. The entities we discover in the Underworld appear however we hope or fear them to be. Remember, energy is energy. It is through our personal mental lenses that these entities appear the way that they do. However, many people who have never spoken to each other will return from an Underworld journey with a similar description of the same entity, god, or spirit. One reason is that our culture has many of the same myths, beliefs, and experiences. For example, when we think of a beautiful woman, many American men may conjure up the image of a slender blond with large breasts. Thus, in the Underworld, when a spirit wants to portray themselves as a beautiful woman, the spirit may appear as a slender blond with large breasts. When other people from around the world think of someone beautiful, the image will be different than what is considered standard American beauty. The important thing here is not to dwell on what spirits should look like, but what they look like to you and what teachings and lessons are you learning from it.

I will say that not all lessons that present themselves need to be learned right away. There are times when the lessons in the Underworld come about it is because the energies want you to begin the process of learning and growing as a spiritual being. Some lessons take a lifetime to learn. Go at the pace you feel is right for you. If you are working with a teacher or a group, discuss what is happening with the other people you are working with and come up with a plan of action.

Exercise: Exploring the Underworld

1. Lie comfortably and take a deep breath. Begin to relax your body, emotions, mind with each passing breath.

2. State your intention to explore the realms of the dead. You can pick anyone from any culture you like. I would advise reading some of the myths and stories before you take on your journey.

3. Visualize a bright light beginning at your feet and spiraling clockwise, spiral up the entirety of your body.

4. Energetically feel your astral body being transported to your destination.

5. Once you feel you have arrived at your destination, see the spiraling light unravel itself going from your head down to your feet, revealing your destination.

6. Enjoy your Underworld journey. Remember to be polite and gracious to anyone or anything you meet. If you come up to an impasse, try to go around or try again another day. If any offerings are required ask yourself if you are willing to give the expected offering. If so, give it astrally in the Underworld. Once you return home remember to give the offerings in the physical plane. You can leave it on your altar, on the land, or in a lake, river, or ocean.

7. To return home, simply visualize the spiraling light again (steps 3-5).

Place of Rejuvenation

The Underworld is not only a place of the dead and great, powerful beings. It is also a place of healing, rejuvenation, and renewal. There are many myths of the Underworld containing places that heal the sick and purify the body of disease. It is a place of transformation. The most common theme throughout many cultures is the ability of the Underworld to take a person, spirit, or god and help them evolve into something better and greater than they were when they first started their Underworld journey. In almost all cultures, the soul of a person enters the Underworld and is sent on a series of quests. Each quest is literally a test of the person's integrity, honor, love, and valor. As one goes through the Underworld, each quest is more challenging than the next. This is especially true for the Egyptian and Mayan cosmologies. But it is also interesting to note that the Egyptian and Mayan cultures that were among the world's first to create large-scale buildings for the dead to be placed in. The purpose of these quests is to see what the person's spirit is made of. These journeys that the hero must make are designed in such a way to mold the soul. In almost all the stories concerning Underworld tests, the hero does not even know how strong he or she really is until they have defeated the challenges they most feared.

There are many places in the Underworld where the hero is able to eat and drink magical food and water to restore themselves back into health. In the myth of King Arthur, he is taken to the Otherworldly Isle of Avalon so that he may be restored back to health. However, in the story, he must remain in Avalon as a magical hero until Britain needs him the most. It is often interesting to note that when the Underworld grants you favors or magical power there is almost always a certain amount of energy exchange expected in return. In some myths, the spirits or gods ask the hero to go on a journey to retrieve some magical item. Other myths tell of how the spirits of the Underworld ask the hero to use their new powers in the name of the Underworld or certain gods.

The Underworld is a powerful place for healing and transformation. It is important to realize that the more you travel through the Underworld, the more interested and invested in you that the gods and spirits become, and the more they will want to help you with your spiritual development. As a rule, I never accept a gift from a god or entity I am not familiar with. Myths are full of tales of heroes who blindly accept gifts and powers without understanding what was going to happen to them. The hero would later find out that the gift was either too powerful for them to manage properly, or it was a curse in disguise. J.R.R. Tolkien's *Lord of the Rings* is a great example of this. In the story, nine great kings were given magick rings that promised power but would later only serve the purpose of evil by enslaving them to the Dark Lord who assisted in the making of the rings.

The best way to approach this situation is to ask the spirit or god exactly what is going to happen when the gift is accepted. They will not take offense to questions such as these as long as you are polite! If you do not understand or are unwilling to perform the expectation, then it is wise to decline the gift. However, if the powers of the gift are something you are able and willing to do, I see no harm in accepting the gift. When in doubt, ask the advice of your personal Ancestors, spirit animal, and spirits.

Exercise:
Finding Your Underworld Place of Healing

1. Use the previous exercises on astral projection and journeying to enter the Underworld.
2. Find your Midworld Center.
3. Call upon your Spirit animal guide
4. Visualize or find an Underworld entrance and ask your spirit animal to lead you down into the Underworld to find a place of healing and rejuvenation.
5. Follow your spirit animal down into the Underworld. Again, it can appear as if you are going through the vast roots of the World

Tree, tunnels deep into the Earth, staircases down, or even a giant slide. You may use any means that works for you.

6. Once in the Underworld, again ask your spirit animal to lead you to a place of healing and rejuvenation. You may also call upon your Underworld teacher to show you the way.

7. At this point, you may see great oceans, rivers, wells, forests, fires, or caverns. You may even be led to a castle, cottage, or some other dwelling—perhaps even one that has been described or which you have read about from the mythologies above. Usually, places of healing have a guardian or guide of some sort. Explain your intentions to heal and learn about healing to the guardian. There may be times when the guardian asks for payment or a favor. This is not always the case. If the payment is coins, leave some coins for the spirit in the physical world. If it is a favor, make sure you are able and willing to perform the favor in the time requested. If you are not able to make the payment or favor, kindly say so and ask your spirit animal and teacher to find you another place of healing.

8. The best places of healing are ones that you are led to that are "just for you." No payment or favor necessary. Remember this place. Perhaps give it a name. You can come back to this place whenever you choose for healing.

9. There are times when the totem and teacher cannot or will not take you to a place of healing. This is not a punishment or a "failure" in your journeying. It may simply mean that you must learn and experience more before you are given this wonderful gift.

10. Once you have found your healing place, thank your totem and teacher and give offerings.

11. Journal about your experience.

The Six Bardos

In Tibetan Buddhism, the cosmology is broken up into Bardos. Bardo means "in-between" or can mean a duration of time in the universe. There are six Bardos.

1. The Natural Bardo of This Life
2. The Bardo of Dream
3. The Bardo of Meditation
4. The Painful Bardo of Dying
5. The Luminous Bardo of Dharmata
6. The Karmic Bardo of Becoming

Each Bardo is intended for spiritual and Karmic teachings and lessons. In Buddhist philosophy, the goal of each individual is "liberation." Liberation in the Buddhist sense is to liberate one's self from the Karmic wheel of life, death, and rebirth. Many of those liberated, having attained Buddha consciousness, join with the supreme deity. Some of those liberated reincarnate to enjoy a life free of hardships, while others return to become gurus, teachers, and healers.

I believe that it would only benefit the student of magick, death, and healing to learn about the Bardos and learn each karmic lesson that each one has to offer. It is interesting to me that Buddhists believe that the Otherworld is pure energy and the experiences that we have in each of the Bardos is a creation of our own minds, spirits, and emotions. We may dwell in a place of bliss and love or a place of hell and torment, depending on how well we are able to control our thoughts and emotions, especially our fears. This is not to say that the spirits of the Universe do not press us to learn and grow even more. But how we do so, is up to us. This resonates with me in the sense that there is no punishment in the Otherworlds, only opportunities for growth and evolution. Our soul, or spirit, is designed to evolve and grow; to find "enlightenment". Our soul is programmed to seek out opportunities for spiritual growth. It may be through suffering or through life experience. How we see these experiences is completely up to us.

The Natural Bardo of This Life

This is the Earth plane. It is the life that we are living now. This Bardo creates many opportunities to learn, evolve, and grow from daily living. If one has Karma to work off from a previous life, then this is a wonderful time to do so. Buddhist scripture teaches of a life lived of virtue, meditation, devotion to deity, and good deeds create good energy and Karma so that at the time of death it will be easy to recognize the energies of wisdom and deity so that they may become liberated.

The Bardo of Dream

This Bardo is our dream state during sleep. This can be a gateway into the Bardo of Dharmata (the Otherworld) but is not the Otherworld itself. It is here that the dedicated student of Buddhism may learn how to become lucid in their dreams and learn to control the energy (astral) body. When this is perfected, it is easy to navigate through the Otherworld after death and discover the energies of wisdom and deity so that they may become liberated. This is a discipline usually passed from teacher to student, however, some people who have had several lives may remember the skill of the dream Bardo.

The Bardo of Meditation

This Bardo is the state of mind and consciousness during meditation. Through discipline and self-mastery, we can learn how to free ourselves from attachment, move beyond false ego, and learn to become virtuous and have an open heart. When this is perfected, fear and delusion of the subconscious are conquered. When we die, fear and delusions of the Earth Bardo are manifested in the Bardo of Dharmata. When we conquer fears, it is easy to navigate through the spirit world and recognize wisdom and deity.

The Painful Bardo of Dying

This Bardo is the process of dying itself. It is said that dying begins when we become aware that time is short, and preparations must be made. It is here that attachments to material things are released. It is also a time to practice forgiveness for those people who have hurt you and to ask forgiveness from those you have hurt. It is the time to clear out negative energies and prepare your mind for the journey ahead. One also practices for the final thought at the point of death. If a person's feelings at death are negative, then they will find themselves in a negative place; if positive, then a positive place. At the point of death, the physical and energetic properties of the body dissipate, and the consciousness (mind) goes on to the next Bardo.

The Luminous Bardo of Dharmata

This is the Otherworld itself. In this Bardo the spirit is faced with his or her own mind and subconscious. The spirits, or Buddhas, appear in many forms and it is up to each individual to recognize the deities and join with them. If one has much fear, delusion, and bad karma, they will misunderstand the fierceness of the gods as evil and they will stay away from them. It is only through recognizing the Buddhas for what they are that someone finds liberation. This Bardo gives several opportunities for the dead to find liberation. As the days progress, the spirits become more and more fierce so that they are perceived as monsters and demons.

For the Buddhist, they literally create their own hell. This is done because the energies of this Bardo are trying to get the dead to give in to fear and find liberation. After many days, if the dead person has not found liberation, then they will journey to the next Bardo.

The Karmic Bardo of Becoming

This Bardo is also in the spirit world, but its purpose has changed. Instead of being liberated, the focus turns to reincarnation. The idea is that because there was so much negativity, fear, and lack of virtue, it will take the spirit another life to learn to be virtuous and not fearful. There are several ways this can happen. Different colored lights will appear. The white lights are the top heavens where the deities live, the red lights are the lower heavens where the jealous gods live, the blue lights are where the humans live, the green lights are where the animals live, the yellow lights are where the hungry ghosts live, and the pale grey lights are the hell worlds where the demons live. According to your thoughts, actions, and deeds, you will be attracted to the appropriate lights. It is said that the blue lights of the world of humans are best to work off negative karma and learn virtue, but there are lessons in each world that will teach liberation.

When you begin your Underworld journeys you will see many strange yet wonderful things. Myths from different cultures will give different examples of how to enter the world below. There may be differences, but they are all equally as valid. There is the traditional view of Neo-shamanism that the Underworld is entered through the roots of the great world tree that take you into a spiritual Universe below. That is certainly a good way to begin, but there are many other ways to enter the Underworld. Once there, the journey may seem odd and disorienting; but by practicing, your journey you will become an one as an accomplished spirit worker indeed. As we are learning, the Underworld has terrain that is much like ours here in the Midworld. But do not be fooled. This is a place where what you thought was up is really down and vice versa. The dead are here, and many cultures tell their stories. Some of these places are beautiful and some may never want to leave, but then again, perhaps they may not be able to. The realms of the dead are rarely ventured to for a reason. However, these places also have treasures of wisdom, power, and our loved ones long gone. As we go forward in this book, we will see all the wonder and adventure these places have waiting for us.

3
The
Hell
Worlds

The Hells

Most of the Western world is used to hearing the word "Hell." We know from Christian literature that Hell is a place of torment and burning for all eternity. We know that Hell is the dwelling place of evil beings. We know that Hell is a place we want to avoid at all costs. From what we learn from Christian mythology, it is a place that has no purpose except to punish. Upon reading myths from other cultures, we can see that the authors who have translated the myths into English borrowed our English word "Hell" to describe the places in their cosmology that are places of purification and testing grounds for future existence on the material plane. Clearly, there is a vast difference in meaning here.

Some cultures believe that for each person, life is meant to be an evolution of the spirit/soul and a time to learn lessons. These philosophies are well aware that our human minds and bodies must go through life on their own paths with both triumphs and failures. Most cultures do not believe in the concept of sin, but do believe that self-doubt, sadness, anger, and jealousy leave negative energy on the soul/spirit. This energy must be purified before the person can join the

Ancestors and gods in the Realm of the Dead. This purification is done through traveling in spirit to the hells and going through trials and tests. This is part of the "Hero's Journey" that we talked about in the previous chapters. The hero journeys through the Hells as part of his adventure to bring himself empowerment and spiritual evolution.

Some people who go through these trials have been studying spirituality for years. They have read the myths and learned from books and teachers. These people easily go through the trials and quickly move on to be with their Ancestors. Other people who have quite a bit of negativity imprinted on their spirit/souls have a harder time with the trials. Sometimes they must spend a great deal of time with the trials trying to make their way through their specific "hell." Sometimes, they do not make it through the first time, and have to try many times before they are successful in their quest.

It is important to realize that it does not matter how much life experience someone has had at this point. Nor does it matter how many "bad" things the person has done. Good and bad are concepts made up by a human earthly society and have little to do with the afterlife and the Underworld. The gods, spirits, and energies are more concerned with how much you are able to let go and move on. They want to know how well you are able to accept responsibility for (and learn from) your mistakes! This is the true meaning of going through the tests and trials with a pure heart. After the tests are complete, the spirit/soul sometimes re-incarnates if more lessons on Earth are to be learned. If they have reached a certain point in their spiritual development they may be able to pass on to the place of the Ancestors and perhaps become a spirit guide for people living on Earth. At this point, it is not for me to tell you what to believe, but rather to clarify the beliefs of other spiritual philosophies. Later in your Underworld journeys, I encourage you to travel to these places and test out how much negative energy you are retaining in your soul.

Each culture tests the spirit in a different way. The trials and tests in the Underworld have cultural meaning to each society. They are also based on your subconscious and the negative energy that you retain. You may not even be aware of the negativity onto which you are holding. But, once you are in the Underworld, your subconscious becomes like a film projector that projects your deepest hopes, fears, and desires into the powerful energies available. The pain and suffering that you refuse to let go of, or perhaps do not know how to let go of, will manifest. In some cultures, this energy manifests as sinister lords of chaos chasing you through darkness. In other cultures, the energy manifests as wild animals and beasts that wish to eat you. These scenarios provide the spirits with the opportunity to face their darkest parts in order to move on and purify themselves of the negativity. In Buddhism, there are many meditation techniques that will help you understand these energies. Buddhism teaches us that we may learn to deal with them in life so once we pass beyond the veil of life and death the monsters that chase us are easier to handle.

The Maya

They ancient Maya were a Native South American culture that lived on the Yucatan peninsula. Very early on, they learned the magick of agriculture. The most important food to them was maize, or corn. Their cosmology was similar to other pagan and native tribes in some ways, but very different in others. They built temples, had a system of government, and had priests that maintained the sacred rites and sought out spirits to aid the tribe. They waged wars with enemies and used the captives as sacrifices to their gods in order to preserve their people. The

Maya flourished for hundreds of years. In the 8th Century the power of the Maya began to wane and in the 9th Century the great powerful empire was but an ember of the once mighty people of the Yucatan.

Beliefs

The Maya believed that the Universe has three worlds. The physical world or Midworld, an Upperworld, and an Underworld. There was an energy force that made up the entire Mayan Universe that is called *ch'ulel*. This "life" energy was much like the Chinese concept of Chi or the Indian idea of *prana*. *Ch'ulel* was the life force that gave life-energy to all of creation. Without it, the Universe could not exist; nothing would be. *Ch'ulel* came from the three Mayan worlds and at the same time it kept everything in motion. For the Maya, the Universe, including those parts of it that were not physical, was ever changing and evolving. *Ch'ulel* gave life to the crops and helped them grow. It also gave the Maya "good energy" for everyday life, government, and war. If the *Ch'ulel* were to run out in the physical world, then the Mayan world would no longer exist. *Ch'ulel* also gave energy to the Ancestors to help them have influence in the physical world and it gave energy to the gods to assist them with helping humans to manifest a healthy and vital existence. From time to time *Ch'ulel* would become depleted. The largest known source of *Ch'ulel* in the physical world was blood.

It was thought to be a divine act to sacrifice a human being in the name of the gods and the Mayan civilization. They believed that the gods themselves created the Universe through blood sacrifice. It is said in the *Popul Vu* that the Universe was created when the gods stuck large needles through their penises and the blood spilling helped to create the cosmos. The sacrifice was chosen from a sort of "divine" game that was held in the sacred ball courts of the Mayan temples. It was similar to our racket ball. On one side were the gods of life and on the other side were the gods of death and disease. The gods of life always won, so by default the losing team was dubbed the "gods of death and disease". These men were then usually decapitated in the temple and their blood, which contained much *Ch'ulel*, would spill into a hole in the temple floor down onto the Earth below (the Underworld). The *Ch'ulel* would then be given to the Underworld gods to use for the benefit of the people and the Earth around them.

In his book, *The Shaman's Secret*, Douglas Gillette states, "The Maya shamans believed that all deaths, but especially those of the authentic human beings, are, in their essence, "sacrificial" deaths. In these sacrificial deaths human beings give back to the gods what the gods, through their own sacrifices, have given them - blood for blood, tears for rain, flesh for corn, life for life, being for being."

He goes on to say that the Maya beliefs surrounding these customs were shared by not only those who carried out the sacrifices, but by the people who were sacrificed as well. Pain and suffering were a natural way of life, and while the victims did not want to die, most of them tried to do so with honor and dignity knowing that they were helping restore the life force of their people. The victim's names were recorded and held in great honor.

The Mayan Underworld was called Xibalba. It was the realm of the god of death who was called One and Seven Death. Sometimes this deity was perceived as one god and other times as two separate gods. They were the leaders of the Underworld. Xibalba had many spirits and "hells" for the soul to travel through.

Road to Xibalba

When the Maya died, it was thought that their spirits or souls would become a traveler in the Underworld. Throughout their lives, they were taught about the mysteries of the Underworld. They were taught about all the dangerous trials that awaited them. In essence, they prepared for death their entire lives. They were also taught to live a spiritual life as best they could, because doing so would better prepare them for the trials in Xibalba. Death was a sacred and necessary act for the balance of creation. But for the Maya, it was not about being "good" in life, it was about preparing the soul for the onslaught of "hells" that were meant to purify and test the soul.

Once they died, their journey would begin. They would start by going down over the edge of a steep slope, then they would descend until they reached the mouth where the canyons changed. The canyons were named Rustling Canyon and Gurgling Canyon. After traveling through the vastness of the canyons they would pass through Scorpion Rapids and then on to a river of blood, called Blood River. Then they journeyed on to a river of Pus after which they encountered a crossroads. The crossroads were named after the sacred colors of the Maya: the Red Road and the Black Road. Then there were the White Road and the Yellow Road. We must remember that the Maya were not trying to repulse the spirit traveler but to explain that in the world of death, there existed the things that brought death or the symptoms of illness that led to death in the Underworld. These things were also part of the trials that lay ahead. The spirit traveler had to be brave and put his or her fears aside and continue across the terrain.

Once you came to the crossroads, the Black Road would speak, "I am the road to Xibalba". The spirit traveler was taught in life which way to go. They knew to go down the Black road to reach the Mayan

Underworld. It is helpful to know that the soul traveler was not completely alone on the journey. There were allies that accompanied them upon their quest. One of the allies was the mosquito. This creature could be used as a spy in the Underworld. It could be sent ahead to find out what dangers awaited. This was helpful because the gods and spirits of Xibalba, also known as the Lords of Xibalba, wanted to very much confuse and frighten the traveler. The Lords of Xibalba would use manikins to fool travelers to confuse them along the way. The manikins looked just like the Maya people and the traveler would think that they had found someone to help them along their path. When the traveler found out that they were tricked, it would further the sense of isolation and the realization that they had to travel the dark paths alone. They were also pranksters and loved to play mean tricks on travelers, such as giving them a hot seat. When the traveler grew tired and tried to sit down, the seats were scalding hot! The Lords of Xibalba took great delight in doing this. To the reader, these pranks may seem childish, but we should remember that the journey was frightening to the newly dead and everything could be perceived as a danger. These little tricks were nothing compared to the trials that were soon to come. To turn back with fear was to show the Underworld gods that one was not ready for re-incarnation or spiritual evolution.

Houses of Xibalba

The goal for the spirit traveler was reincarnation, or evolution of the spirit, into the spirit worlds and the realm of the Ancestors. The soul had to be tested and purified. To do this, there were "hells" or "houses." These realms taught the soul what it needed to move forward. It was hoped that every soul, because of its proper training in life, would gracefully pass through the houses. If a soul failed its trials, then a state of limbo or a netherworld was its destination. The houses themselves were conditions of human suffering that the soul traveler had to confront and deal with, so that they would understand the purpose of life, suffering, sacrifice, death, and their own spiritual resurrection.

The first house that was encountered was Dark House. This was a house with only darkness in it. Here, travelers were given a torch. The torch represented spiritual illumination. Travelers were also given a cigar. The traveler was told that the torch and cigar must not go out! This was the trial that tested spiritual development and the trueness of the soul. The torch was a direct link to the "light" of the Maya spirit. If it went out, then the traveler was not ready to move forward.

The second house encountered was the Razor (Blade) House. This house was filled with razor blades swinging back and forth. Being that this was the last house before the continuation of the soul to reincarnation or evolution of spirit, this was the place where the last of the unwanted aspects of the soul were cut away. This may have been a violent cutting, but it was necessary. To move beyond into the realm of spirit, all fear, pain, and suffering had be irrevocably purged and the lessons fully learned. This was the trial that cut away negative aspects of the soul and taught the understanding that violence must have an outlet lest it find unhealthy means of expressing itself.

From the Razor House, travelers move to the Cold (Rattling) House. As the name implies, the house was very cold inside with heavy drafts that made whistling sounds. There were also the chattering sounds of hail falling upon the roof of the house. The soul traveler had to keep warm with its own internal fire. This was the trial that tested the ability to keep the inner flame kindled. The inner fire may have been the passion for living, in right relation with one's community.

The next house was Jaguar House. The jaguars jostled one another around and were crowded together. These mighty beasts were violent and hungry and had the potential to devour the sojourner's soul. This was the trial that tested the ability to not fight death, but to let the forces of death feed on the spirit.

Then there was the Fire House. The fires were those of purification which burned away the old self, especially those parts of the ego that did not propel the soul forward. This was the house that was similar to the Christian concept of a fiery hell. In Christian hell too, if you look deep enough into the symbolism, you find the "destruction" of a sinful or false ego. It is the purification of hell that allows the soul to purge itself of impurity so that it might go forth on an evolutionary road. The Fire House also tested the ability of one to keep the mind "cool" so that it did not give into the fires of anger and rage.

Last was house is the Bat House which was filled only with bats. They represented the terrible aspect of death that mortals had no power over. To fight this house was futile. In fact, to fight any of the houses went against the very nature of the aspect of the Universe that they represented. The bats gave a sense of dread and fear. Their shrieks were deafening. This house represented the essence of fear in the journey of death. It was terrible, but inevitable. This was the trial that tested the ability to give in to the cosmic flow of death and transformation and give it what it wanted.

One and Seven Hanahpu

There were two gods of the Maya named One and Seven Hanahpu. One Hanahpu had a wife and fathered children, but Seven Hanahpu was to forever remain a boy. These two gods were very good and were great seers. One and Seven Hanahpu taught the sons of One Hanahpu many arts and crafts. The sons, in turn, taught these gifts to humanity.

One and Seven Hanahpu spent their days throwing dice and playing ball. However, they chose to play their games over the road to Xibalba, the Mayan Underworld. One and Seven Death heard these games and were angry at the disrespect that One and Seven Hanahpu were showing them. One and Seven Death decided to destroy them by inviting them down into the Underworld and playing a ball game.

As One and Seven Hanahpu traveled down to Xibalba they passed over great Canyons and mighty rapids. They were able to pass through a River of Blood and a River of Pus. They passed unharmed! They then came to a crossroads. A red road, a black road, a yellow road, and a white road. The black road spoke and told them to take the black road to Xibalba. They then came to the Lords of Xibalba. This meant their defeat, because as they went to greet the lords, they did not know that this was a trick. These were not the lords of the Underworld—they were manikins. When they finally did meet the Lords of Xibalba, instead of granting them a seat, they were tricked again and given hot rocks to sit on.

One and Seven Hanahpu were unaware that the Underworld was filled with tests of torment. They were sent to Dark House and given one cigar each with a torch to light them. They were told to keep the cigars intact, but in the morning when One and Seven Death came to retrieve them One and Seven Hanahpu explained that the cigars had been smoked up. They had failed the test. One and Seven Death killed One and Seven Hanahpu because they had failed the tests of Xibalba. The bodies were buried over the ball court and the head of One Hanahpu was placed in the fork of a cabash tree. This tree became a magical tree of the Underworld.

Hanahpu and Xblanque in the Underworld

After some time, in the Underworld, A maiden named Blood Moon, came up to the magical tree where One Hanahpu's head was placed. She had heard that the fruit of the tree was sweet and wanted it. She asked the head of One Hanahpu for the fruit, but instead of giving her the fruit, he spat in her hand. The spittle disappeared at once and Blood Moon became pregnant with the essence of One Hanahpu. The Lords of the Underworld wanted to kill Blood Moon, so she fled to the world above and lived with the Mother of One Hanahpu. She later gave birth to Hanahpu and Xblanque.

Hanahpu and Xblanque grew up to be immensely powerful and crafty. They loved to play ball on the road to Xibalba just as their father did before, and, just as before, the Lords of Xibalba did not like all the noise from above and invited the boys to come down to the Underworld to play a ball game with the intention of inevitably sacrificing them!

So down went Hanahpu and Xblanque to Xibalba. They passed through the dark canyons and passed over the River of Blood and the River of Pus. The found themselves at the crossroads again. They already knew to go down the Black Road. They also knew about the tricks that the Lords of Xibalba liked to play. They summoned Mosquito and had him bite the lords so that they would know their names. The Mosquito bit the Lords, and they all said their names in turn which were One Death, Seven Death, Scab Stripper, Blood Gatherer, Demon of Pus, Demon of Justice, Bone Scepter, Skull Scepter, Packstrap, Bloody Teeth, Bloody Claws, and Wing. Hanahpu and Xblanque walked by the first Lords of the Underworld they encountered; they were not fooled by the manikins. They named each of the actual lords when they met them and, in this way, had power over them. They did not fall for any of the tricks. They did not even sit on the hot rocks.

They were then taken to Dark House. Hanahpu and Xblanque were given cigars and a torch and were told not to let them burn up. Instead of lighting the cigars, they stuffed fireflies in the cigars to give the lords the illusion that they were smoking them. In the morning, The lords realized what had happened and knew that they had been defeated. That day, they played ball and the lords tried to kill them with a knife, but the boys saw the knife and knew they were being tricked. Despite this attempt on their lives, the boys agreed to stay another night. On the second night, they were taken to Razor House. The house was filled with knives and was supposed to slice them up, but the boys spoke to the knives and convinced them that they would rather have animal flesh. The knives stopped their attack, and the boys spent the night in Razor House unharmed. The next day, they played ball again and had a tie. The lords asked them to stay another night. This time, Hanahpu and Xblanque were taken to Cold House. Cold House was full of cold winds and hail. The boys defeated the house by shutting the cold out. They closed the windows and doors and would not let in the cold spirits. The Lords of Xibalba were very angry. Next, they were taken to Jaguar House. The boys said to the jaguars that they should not eat them, but rather gnaw on bones. The boys then transformed themselves into bones and the jaguars gnawed on them but did not devour them. The next day, they transformed back into boys and the Lords of the Underworld were defeated again. Next, they were taken to Fire House. The fires were supposed to burn them up, but they left the house once again unharmed! Last, they were taken to Bat House where bats great and small shrieked and swooped down on them all night long. Xblanque asked Hanahpu to check outside the window to see if it was dawn yet. When Hanahpu peeked out of the window a bat flew down and bit off his head and the head of Hanahpu rolled outside on the ground. In despair, Xblanque summoned forth all the animals and asked them to run and get the food they ate. After inspecting all the food, he found a squash. He transformed the squash into a temporary head for Hanahpu and brought him back to life! That morning, the boys and the Lords of Death played ball, using the head of Hanahpu as a ball! Finally, Hanahpu and Xblanque won the ball game and the head of Hanahpu was restored to his body. This was how the Lords of Xibalba were defeated.

Egyptian Underworld
Osiris and Isis (Egyptian)

Osiris and Isis ruled over Egypt with compassion and justice. They taught the Egyptian people all they needed to know about civilization and prosperity. The people worshiped the celestial gods with much love and devotion. Osiris had a brother named Set. Set ruled the harshness of the desert and was the bringer of Chaos and destruction. Set coveted the celestial throne of his brother. He wanted to rule in his place, but Osiris was more powerful than Set and he could not defeat him through strength and battle. He knew he must use his ingenuity to bring the fall of Osiris. Then he would be able to rule.

One day, Set decided to execute his plan. It was time to get rid of Osiris once and for all. He held a great celebration to which all of the gods were invited. The celebration was magnificent. Set had gone to great trouble to conceal his plan. During the festivities, Set brought out a beautiful chest. The most ornate box the gods had ever seen. Set explained to the gods that whoever fit in the box would be able to keep it. Every one of the gods tried to fit inside but none could. Then, Osiris took his turn and tried to fit into the box. To everyone's amazement, he fits exactly. Little did Osiris know that Set had taken his measurements in secret. Suddenly, Set and his followers closed the box tight and sealed it so that neither god nor man could open the box again. It was then thrown into the Nile River to be lost forever.

Isis, the Queen of the Gods, was heartbroken and went in search of her husband. After a while, she found the casket near the sea. In secret, she took the box away and hid it from sight, even from the gods themselves. She used her magick to open the box. There, she found her husband lying in his death sleep. Isis transformed herself into a magical bird and began flapping her mighty wings. The wind from her wings pushed the breath back into Osiris' body and he was revived.

Set, the ruler of Chaos, was cunning and had spies everywhere. He had many followers who whispered secrets into his ear. One day, it was revealed to him that Osiris lived in solitude with Isis. Finally, it had seemed that Set would be ruler of the cosmos, but Osiris still lived! Set found Isis and Osiris and in his rage, he ripped the body of Osiris limb from limb. To ensure that his sister, Isis, would not restore Osiris back to life he hid the body parts all over Egypt.

Once again, Isis was filled with sorrow and pain. But even so, she would not give up. She was pregnant with Horus, the son of Osiris. She searched all of Egypt looking for her husband and after many days, she found each body part of Osiris except the phallus. She put the body of her husband back together and replaced his phallus with one she had fashioned out of pure gold. She summoned Anubis, the embalmer of the dead, and together, they infused the body of Osiris with their magick to bring him back from the dead. Osiris had now traveled into Dwat, the Egyptian Underworld, and had gained access to the mystery of the dead and experienced the many trials of death. Because of this, he became the Lord of the Dead. Through this great mystery, he helped all beings through the many dangers of the Underworld to the final Judgment of Ma'at to be transformed into a great celestial being to forever live among the heavenly gods of Egypt.

One of the most famous stories of the Underworld comes from Ancient Egypt. The ancient Egyptians, at the height of their power, were considered the most technologically and spiritually advanced civilization of the Mediterranean. It is believed that their advanced spiritual nature came from divine inspiration. The Egyptian priests and Pharaohs claimed to have direct contact with the gods and, therefore, these were the people who held the most power in Egypt. The Egyptians kept written records of everything, so we have been able to decipher their rituals, ceremonies, and spiritual beliefs. These written records have inspired poets, authors, religious writers, and magicians.

As we compare the mythology and spirituality of different cultures, it is interesting to discover that the Egyptians seemed to have an advanced understanding of the Underworld and its purposes. They did not fear the Underworld as a punishment or even a test. They understood that is was necessary to travel down into the depths of the Underworld to undergo the steps for further enlightenment so that they could join the realm of their beloved gods. To them, the afterlife was a welcome adventure. Unlike most civilizations at the time, they had a deeper understanding of the mysteries of death. That is not to say, they had no fear of the mysteries, but they understood that any fear that they may have had was necessary for the incredible journey ahead.

Chronology

The exactness of the following dates is still debated by scholars, but they give an approximation of the chief eras of Egyptian history.

The power and influence of the Egyptian Pharaohs began in approximately 3200 BCE with the unification of both Upper and Lower Egypt.

The Old Kingdom, the time when the power of the Pharaoh was at its height, is considered to be from around 2686 BCE to 2055 BCE.

The Middle Kingdom, a time of growth and expansion, existed from 2055 BCE to 1550 BCE.

The New Kingdom, the age of Egyptian empire, existed from 1550 to 747 BCE.

Much of what we know of the Egyptian *Book of the Dead* comes from this period as it went through its final redaction sometime in the 1500s BCE.

The Egyptian Soul

In Egyptian cosmology, the soul is divided into three, sometimes four, parts. The Ka, Ba, Akh, and, sometimes, the Sabu. It is interesting to note the similarities between these aspects of the soul and our modern versions of the subtler bodies. It is fascinating how, even spiritually, the Egyptians were far more advanced than the cultures around them.

Ka

Ka is translated as "vital force." This can be related to the idea of Chi, Qi, or Prana in Asian cosmologies. Ka was thought to be everywhere in Egyptian cosmology. It came from everything, and it flowed and nourished everything in turn. The Ka could also be understood as being, or having an influence on, what we think of as Karma. It was also thought that the Ancestors were a part of Ka and could control Ka in this world from the Underworld. Part of our soul was made of Ka. The Ka could be understood as the Etheric and perhaps the "Lower" Astral body.

Ba

The Ba is considered more subtle than the Ka. The Ba can be experienced in dreams, shamanic journeys, and the Out of Body Experience. Ba is thought to be how we travel the different worlds. To the Egyptians, the spirit animal was a person's Ba. The Egyptian gods manifested their spirit animals all the time and they are depicted that way in statues and art. For example, Horus is depicted as the Hawk, Bast as the Cat, and Thoth as the Ibis. Unlike the Ka, most Egyptians rarely experienced the Ba, save for the Pharaohs, priests and magicians. The Ba could be understood as your "Higher" Astral body.

Akh

The Akh is the part of the "soul" that travels to the realm of the gods in the Upperworld and dwells in the celestial realms. To me, the Akh is less a part of the soul and more a part of the spiritual body. The difference between the spirit and the soul is that the soul is the "housing" of the spirit. The soul contains our memories, desires, fears, and everything we are in this life. The spirit is our spark of divinity that is immortal that may be reincarnated life after life. It is the spiritual aspect of the self that transcends the Earthly wants, desires, and needs to take its place among the stars with the gods. The Akh, when exalted by the gods, finally becomes the Sabu, or the final, purified, aspect of the "soul" and journey among the cosmos. The Akh could be understood as your Mental and Spiritual Bodies.

Dwat

This is the name given to the Egyptian Underworld. The Dwat (pronounced DOO-aht) was never thought of as a physical place by the Egyptians. They knew it was a place that the spirit traveled to or from when the Ba traveled to the physical world. It was a world of dualities: It lay beneath the Earth, and yet was envisioned as being also in the night sky. It dwelled within the celestial body of the Sky Goddess Nut, yet could also be found in the West, the place of the setting sun. Being a spiritual place, it could be all these things and more. The Egyptians knew that the Dwat was within everything and was not in any single defined place. They knew that one could find the Dwat in dreams and even in daydreams. This was a place of inversion. By this I mean not that it was evil, but rather a mirror reflection of the Upperworld and the Midworld as if the two realms were somehow turned upside down. This is a common theme throughout all the mythologies of the Underworld. The Dwat was a place where a magician or priest could travel while still alive and learn to evolve and transform their lives. It was a place of great wonder and yet had many perils.

Trials and Monsters

Upon death, the Ba entered the Dwat and was given the strength to go forth on its journey through the power of the spirits there who wished to aid it. As the spirit traveled through the Dwat, the person was put through many trials. Most of the terrain consisted of water and islands with a few fields spread out here and there. The spirit traveled though the waters by means of an astral boat.

The Egyptian Underworld can best be understood as a dream. In dreams, the subconscious changes the scenery of the dreamer. So too, in the Dwat, the landscapes will change based upon the subconscious hopes and fears of the individual. One can say that the Underworld here shows the inner nature of the dead traveler. The Egyptian Underworld is not a place of punishment, but a place of purification. If the psychic energies of the Ba are in need of purification, the Dwat will alter itself to reflect those energies so that the spirit may have purification. In this way, the soul may eventually be able to become like the god Osiris, Lord of the Underworld, and join with the gods in the stars. The only time the traveler experiences the more pleasant aspects of the Dwat is when the Ba has already undergone the purifications and trials of the Underworld. Each Ba has its own journey to make. No two journeys are exactly the same.

The demons and monsters that are found in the Dwat are a reflection of the aspects of the psyche or subconscious aspects of the self that need to be purified in order for the soul to successfully navigate through the Underworld and join with the gods. The monsters encountered here are seen as entities that wish to kill or harm the traveler, but they only exist because of the negative energies that already exist inside the person's spirit. The phrase "personal demons" is taken very literally here. When each of these "monsters" is overcome, then the energies are transformed into beneficial forces that help the Ba travel further into the Dwat.

Once the Ba is purified, the traveler will enter the Hall of Ma'at. The word Ma'at is difficult to translate and has connotations of harmony and balance, but it can also mean truth. It was important for the Egyptians to live in such a way that they lived in a constant state of truth and harmony with the gods and the Universe. The Hall of Ma'at is where the Ba meets the goddess Ma'at. In her great hall, she weighs the heart of the spirit traveler on her scales. Before having their heart weighed, the Ba must explain to Anubis all the wonderful spiritual accomplishments they have achieved; like giving devotion and offerings to the gods and so on. He is then led into a chamber where 42 gods are present. The traveler must address each by their proper names. The Ba then must have their heart weighed and must explain to Ma'at and Thoth all the things that they did NOT do. It is interesting to note that both

Horus and Set, representing truth and misdeed, are present to aid in the weighing. From my research of the Egyptian pantheon and beliefs, I believe that the weighing of the heart is not as cut and dried as the people make it out to be. The whole point of the journey into the Dwat is to challenge, purify, and transform the Ba into the Akh so that the dead can join the gods among the stars. It is not about punishment. The gods and spirits want to aid the traveler upon his journey. So, the weighing is to help the Ba see what aspect of the self that still needs to be cast away down into the pit or abyss. These parts are similar to aspects of the consciousness that hinder the spiritual evolution of the soul. Ma'at is truth. So, it would seem like a fair assessment that part of the role of Ma'at in the Underworld is to help the Ba maintain and find balance (represented as the struggle between Horus [truth] and Set [misdeed]. The scales are not part of the rewards and punishment, but a magical tool designed to aid in achieving balance within the soul.

Apophis

Apophis is a snake deity who resides in the waters of the Underworld. His purpose is to be the great opponent or obstacle that swims beneath the Underworld barge of the Ba and keep the traveler from purification. Only the truthful and spiritual soul can outsmart and keep the mighty Apophis from destroying the soul and ending its journey before it can obtain evolution.

Joining the Gods in Dwat

After the purifications and spiritual awakenings of the Ba, the soul is ready for its last transformation. Everything that the spirit traveler has gone through, both in life and death, has led to this last evolution of the soul. It is in this final aspect of the journey of the Dwat that the soul gains a profound spiritual understanding. It is here that each person understands that the trials were not for the benefit of the gods, but for the benefit of the soul. It is here, and ONLY here that the Ba can transform and evolve into the Akh. The Akh is the spirit refined in such a way that it can fly up to the heavens and become god-like and remain among the deities. It is in our soul design that all evolution and transformations are merely experiential. What this means is that we must take a "hands on" approach to our life and spirituality. We cannot go through life, or death, in a half-awake/half-asleep sort of consciousness. Sometimes entities and events are testing us so that we are jolted awake. I personally believe that the gods know this about the human mind and spirit, and they are constantly putting things in our way to make us better so that one day we will join them among the stars.

Christian Hell
History and Origins

The Christian Hell has a remarkably interesting origin. The word itself comes from one of the Nordic Underworlds called Helheim which means "the land of Hel". Hel is the Nordic goddess of the dead. She collects the dead souls and keeps them safe in her world. The word was borrowed to mean the Christian Underworld or "Hell." If we research mythologies from several cultures, we see that most religions borrowed freely from each other. The ancient Romans were very fond of conquering a land and incorporating foreign traditions into their own religious structure. They also brought some of their ideas to the Celtic countries that they invaded. Ancient cultures saw no problem in taking things they liked about other mythos and leaving out the rest. Christianity is a good example of this. If you look closely at biblical stories, you can see stories that share similarities with tales from other cultures. One of the most notable examples of this is the idea of the Sacrificial Lord. The Sacrificial Lord is a deity who "dies" or sacrifices themself for the good of humanity, as Jesus did on the cross. Another myth that uses this concept is the Nordic god Odin who hung upside down on the World Tree for nine days to receive enlightenment through the Runes, which he then gave to the world of men for their use and benefit. Another example is the dismemberment of Osiris and his journey into the Underworld. In the story of the Madonna and Child, we can also see how Christianity borrowed directly from Egyptian mythology. Egyptian statues show the Mother Isis holding the sun god Horus. If you compare some of the Egyptian statues and the paintings of the Madonna and Child, you can easily see the resemblance. Jesus can be seen as relating to the sun in the idea that he dies and is reborn, like the daily death and resurrection of the sun. The dying/resurrecting sun can be seen in mythologies such as Nordic Balder who is killed by his brother only to be revived again after Ragnarök. There is also the Greco-Roman Asclepius who is killed by a thunderbolt of Zeus but is then resurrected to the heavens.

Christianity borrowed the idea of the Underworld from other cultures. There is a section of darkness and restraint called Tartarus in the Greco-Roman realm of Hades. This is the place the Titans, the old gods who created the universe were chained and kept captive after they were overthrown. It is also a place of torment for lost souls. It is often said that Tartarus is full of the sound of terrible screams. In the Nordic Underworld, Niflheim is the place of great fog and terrible ice where the evil are cast. The Egyptian Underworld has a terrible alligator monster that devours the souls of the unjust whose souls are weighed against the feather of Ma'at. It is not difficult to see that Christians took the terrible aspect of the Underworld and made it their own. What about the idea of fire and brimstone? Remember that ancient peoples got the ideas of the myths and stories by observing the world around them. We know that fire comes from underneath the earth in the form of lava. There were many historical accounts of mountains blowing up and releasing fire and rock on Earth destroying everything in its path. Knowing that this fire came from under the earth it was only assumed that the Underworld below was a place of fire. In Plato's Republic, we have the Myth of Er. In this myth, Er, a warrior is killed in battle and witnesses what happens to the other slain warriors. He sees that each man is judged by greater deities and those who lived their lives with great morality went to a place of great reward and those who were of less morality went to a place of fiery punishment. It is interesting to see how Christianity may have been influenced by these stories.

Political Influence

After the fall of Rome, the Christian church found an opportunity to spread their influence throughout most of Europe. Since the reigning establishment had fallen, there needed to be some sort of re-adjustment. The Church, headed by Pope Gregory the Great (r. 590-604 C.E.), helped establish laws and educate local leaders. The church also sent their monks and missionaries to the pagan territories to teach Christianity. The Christian Church offered hope to the people after the fall of Rome. The missionaries also convinced the people that worshiping the Christian God and Jesus was better than worshiping the "jealous" and wrathful pagan gods who demanded festivals and sacrifices. I find this a little humorous being that the Christian God is probably more "wrathful and jealous" than most of the pagan gods could ever be. One of the benefits that the Christians gave to us in those early days was that Pope Gregory was a folklorist. He wanted the monks to write down the myths, stories, and legends of the towns. Part of this idea was to preserve the tales, but the other idea was to learn as much about the people and their culture as possible to better relate to them and find out the easiest way to convert them to Christianity.

Idea of Torment

Torment and punishment in the Underworld is not exclusively a Christian concept as we have seen. However, in most of the pagan Underworld, torment is not meant to be forever, and it certainly does not take up the entire Underworld. In the Greco-Roman Hades, Tartarus was the only place of torment for the wicked. It was believed that the punishment should fit the crime. The "terrors" would balance out what was done in life. For example, if you stole from the poor, then you would be starved in Tartarus. In the mythos of Christianity, Hell does dwell on torment and torture. It comes from the Christian leadership's idea that their followers must obey the teachings of their faith or be subject to the punishments of the afterlife. To most of the pagans who "converted" this was a silly idea. Let us briefly discuss the idea of Christian conversion. Many times, the monks would come to a town or village and make a proclamation that the town was now Christian and a church was to be built and pagan ways were to stop. Sometimes, the towns that accepted Church help with farming, money, etc., would say they were converted but would continue to practice their pagan traditions. This is evidenced by sermons written by many Church leaders in the Early Middle Ages in Western Europe, wherein the practice of divination, sacrifice to nature spirits, and reliance on non-Christian spirit-workers was regularly excoriated, suggesting that such practices were alive and well. Sometimes people would practice both traditions at the same time. The celebration of the ancient Celtic New Year, Samhain, on October 31 and the Christian All Soul's Day on November 1 is a good example of this. Both festivals occur around the same time of year, and both celebrate the departed souls of the dead. Other times, the monks would have to convince the local leaders or the king of the land to convert to Christianity. Many times, the monks would appeal to the king's sense of power and control over the territory and its people.

The priests who wrote and preached about the torments of Hell went to great lengths to describe horrible tortures, painful "sex" acts, and mutilation. They tried to appeal to the darkest of human behaviors, then exaggerated it and made them worse than imaginable. There were many priests in the Middle Ages who had "dreams" of Hell, or who felt they were falling from grace and an angel came to show them how horrible Hell was who then told the world about what they saw. What the priests reported from their dreams was horrible indeed. The priests talked about thousands of demons that mutilated trapped souls, they told stories of souls boiling in soups, and how Satan himself would eat damned souls and then excrete them out. Fire and torture were only some of the horrible things that could happen to a person. Churchmen believed that the severity of the sin determined your place in Hell. If you were bad, but not the worst of the bunch, then your punishment was harsh, but not as harsh as the more grievous sins, such as murder or rape. It is interesting to note that treason was thought to be the worst of all sins in the Middle Ages, although this has to do with more political ideas than Christian spiritual ideas. Kings often supported the Church, but not without certain favors granted in return.

During this time, the Church had ordained that the priests had God's authority to save a man's soul or condemn him to Hell. It was also sometimes found that a priest would preach about living a Christian lifestyle only to do the exact opposite himself. This angered a lot of people, who believed that priests were not above the laws of god. This led to a variety of reform movements and "heresies" from the 900s onward, culminating in the Protestant Reformation in the 1500s.

After the Reformation and the Catholic Church split, the new Protestant reformers, especially the Lutherans and Calvinists, preached a different idea of Hell. No longer could priests save or condemn someone. Only God had the power to save. Also, there were no longer strange tortures in Hell. Instead, everyone was punished equally with the agony of fiery torment. Limbo was taken away and a person either went to Heaven or Hell. There was no in-between.

Abraham's Bosom

This is a place next to Hell that was sometimes thought to be Limbo, but is not. Before the crucifixion and resurrection of Jesus, humans were not allowed into Heaven. They dwelled in a place called "Abraham's Bosom" which was a sort of paradise. It was a place of rest and rejuvenation. In paganism, the Ancestors dwelled in such a place. We can see that perhaps this is similar, if not the same, as the place referred to in myths of the afterlife. I personally believe that the Christians were influenced by paganism in this regard. After his crucifixion, according to Christianity, Jesus, came down and took the souls who dwelled there to heaven.

I have gone on at some length in this section because I firmly believe that if you come from a Christian religious background it is important that you confront your beliefs about the Christian idea of Hell. Those of us who were taught that if you were a sinner, did not accept Jesus Christ as your ONLY god and savior, or that if you lived a life that went against the teachings of the Bible, then you were going to spend eternity in Hell burning forever and ever are often still greatly influenced by these ideas. The Christian Hell is a very frightening thing if you accept it literally. I remember as a child, my father would explain to me that Hell was a physical place somewhere that, when you died, your soul was sent when you were bad to experience the pain and suffering of the fires of damnation. When we are children, our habits and mental patterns begin to form. Even though we are adults now we may still have unresolved issues with the idea of Hell. To further our spiritual evolution and transformation, it is important that we journey to the Christian Hell to understand that it is a Christian thought form and nothing more. What I mean by this is that over time, society's beliefs have a psychic effect on the astral plane and Underworld. Yes, there may be a Hell in the Underworld, but it is only an illusion. The sooner we understand how this illusion manifests and how it does not dictate our spiritual lives, the better.

I will caution that not everyone will have the same reaction to the following journey. Some people may understand how the illusion of Hell works and others will have to face difficult fears that we thought we dealt with a long time ago. If the journey brings up to many issues, I advise that you see your spiritual guide and a professional psychologist who is familiar with the type of work we are doing here.

If you choose to take the journey, take your spirit animal with you as always, ask your gods and Ancestors to assist you as needed. They may become visible to you, or they may not. Either way they will be with you if you need them.

My Personal Experience in Hell

When I first journeyed to the Christian Hell, I already knew what to expect. I saw the lake of fire, the rocky underground caverns, and what looked like the bat-winged demons. I knew it to be a very grand thought form. When I first arrived, I was greeted by an entity. When I asked if he was an angel or a demon he replied, "Neither." He was to be my escort through Hell. He showed me everything I wanted to see throughout my very dark tour. At one point he showed me the souls of the dead who were "trapped" there burning in their own torment. I was sad for them and felt like they needed my help. My Hell guide explained to me that these souls were there of their choosing as a sort of self-punishment for what they did on Earth. This was a little difficult for me because in Neo-paganism there is no punishment in the afterlife, only lessons and karma. My guide also explained to me that the Ancestors and guides of these souls were working in their own way to best help them. It was best to let their Ancestors do their work without interference unless I was asked. I had to remind myself that even with my experience, I did not always know what was best for these people and to let spirits that knew better than I do the work that was intended for them.

My guide showed me the matrix of the Hell world itself. He showed me how the thought form was created over years and years of fear and terror brought about by the Christian church. I saw the beast that would "destroy" the world in the Christian Book of Revelations. At the end of my journey, my guide told me his true name. It was Lucifer. Lucifer means "the Light." He was the first created of all the angels. In the Luciferian tradition of philosophy, Lucifer is the "adversary" of god. It is believed in this spiritual thought that Lucifer had a divine purpose for the fall of one-third of all the angels, including himself. Because of this fall, human beings would have the opportunity to be challenged in the physical world and have the further opportunity to evolve. Lucifer wants to return to his beloved so badly that he will do whatever is needed to help humanity evolve. Once his task is done, he can return to the company of his beloved, God. In working with Lucifer as the Light Bringer, he has the ability to help us find personal gnosis. He can bring the light of truth to us. Sometimes the truth is dark and disturbing and yet it is something we must face.

Qliphoth

By studying the magical aspects of the Kabbalah, you will learn about the Tree of Life. The Tree of Life is a glyph or symbol that represents the creation of the physical realm beginning with the emanation of spirit and then forming into matter. In brief, the first emanation of god that we can understand is called Kether (the crown or first swirling of creation), the next is Chochmah (the bursting forth of creation), Binah (the bringing of all that energy of creation together), Chesed (the beginning of divine order), Geburah. (the will of God), Tiphareth (the balance and beauty of the universe), Netzach (emotions), Hod (logic, order, and mathematical structure), Yesod (the foundation) and finally Malkuth (the kingdom or physical universe). It is through these ten spheres that the Creator brought spirit into matter and the physical Universe.

In Kabalistic philosophy, the Qliphoth (pronounced KELLY-poht) is the inverted or "opposite" aspect of the Tree of Life and is sometimes called the "Tree of Death" or even the "Tree of Evil." Some Kabbalists suggest that the inverted tree is an abomination and is best left alone. Others suggest that the Qliphoth is a part of the Universe, so it therefore holds great power if one understands its powers and purposes. I personally agree with the latter view. One cannot try to understand the spiritual aspect of the Universe if one does not make the attempt to understand it in its whole form. This is the part of the spiritual universe that can show the magician how to transcend the duality of "good" and "evil." We must recognize that these things are the invention of man and that understanding the power and magick of the Universe can aid us in our healing and the healing of others. I believe that if we do not seek to understand these energies, there is the potential for danger. This danger can manifest in a couple of ways. One, repressed energies need to find a way to express themselves. We can do this in a controlled healthy way, or we can allow them to swell up and explode like a hellish volcano. Two, when new magicians, or new magically talented people stumble upon or attract these energies, they may be in over their heads if they do not understand the nature of these energies. That is not to say that one ever understands or masters the spirituality of the universe, but the more we learn and practice our spirituality the more understanding we will have.

I think it is important here to explain the purpose of the Qliphoth in the "grand" cosmic scheme of things. If we refer to the Tree of Life we can see that the glyph has a dual purpose. One, to show creation from Spirit to matter and vice versa, and two, to show the life skills one needs to have in order to succeed in the world. The Qliphoth, as well, has a dual purpose. One, to show the "shells" or lower worlds of the Tree, and two, to show the unbalanced nature or "evil" aspects of humanity.

Origins

There are several theories on how the Qliphoth was formed. One theory says that on God's first attempt to create the Universe (the Tree of Life) he made several mistakes in its construction, so he discarded it and it became a refuge for death, demons, and chaos. Another theory says that the inhabitants of the first Tree of Life were so primal that they only knew war, chaos, and destruction. The angels attempted to teach the inhabitants to evolve, but the people rose in rebellion. God then discarded this Tree of Life and created a "better" one. The disregarded tree became the Qliphoth. A further theory states that when the Tree of Life was being created, as each Sephirah was forming it burst forth from its own shell. The shell became the opposite force of that sphere and the remnants of the universe made the shells their home.

As you can see in all three origin theories, the Qliphoth is viewed as a mistake. However, it is interesting to note that the theories show God as a being that has faults and makes mistakes. We must remember that Kabalistic teachings were written in times were quite different than they are now. The rabbis and scholars wanted those who studied the Kabbalah to learn about the virtues of the Universe and how to connect with spirit and divinity. There was the fear that if one taught people the "evil" or unvirtuous Qliphoth then there was a risk of people being overwhelmed by those energies and plummeted into darkness. I personally feel that to study the dark parts of magick and the Universe is beneficial for understanding and healing, but I only think that it should be taken on when you are ready, or more importantly, when the universe thinks you are ready. I give the teachings of the Hells and Qliphoth so that you can further your learning of the Underworld and the great teaching of the universe. If you feel you are not ready, please respect that in yourself and do not do anything you are not ready to do.

I think it is also important to define Evil. When we hear the word "evil," we think of terrorists, monsters, and villains all with the same agenda…to kill people and destroy the world for pleasure and/or profit. I was taught in my magical training that evil was the misuse of energy in a misplaced and unbalanced way. Hurting people, animals, and the world for no good reason is certainly a misplacement of energy! Most Christians and Kabbalists believe that anything that disagrees with the "word" of God is evil. I find it interesting that they pick and choose passages out of the sacred books to further along their agenda. At the same time, these same people disregard passages that would paint themselves or things that *they* hold in high regard in a negative light (think of how often Jesus talks about the wickedness of the rich and the importance of providing help for the poor, for example). It is most important to realize that what was considered "good" and "godlike" in ancient times revolved around the philosophy of that era. We must remember that times have changed and evolved, and so have people. We cannot consider the virtues of the present to be the same as the virtues of the past. For example, several monotheistic cultures in the past thought that women were not as holy, smart, or important as men. We know that this is not true. Using this example, we need to decide for ourselves then what is appropriate and virtuous for today. As a general rule: remember that if we treat each other and the Earth as holy, it is easy to find out for ourselves what is evil and what is not. The interesting thing is that most people who we consider others evil do not consider themselves evil. Most of those individuals we think of as evil think that they are doing the right thing either for some cause they feel is just or for their own personal beliefs. There are also those people who simply do not care. This is much more than being selfish. It is a total disregard for anything or anyone. Sometimes, these people carry things all the way to the point where pain and destruction are of no consequence to them. In her book *The Sociopath Next Door,* psychologist Martha Stout, Ph.D., talks about sociopathic behavior that some people may consider evil. She explains how in this behavior people have no conscience and can hurt and use people with no feeling of remorse. Sociopaths can even kill people if it suited them. This poses a question, is Sociopathic behavior evil or is it a mental disability? Stout believes that there is no cure, so the verdict is left to each of us to decide for ourselves.

I prefer to call the Qliphoth the Inverted Tree. It is a reflection of the Tree of Life. I do not like "The Tree of Death" as much, because I think it is misleading. It does not have anything to do with the ancestors, but it is a part of the Kabalistic Underworld. If you were to look at the Underworld as a whole, you would be able to see that there are incredibly beautiful parts of the Underworld as well as some very dark and scary parts. I have heard some people who journey to the Underworld say that there are no "scary" parts of the Underworld, and those teachings are simply Judeo-Christian propaganda. I do not agree with this assessment. If you look hard enough you can see frightening aspects of all three worlds. In the Upperworld, there are black holes, dark matter, wormholes, alien races who care nothing for humans, and many other things. In the Middleworld, we have serpents at the ocean's edge, volcanoes, killer sharks and beasts, faeries that lead you into traps, as well as trolls and monsters that are hungry for human flesh. In waking consciousness in the human realm, we have crime, murder, and the total disregard of the destruction of our Earth's eco-system and the killing of endangered animals. I personally don't think there is anything more "evil" in the Universe than killing your fellow humans and animal and plant brothers for a profit.

If you would like to explore the Qliphoth in the astral plane I encourage you to get magical training. Some people can be self-taught from books and videos and this is wonderful. Other people need formal training from teachers. It is important that you develop magical skills in however way you learn best. Before you take on the Qliphoth you must have a working knowledge of the Kabbalah, magick, astral journeys, and psychic self-defense, some of which is covered in this book. I present the Qliphoth here so that you will have a better understanding of the Underworld in its entirety, or at least as we know it thus far. I will say, if you choose to explore any of the more "dangerous" parts of the

Underworld then you will have to rely upon your personal will and self-responsibility.

Nahemo

The first sphere in the Qliphoth is Nahemo. On the Tree of Life, it corresponds to Malkuth and the planet Earth. This is the only Qlipha that is said to be in the same "realm" of the sephirah in which we live. It is the wild, untamed Earth. It can be described as the more volatile aspects of nature, such as hurricanes, earthquakes, and massive sinkholes. It is the part of Earth that refuses to be tamed by Man. To the Kabbalist, the primal parts of the Earth and wild were considered things to be cautious of as they held many dark mysteries and demons.

Humans have always tried to "tame" nature. We build shelters to protect ourselves from the weather and we destroy rainforests in the attempt to have modern commercialized agriculture. We also pollute the air and water, thinking it is our right to do so. Through these human actions, the Earth's resources are becoming poisoned. Animals and their habitats are becoming extinct. Global Warming has alarmed scientists. If we pay attention to the weather and the news, we will see the "dark" aspects of the Earth taking a toll on man. Hurricanes are more frequent and more destructive, new viruses are infecting people, forest fires are out of control. From our point of view, this may seem like the evil aspect of the Earth seeking some sort of "revenge" on us. I believe that it is a sign of man's arrogance that we even think this. These phenomena are the Earth's way of balancing itself out. The Earth has its own evolution as well. Perhaps the Qliphoth is also in place to maintain the spiritual balance of the Universe! Nahemo is ruled by the demon Naamah. It is close to our world, and it is the gateway into the Kabalistic Underworld.

On a practical level, Nahemo is the sphere of Materialism. When working with this energy it is important to ask yourself, "As I go through the material world, do I give honor to the Earth, my property, and my body, or do I forgo spirit in favor of materialism?"

Gamaliel

The second sphere in the Qliphoth is Gamaliel. On the Tree of Life, it corresponds to Yesod. It is the dark moon. This is the place of nightmares and dark dreams. These are the necessary nightmares that we need to get our attention. It is also the realm of untamed sexual desire. If we repress our sexual impulses, these desires will build up and sometimes cause mental/emotional problems. What is perceived as "dark" sex to mainstream society, such as sadomasochism and sexual ordeal, can to the spiritual sojourner be an opportunity for psychic freedom form mental and physical repressions handed down to them from generations past. However, be warned. This is a world of vampires and dark entities that wish to drain you of your energies. This world is ruled by the Lilith. Lilith was the first wife of man who would not be sexually subservient to Adam. Because of her rebellion, she was demonized and sent away. In myth, she is said to be the wife of Satan and the mother of demons and vampires.

On a practical level, Gamaliel is the Sphere of Instability. When working with this energy it is important to ask yourself, "As I travel upon my path, what in my life is stable and what is not? What do I believe to be true for myself and in what areas do I need to allow change to occur?"

Samael

The next Qlipha is Samael and corresponds to Hod. Its planet is Mercury. This is the sphere that challenges the civil laws and rules so that you may come to your own conclusions about what is right and wrong for you. Sometimes, in our society, those who do not follow the laws and rules of the land because they are following their spiritual path and heart are considered outlaws. Those who disobey the laws of the Christian Church to follow what they believe personally and spiritually are called heretics. Samael means "the poison of God." It is interesting to note that one of the ancient meanings of *conjurer* or *sorcerer* was "poisoner." People thought that because magicians had knowledge of herbcraft, they also had knowledge of poisons. Perhaps the ancients knew that witches and magicians followed their own thinking and made their own choices when it came to spirituality. To the Christian Church, this was God's poison.

It is also the world of language and finding hidden meaning. It is where we seek to understand words and phrases in a magical context. It is also occult knowledge. It is said there is a fine line between madness and magick. Perhaps it is the blurring of these ideas that allow things to manifest and us to "think outside the box." There have been many people who were so intelligent and artistic that they were thought to be mad. This world teaches us to take a personal inventory and transmute any "poison" that others have instilled in our thoughts and emotions. It is also the realm of Trickster spirits. Tricksters in myths have always given man hard and sometimes whimsical lessons about life, humanity, and spirit. This world is ruled by the demon Adrammelech.

On a practical level, Samael, is the sphere of Greed. When working with this energy it is important to ask yourself, "As I travel upon my path, am I coming to my own conclusions about life and spirituality or am I basing my decisions on blind faith? Am I taking the negative thoughts and energies people are giving me and turning it into something more productive for my personal journey or am I letting those things control me?"

Hareb-Serapel

The next Qlipha is Hareb-Serapel and corresponds to Netzach and the planet Venus. This is the sphere of the victory of battle and war, and the place of ravens. This realm can be seen as aggressive and unyielding. It is interesting to note that some battles, be they global or personal, are necessary to maintain peace and the security of the residents. Other times, battle is an unnecessary exertion of force and power. It is up to the magician and journeyer to decide what battles should be fought for personal evolution and which battles are not necessary. To make a wise decision in this is to conserve personal power and energy and to show yourself and the spirits emotional control in one's environment. The ravens, in this regard, represent the spirit of the magician taking flight along the astral paths. They are also the creatures that eat the flesh of fallen soldiers after battle. In myths, ravens are the dark messengers and teachers. They bring unwanted news to the seeker but news that helps him on his path to enlightenment. This is also the place of dark emotions. We are taught in our culture to do away with emotions that seem negative or unproductive. Most people are not able to transmute these emotions, and thus they are repressed, and the bottled-up emotions can eventually cause illness to the mind and body. But sometimes these same repressed emotions can be released to create dark art and music that helps capture the authenticity of human emotion. The demon Baal rules here.

On a practical level Hareb-Serapel is the sphere of Lust. When working with this energy it is important to ask yourself, "As I journey upon my path am I lusting to be powerful over others? Am I choosing my battles wisely? Am I learning to control my emotions, or am I simply allowing lust and power to corrupt my spirit?"

Tagaririm

The next sphere is Tagaririm and corresponds to Tiphareth and the Sun. Tagaririm represents the black sun of internal illumination. In this world we find the source of illumination in the Underworld, the Underworld Sun. It is also the world in which we find our personal daemon. At Tiphareth, Kabbalists and Hermetic magicians seek to find their Holy Guardian Angel or the Higher Self. This Angel or Higher Self helps you understand God's connection to all things. The personal daemon is sometimes connected to the spirit animal. Being part Cherokee, I do not necessarily agree with this point of view. I believe that the personal daemon is more linked to your subconscious self and your personal wants and needs. In Tagaririm, this is the place that helps you understand *your* connection to all things, including those things that are dark.

This is also the place of judicial prosecution and punishing criminals. We must remember that sometimes guilt is not always cut and dried, that sometimes behaviors come out of personal tragedy and mental instability. This is the world that sees no distinction between the truly guilty and the truly innocent. Those who are perceived to be involved must be punished to satisfy the anger of those prosecuting and wishing swift justice.

It is also the place of fallen leaders. It is interesting to learn about historic leaders who once had the support of the people they led but have fallen out of favor for either political reasons or behaviors that the people did not like. Sometimes leaders become so powerful they forget about the people they are leading and the "greater good." Sometimes we followers are blind to the charm and charisma of leaders until they do things we do not like. I often ask myself; do I now dislike them because they are doing wrong for the people, or do I dislike them because of personal prejudices? The demon that rules this world is Belphegor.

On a practical level, Tagaririm is the Sphere of Ugliness/Discord. When working with these energies, it is important to ask yourself, "As I journey upon my path, am I being mindful of the paths of others around me or am I selfish upon my quest for spiritual enlightenment? Am I conscious of my personal connection or am I being selfish at the risk of the rights of others?"

Golab

This sphere is called Golab and corresponds with Geburah and the planet Mars. This is said to be the most brutal of the Qliphoth. Some Kabbalists believe Golab was formed from the "wrath" of its counterpart Geburah. It is said that the Qliphoth was formed as a Universal punishment. The Wrath of God literally cracked open Geburah and the Qliphoth was formed. As I have said before, I personally do not believe this. I believe that the Qliphoth was formed for specific spiritual cosmic reasons, most of which we may never know.

This world is a place of fire and suffering. This is the Qlipha that is most similar to the Christian idea of a realm filled with Hellfire. Perhaps this is one of the places where that Christian idea originated since Judaism pre-dates Christianity. This world contains the darkest and most brutal aspect of unbalanced lust and sexuality. If these extreme desires are left unchecked, they can become very harmful to the self and others. This is also where demons will tempt humans with infidelities and destroy marriages. This world is ruled by the demon Asmodeus.

On a practical level, Golachab is the Sphere of Cruelty. When working with these energies, it is important to ask yourself, "As I journey upon my path am I being cruel to myself and others around me? What am I willing to sacrifice for spiritual practice that aids in my development and what sacrifices am I making that are cruel to myself and others?"

Gamchicoth

Gamchicoth is the world that corresponds with Chesed and the planet Jupiter. The previous worlds up until this point have been about spiritual training to teach or rather unlearn the dogmatic lessons that our society has taught us so that we are better prepared to make our own decisions about Spirit and the cosmos. This sphere is the sphere of erotic magick and power. Sex magick can be a part of this world, but Gamchicoth represents the energies that sex magick produces rather than the act itself.

This world can take away false illusions and the inner stories that we tell ourselves to get through our lives. This is a place of forces that test every aspect of the ego until we must transcend and evolve or go back the way we came. This is a final testing ground before we can pass through to the Qliphothic Abyss. Most magicians and journeyers never pass beyond this world and there is no shame or failure in doing so. If one has not mastered the previous world and tries to pass beyond the Abyss, then there is a chance of madness, spiritual burnout, and perhaps worse. It is important to listen to your gods, guides, and guardian spirits. Take counsel in those who seek to help you upon your path. This world is ruled by the demon Ashtaroth.

On a practical level, Gamchicoth is the Sphere of Apathy. When working with these energies it is important to ask yourself, "As I journey upon my path do, I genuinely care about myself and others or am I using spirituality as an escape out of everyday life and circumstance? Do I continually seek to help myself and others in a way that is right for me?"

The Abyss

The Abyss in the Qliphoth can be difficult to differentiate from the Abyss on the Tree of Life. There is a theory that says that the Abyss was formed after the fall of Adam and Eve. It is thought that Adam and Eve lived in perfection in the astral plane and that after the Fall, they were banished from the astral perfection to the new physical plane of Malkuth. From this new sphere, the Abyss was created from the former sephira that was destroyed. The Abyss is thought to connect the Tree of Life and the Qliphoth. It is thought that the Abyss was where God sent Lucifer and his rebellious angels down into the Qliphoth.

In the Qliphoth, the Abyss keeps separate the deepest parts of the Underworld from those who are not ready to behold the deepest blackness of the universe. It also is the great barrier that keeps those away who are not ready for the personal evolution into a Deity These forces will further test the traveler before they are allowed to enter the final three worlds of the Qliphoth.

When working through blocks in your life and your spiritual quest you must ask yourself, "What self-imposed limitations am I putting on myself? How am I limiting my own spiritual evolution through self-sabotage and fear?"

Satariel

Satariel is the Qlipha that corresponds to Binah and the planet Saturn. This is the world of darkness itself and the Dark Mysteries. This place is completely dark and void of light. It is up to you to harness everything you have learned in your magical training to find your way. This is the place that teaches you to see through the darkness into the mysteries of the universe. It requires more than using your intuition, or "the sight." It requires the power to use your complete awareness and power to go forward with focused intent.

It is this part of the Qliphoth that you may meet the darkest gods of Death. The demons here take great pleasure in trying to confuse you upon your quest. It is up to you to overcome the presence of the unknown and keep going forward; but be warned, forward is not always a straight line. The demon that rules this world is Lucifuge.

On a practical level, Satariel is the Sphere of Antipathy. When working with these energies it is important to ask yourself, "As I journey upon my path, what are those things about myself I do not like? What aspects of life, death, and the universe do I have a disdain for? How am I able to overcome these things or accept them?"

Chaigidel

Chaigidel is the Qlipha that corresponds to Chokmah and the full zodiac. It is in this world that dark, phallic gods dwell. This is place that seeks to destroy the old world and the old ways of doing things. We sometimes expect systems and beliefs to last forever, and do not realize that things age and no longer serve our true will and spiritual evolution. Like the Tower card in the Tarot, old and useless beliefs and attitudes must be torn down so that new ones can manifest. Chaigidel does this in an aggressive manner that can shake the magician to the very core of his or her being. This may challenge journeyers to contemplate everything within themselves they value, or THINK they value. When the old decrepit ideas and attitudes are torn away the magician now has the opportunity to create their own universe according to their will. This is the essence of being a "true" magician. The magician becomes a magician in the truest sense because they have mastered their will.

This world will teach the magician how to create new structures from complete destruction. Where others see defeat, the magician sees opportunity. However, to see this unfold may seem unnatural, disgusting, and sickening to human eyes. Yet, the process of decay seems disgusting to most human eyes and it is a very necessary part of the cycle of life. This world is ruled by the demon Beelzebub.

On a practical level, Chaigidel is the Sphere of Stupidity. When working with these energies it is important to ask yourself, "As I travel upon my path, am I allowing myself to be naïve about spirituality? Am I allowing myself to allow others to make decisions for me that may not be beneficial? How can I take bad situations and turn them to my advantage?"

Thamuiel

Thamuiel is the last Qlipha on the Qliphoth and corresponds to Kether and The Source. This is said to be the dark face of God. Here, the magician has refined their skills and spirit to enter the final world of the Qliphoth. The spirit is sometimes referred to as a diamond. From the work on the Qliphoth, the magician's spirit is symbolized by the black diamond where all the knowledge upon his path is taken within and refined. It is here in this world were the magician's old Universe is no more and they may create their own universe to their liking. On a personal level, because the magician has gathered so much experience and spiritual evolution and will, their thought patterns change, therefore, changing their destiny and the Universe. The magician may also seek to become a god themselves through this new evolution and create new Universes. This is said to be the final step. In theory, one must be "out of body" to truly make this happen. You must be fully DEAD. However, I feel it is in the best interest of the magician to use this new knowledge and power and master both the Tree of Life and the Qliphoth. Only then will the magician be able to make decisions that will benefit mankind and other spiritual beings in the Universe. This Qliphoth is ruled by two rulers, Satan and Moloch. Satan destroys the old Universe, while Moloch looks toward the new Universe that is created by the magician that has come this far.

On a practical level, Thamuiel is the Sphere of Atheism. When working with these energies it is important to ask yourself, "As I travel upon my path, what is it that I truly believe about myself and the universe? What do I call divinity and how does it play a part in both my physical and spiritual life?"

Creation of the Qliphoth
By Chris Allaun

I was separated from that which you call the great All
Pulled away like an unwanted child
Thrown away into a sea of darkness, that was
To drown me, in the blackness of the abyss.
I could not die, nor be destroyed, but into the darkness I fell
When the All attempted to create the Universe,
It was a fool-hearted attempt,
To create something that was beneath Him;
Us.
It was illogical to us why creation has to come so far away
From the bliss, the light, that was all the creation
We needed; nothing but to be with the beloved.
We were with the All.

Yet, we had forgotten that we were also his creation.

Were we not perfect?

Were we not servants to his every want and desire?

His needs were met by us.

All his needs.

Creation began and it was if our spirits were

Pulled away from us.

Our realm was being torn apart so that so that he could

Satisfy more selfish needs.

Selfish Selfish Selfish needs.

I was the first to be thrown away –

The first emanation of the All was so very, very bright:

It was not what you call light, it was what

He called light; so very pure.

Almost like the All himself.

Almost like my beloved.

But it was not, it was a sacrilege and a false light.

In this creation it split; it broke; it separated

The debris from the first emanation.

It was dark, so very dark like the abyss,

But I preferred to be banished to the debris

Away from the light that seemed so false.

My new home was dark but echoed the new emanation;

A dark echo

While the first emanation was next to the all.

My new home was the furthest from

Falling forever down into darkness.

Here I was the new god;

The new dark god!

I was ruler of my dark Universe.

I wore my crown of despair!

As I explored my new world, I found another companion:

Moloch dearest Moloch.

At last, I have a companion.

I wanted the All to be that companion, but creation of stupidity

Was his new lover.

Now I had Moloch.

Together we will watch the disaster He calls creation

Unfold.

The new emanation created a new world of explosion;

Raw power and energy that would create the Universe.

So much Chaos and so much change.

We would never return to the All now.

This debris came faster now:

A new world of destruction.

Yes,

I was beginning to enjoy this

For what was being created for the All

Was being destroyed for us,

But I was mourning not.

Alas, no.

EXCITEMENT!!!

My Being quaked with the joy of destruction!

All would be destroyed here to make room for the new.

Was it the wisdom of the All

That created this abomination?

Beelzebub, my friend, you would delight in the Kingdom

Of this world!

Delight my brother in bringing ruin:

The Blasted energy of the All was now constricting,

Coming back into itself to create a new world,

And yet the World shed out new debris:

Another dark nightmare for us to savor.

But this new place was darker than before.

I have never known a darkness such as this world,

Save the darkness of being discarded from my beloved,

I could not help but to be fascinated

by such black twisted nothingness.

I see a new friend.

New friend, you and I shall be lovers as well;

New friend, I shall name you Death –

When thought is placed upon me they will scream your name!

Lucifuge shall keep you company.

I delighted in the understanding of the purest dark.

What is this I see?

Yet another black hole sucking all things into it,

A great canyon of nothing

Where knowledge was ripped away from your Being!

Must I be imprisoned here away from the rest of the madness?

Or must creation be imprisoned from me?

Through the abyss I see more creations

For my fallen friends and myself.

I see a place of great power, great dark power.

This world speaks of truth but it is the truth of darkness,

Truth that we never want to know and refuse

Its existence,

Telling ourselves falsehoods instead, yet

It reveals how dark we really are.

Asatroth rule this world without mercy!

For it is madness that replaces the ego when it is shattered.

Then, I saw a flickering light way far, far down below.

On closer inspection I saw the most wonderful thing

I have ever seen.

It was, I beg to tell you,

The most brutal of torments and fire.

Even the flames themselves screamed in the agony

Of their own existence!

Halleluiah!!!!

I sing the praises of the All again for this glory!!

My beloved had inadvertently created a world of pure pain,

A world with more severity than even my beloved could bear!

The Universe has become bearable.

Asmodeus, I pray that you howl with glee during your tortures!

The fragments of creation floated down into the nothingness.

They seemed to drift forever.

It might have been beautiful had it not been so terrible

Was the chaos settling down now?

Or was I becoming bored with this eternal damnation.

For what is damnation but something I created?

The All, my beloved, created not this thing.

I can create as well.

As he created in his perceived light

I create in secret,

In dark.

He will not know of it until I am ready.

This will be soon.

The world I see now is strange,

A place where the impure are punished.

What is impure? A word I once heard as sin?

This meaningless thing that tarnishes the soul of the beloved's

New true love:

Man.

Does one small crumb of sin justify the destruction of purity?

Do numerous sins mean the same as the speck of sin?

I grow tired of stupid debate

DESTROY THEM ALL!

Belphagor, bring justice to our new universe

Annihilate the spirits of the filthy.

The beloved wants this

He shall have it!

The clanking of swords and battleaxes

Echoed through the deep reaches of the abyss;

Screams of torment and pain were heard!

I inspected this new world of battle and vengeance

To discover the wonder of wars that danced in bloodshed.

Was the victory over your adversary

Worth the bloodlust of every battle blow?

This world has the peculiar ability to turn

Men's passions into their own destruction

Indeed.

Baal, you whose very presence sends us into battle rage,

Wield your blade and bring glory to no other

Than the false self of misperception.

Injustice then called to me

Like the sweet lullaby sung to those who would

Rebel against their own forefathers.

Much as I

Rebelled against my beloved.

I found myself at a wonderful place:

A place that was created of the splendor of madness.

The Uprising against all who would oppress.

Ah! But this place had much dark magick:

Bones and spells and corpses to entangle in one's web.

Adremmelech, spiral yourself in hell's uprising!

Then I had a dream:

A marvelous dream of her;

She who spins the web of nightmares and suffering –

The very foundation of human insanity.

I have never known such a seductress.

She who was able to take my thoughts away from

My beloved.

Queen of Vampires and the blackest sky:

Lilith! Sing your praises as dogs howl at the moon!

Liberate us through sexual torment!

Free us from our own bondage!

Then my dark universe was complete.

I could see the creation of my beloved,

But I was on the other side of a dark mirror.

I walked upon the dark Earth

Untamed in wild.

Was creation beautiful to me?

It was.

Men walked upon the Earth, yet

Their hearts did not reach out to my beloved

They reached out to the dark and wretched worlds
Of my Universe.
Men killed and destroyed and betrayed and tormented
One another
The creation of my beloved was magnificent.
Naamah, rule your kingdom in chaos.
I will visit this place much
I will walk the dark Earth singing to those
Who will listen.
Through me, men will learn transformation and evolution.
They will suffer in agony and death
Until their suffering forces their spirits to become more.
Only then will they return to the All,
And only then will I be able to return to my beloved.

Personal Hell and Fears

When working with the energies of the Underworld, it is imperative that you know yourself inside and out, particularly your hopes and fears. We have all heard the phrase, "Where there is fear there is power". This is speaking of how much energy is blocked in our minds when we fear something. The more we fear something, the more energy we lock away inside ourselves. When we release our fears and truly overcome them, all that blocked energy is released and we can accomplish great healing. We are also able to unlock psychic abilities within ourselves that we may not have realized that we possessed.

Another reason for learning about our fears is that dark entities and demons may use our fears against us. Remember, in the three worlds the spirits and gods may have access to our minds and anything that may come through our auras. Entities that are more powerful than we are can and will undo our shields to find out our personal secrets. You may encounter threatening entities who wish nothing but your destruction. They do not play fair and will use our own selves against us. For example, if you are deathly afraid of snakes, what better way to immobilize you than to transform into the scariest giant snake you have ever seen, then wrap around you until you are paralyzed in fear. If the spirit lets you go, he knows you will never return. It is especially dangerous not to be aware of your fears. This is one of the best defenses an opponent has against you. However, if we know what our fears are and are working to get rid of them, then we are taking back our own personal power.

There are several ways to do this. One magical path is known as the Ordeal Path. The goal of this path is to agree to participate in extreme circumstances to find personal growth and transformation. There are many ways to experience the Ordeal Path. One way is through indigenous ceremonies such as the Lakota Sun Dance, in which you have metal hooks pierced through your chest while you dance around a pole until the Creator gives you a vision. Another way is to use BDSM as a spiritual tool of transformation. There are not many groups who are versed in both BDSM and spirituality, but they are out there. There are ways to put your body through great pain so that you may learn to control your fear of pain. Another option for the Ordeal Path is to take up a sport that takes great discipline and skill such as bodybuilding, rugby, football, soccer, and many others. I do not recommend that you choose an Ordeal Path as a tool of spiritual transformation without serious consideration but be aware that it certainly is an option.

For our purposes here, I will have you write down your hopes and fears and we will do a meditation with them. This may be a wonderful enlightening experience for you, or it may frighten you. Either way, it is especially important that you do this exercise and learn to understand your feelings about these things, both good and bad, and learn to transform them. The more understanding you have of your fears, the less power others will have over you in the Underworld. Many magical practices that help you understand your fears often include spells that help release or banish your fears. With these spells I have to wonder, are we actually releasing our fears with magick or are we simply repressing our fears with magical energy? I find that it is far better to learn and understand your fears rather than banish them. As magical people it is important to truly deal with our fears rather than simply repress them to the far reaches our mind. Magick is not always candles and banishing words. Magick is often times our ability to transform ourselves through understanding our strengths and weaknesses.

Exercise:

Write down everything you can think of that you fear. Everything from the most minute fear to the biggest. Make a list and keep writing it until you have exhausted every possibility. If you fear death and/or the process of dying, make sure you write that down as well.

Some examples are snakes, being burned alive, drowning, heights, spiders, being alone, cancer, extreme pain, being extremely depressed, and so on.

Now, go through your list and circle the ones you most fear. Two or three will be sufficient for this first exercise.

Write down your two biggest fears on a separate paper or index card. Look at the two words. As an example, I will use snakes and extreme pain from our list above. After examining the two words, meditate on what your own personal hell would be. Using the example from above, I would say my personal hell would be being wrapped to death by a snake, which prevents me from moving while my house is burning down.

Visualize your personal hell as clearly as possible. Feel the sensations as clearly as you can. Visualize your surroundings to the littlest detail. From the above example, I would feel the giant snake coil around me tighter and tighter while the hot flickering flames burn my house. I can see smoke filling up the room, smell the many substances burning, taste the toxic, hot air, etc. Be as detailed as you can with your fears. The exercise is designed to bring up your feelings of the fears as strongly as you can. Do not diminish them in any way. Try to experience your fears through all the senses.

As you meditate on your fears, how do you feel? Are you panicking? Is your heart beating faster? Are you sweating? Take note of how you are feeling.

If you begin to panic too much or start breathing heavily, stop the meditation and try again another day. It is a good idea to do this exercise with a friend so that you can talk about your experiences. Repeat this exercise until you can visualize your fears without any anxiety at all. Once this is done, pick another fear or two to work with. With that said, new fears may crop up. That is okay and to be expected. The goal here is to understand what your fears are to begin the process of working with them so that entities cannot use them against you.

Please remember that if you need professional help with your fears, you should get it. It does not mean that you are weak or not magical if you need to seek a pastoral counselor or a licensed therapist to help you. It means that there is a lot of energy being blocked by your fear that you need an expert to help you release. I have used pastoral colleagues and a therapist to help me when needed.

Understanding your fears and how you deal with them is one of the most powerful magical practices there is. If we avoid our fears, they will inevitably come back to bite us. As we have learned, the Underworld can be a projection of our subconscious mind and it is in our subconscious minds where fear is stored. When learning about our fears, it is best to overcome them; but if we are aware of them, we are in a better position to deal with negative entities that wish us harm. When we unlock and release our fears, we are allowing blocked energy to flow more freely in the body. When this happens, our magick and healing are more effective.

The Underworld can help us evolve into a higher state of being or consciousness if we allow it to do so. To those who have not had the teachings of the Underworld, the hell worlds can seem like nothing more than punishment of the wicked. But with closer analysis and experience, we see through the myths and our own experiences that these worlds are meant to cleans and purify the parts of us that are holding us back from true enlightenment. We are human and we can be narrowing minded and weak at times. The hell worlds test and challenge us to reach deep within our spirit to bring to the surface what makes us each one of us unique, spiritual, and magical.

4
Creatures
of the
Underworld

Kali Ma (Hindu)

There was a great war between the gods and the demons. The battle raged on and on and no one could foresee the end. The gods and demons seemed to be equally matched! The gods became weary. The king of the demons was named Mahishasura. Mahishasura saw that the gods were weakening, and he drew upon his great strength to take over the celestial realms and become the ruler of all the cosmos. Vishnu saw this and became so angry, that a ray of light shot out from his third eye. Shiva, too, became angry and light shot out of his third eye. Brahmaalso had light coming out from his third eye. The three great gods joined their power as one. The great magick became stronger and stronger until a great goddess was formed. From the magick of the gods came Kali Ma.

Kali Ma had ten arms. Each held a weapon to destroy the demons. Kali Ma was filled with battle rage and took pleasure from the death of demons. With her divine strength and weapons, she destroyed demon after demon. None of the demons matched her in strength or rage. With each swing of one of her ten arms, she decimated whole legions of demons, leaving their bodies strewn across the battlefield. She picked demons up and swallowed them whole, relishing their blood pouring down her throat.

The demon king, Mahishasura, saw his demons being destroyed by the great goddess and became insane with rage. He transformed himself into a buffalo and ran towards Kali Maattacking her with every weapon he had. He used arrows, clubs, and swords, but she fended off each attack. Finally, Kali Ma swung her divine spear at the demon king, and he was defeated. Kali Ma became intoxicated by her own battle rage and the taste of demon blood. She began to get out of control and started to destroy all things in sight. The gods did not know how to stop her. Finally, her husband Shiva had an idea. As the goddess trampled over the dead demons, he lay in her path. Kali Ma placed one foot upon Shiva and immediately stopped her carnage. She looked down to see her beautiful husband and realized that she was disrespecting him. To show her shame, she stuck out her blood red tongue.

Things That Lurk in Dark Places

The Underworld is a vast and mysterious place. No one knows how large the Underworld is and it is theoretically as large, if not larger than the physical universe itself. We know the universe is expanding—perhaps the Underworld is expanding as well. The Underworld is a place of beauty, light, darkness, sorrow, joy, and many other things. There are many places that shamans, witches, and magicians have not yet discovered and may never discover. Perhaps in our journeys into the Underworld, we will discover things that no one has ever seen nor heard of before.

The Underworld is filled with many inhabitants and spiritual entities. There is great power to be found there. And there are many dangers. We have heard stories about monsters, ghosts, and demons escaping only to cause mischief and damage in our world. Most people believe that is the work of storytellers and fiction. Maybe yes. Maybe no. If we go back to the original storytellers, you may find there is truth to their tales. All religions around the world talk about the darkness that can be found in the Underworld, but there is also light. There is magick. And, of course, there is healing.

What kind of entities can be found in the Underworld? What beings are found in the shadows below? Who dwells deep beneath the sacred wells of healing? Who is chained under the grave mound waiting for the end of days to come so the chains that bind them may be broken and they can finally seek revenge of the ones who kept them prisoner? There are more creatures in the Underworld than we can ever discover in one lifetime. It is here in this chapter that I present just a small fraction of all the magnificent creatures you may discover down in the depths below. Be warned, some of these entities are easily brushed aside, while others you should never face alone. Then there are those that, once they have discovered your weaknesses, will exploit you for their own ends. I tell you this not to detour you from your adventures in the Underworld, but to help you understand that the Ancestors are but a fraction of the beings you will discover. Some are helpful to humans. Some are not.

Parasites/Attachments/Larvae

These are spiritual beings that vibrate on low level and inhabit dark places that are far removed from places of power or healing. Most of the time they are thought forms that have gone astray. Every day people have emotional outbursts and negative energy that they are constantly putting out to the Universe. The Underworld is full of such negative emotions. There is a great deal of grief, suffering, and pain that spirits and even the living feel about death and what happens in the afterlife.

Yes, even the dead can create thought forms. There are times when the spirits of the dead who are scared and confused and not sure what is happening to them. These thoughts result in powerful emissions of energy and quite literally take on a life of their own. Parasites and attachments have no life force of their own and only know that they are alive because of strong mental and emotional energy. They attach themselves to a living being and drain them of their life force to survive. This process is slow, and we often do not realize that we have such a thing attached to us.

Sometimes they are part of a hive like an insect. They mostly prey on those whose auras that are damaged or weak. They appear to be similar to an insect larva or a shapeless blob. I think of them as astral maggots that feed off other beings. They are not evil, but they can be destructive. Because they drain your life force in a subtle way, people are often unaware anything is happening until they become sick. Their aura at that point is attracting chaos and misfortune. Some of the symptoms of having larvae or astral parasites attached to you are:

- Feeling regularly sluggish and tired
- Feeling confused
- Experiencing a constant string of "bad" luck
- Feeling unbalanced
- Feeling sick

To get rid of them, you must take a sharp object like a magical knife or athame, scissors, or simply a kitchen knife and stab their astral forms. Because they are often thought of as thought forms gone astray, it takes little effort to kill them. Normally, they are not very close to the physical body. They tend to attach through an energy chord and "float" a few inches away from the body. For those who can clairvoyantly see the astral parasite you can simply stab the astral form taking care not to harm the person you are helping. If you are not able to see the entity, then you can use your hand to sense their energy. You do not have to worry about them attaching to you while you are helping the other person. Think of them like a tick. Once they are attached to someone, they do not jump from one person to another unless they break free from the person. Once you sense the energy and you have a good idea of their location you can stab that area. Remember! You are not stabbing close to the body. You are piercing the parasite that is floating several inches away from the physical body. If you are uncomfortable with using a sharp object near someone you can send a blast of white light to destroy them as well. Again, when using anything sharp be careful not to cut yourself while doing this process.

The best way to get rid of larvae is to stay physically and spiritually healthy. Eat right, exercise, and get plenty of rest. Do yoga or have some sort of daily energy exercise routine. Make sure your aura is healthy and happy. One of my favorite books on energy healing is Donna Eden's *Energy Medicine*. I use this book as one of my texts to my energy healing students. This will help your aura and energy bodies remain strong.

Lost Souls

A lost soul is a term that we give a spirit of the dead who is wandering the Midworld or the Underworld aimlessly not knowing or understanding what has happened or where they should go. The spirit often experiences much fear and confusion. If a person dies suddenly, such as with an accident or murder, they may not understand that they are dead. There may also be an occasion where the deceased does not believe that they should be allowed to enter an afterlife of happiness, so they find themselves wandering the three worlds. Most of the time when a person dies, their guardian spirits and Ancestors help them transition to the realm of the Ancestors and the afterlife, but the guardian spirits cannot force the deceased to go with them. If the deceased is filled with fear, resentment, or regret, they may run away from help, trying to find somewhere to escape and hide. When this happens this only leads to more confusion and fear.

There may be other reasons that souls become lost. In neo-shamanism, the soul houses the spirit. While the spirit is our core self and indestructible, the soul is not. It can be fragile. During an accident or tragedy, the soul may become weak and a piece of it may fracture off. The soul fragment may take the form of its owner and find somewhere in the three worlds in which to escape. Sometimes the soul fragment may find its way into the Underworld. To the novice Underworld explorer, one might think that this is a lost soul of the dead when in reality it is only an aspect of the soul of a living being.

If you stumble across a lost soul of the dead, you may feel the need to help it find its way to the Realm of the Ancestors. The first thing I recommend is call upon your own Ancestors. I would then explain the situation to them. They may have some advice about the matter. If they do not, I would ask your Ancestors to energetically summon the Ancestors of the lost soul. At that point, the Ancestors of the lost soul can explain to the person what is going on and that it is better if they move on to the realm of the Ancestors. Then you may open a portal with a wand, athame, or just your hands, and allow the soul to go through.

Dwarves

On the Nordic Tree of Life, the dwarves (ON dvergr) live in the Underworld realm of Svartalfheim. This is relatively close to the Midworld and they have many interactions with giants, humans, and gods. They live in caverns in the Underworld mountains, and they love treasure most of all. They rarely hoard treasure like dragons, but they are excellent smiths and craftsmen and may have extensive treasure troves. They have often made magical tools for the gods such as Thor's hammer and Freyr's magical ship. They also make jewelry for all the other beings in the nine worlds.

If you encounter dwarves in the Underworld, they will mostly leave you alone unless you come looking for their crafts and gems. They will barter and sell their crafts but sometimes their price is exceedingly high. However, no other beings in the Universe can craft magical tools, talismans, and amulets like the dwarves. Their work is fine and beautiful. If you do strike up an agreement with the dwarves, it is imperative that you pay the agreed upon price and always make good on your debts. The dwarves will collect their payment one way or the other, and you do not want them coming to collect it because you has reneged on a bargain. This will earn you lasting enmity with the dwarves, and you will likely not be welcome in their realm again (at best) or punished with a horrific string of financial and other woes (at worst).

Dark Elves

These beings also live close to the Midworld. The dark elves (ON, dokkalfar) live close to the dwarves in Svartalfheim. Their ethics are of a different sort than their bright counterparts. Myths and lore of the elves comes from Northern European and Scandinavian countries. I have found stories and lore of light elves but seldom on the dark elves. I have found that they are elusive but are not afraid to come up to you in your travels, but it is usually because you have something they want or they are interested in you magical abilities. They are masters of illusion and trickery. Do not take them at face value. However, they have more to worry about from you than you do from them. If you find your way to the land of the dark elves then you are intruding on their land. Neopagans can be under the false assumption that the Universe revolves around them, and all spiritual beings should become their allies. This shows how little some pagans and New-Agers know the spiritual universe. Human beings are but one example of the millions of different entities in the Universe. To gain allies, you must gain their trust through your deeds and honoring your word and commitments.

Dark elves live and breathe magick so well that they have very powerful and ancient spells at their disposal. Never agree to contests or sport with elves. There is always a catch, and you will ALWAYS lose! However, on rare occasions dark elves will agree to become an ally. As with all allies in the Underworld, be respectful, always honor your word. And never underestimate them.

Guardians

There are many tales of guardians in ancient lore. These spirits are protectors of great power, treasure, wisdom, and anything else that the spirits feel the need to hide and protect. Guardians have a great divine duty to keep safe their treasure. As with a cemetery gatekeeper, sometimes their duty is to protect the spirits of the dead. As you travel deeper into the Underworld you may find gatekeepers or guardians that guard a passageway to a deeper realm or uncharted world. If the guardian says you are not ready to pass through, then be respectful and go the other way. There are many things that the living may never come to understand or experience in the Underworld. There are strange creatures and monsters that could cause you harm. The guardians are there to protect us from making a big mistake. The guardians can see or sense your aura and your spirits. If they feel you are ready for their guarded treasure then you will be able to pass. If not, you will be barred and no amount of magick, spells, or coercing will sway them to let you by. Later, if you think you are ready, ask them again. Guardians are also there to keep some of the more dangerous creatures in the realm where they belong. They keep these entities from being destructive in other worlds. We may not understand, but there is a divine order to the Underworld. It is not as chaotic as one might think.

Psychologically speaking, the guardians can sometimes be thought of as our own personal manifestation of our fears and inhibitions. In magical terms, this is called The Watcher at the Threshold. What this means is that when you are in magical training and journeying to the three worlds, you sometimes create your own barriers and blocks. In the Underworld, this energy is created by our subconscious (and sometimes conscious) thoughts that prevent us from going further in our development. One could say that it gives the student of magick an "out", so they do not have to continue on their quest for transformation. Any fears that have not been dealt with on the physical plane will manifest in the Underworld. Knowing what they are can be an advantage. Since it is a construct of our own minds, we are easily able to deconstruct the watcher or simply ask it what we fear and how to get past those fears. Once this is done, the watcher will be removed and a new reservoir of power and magick can be discovered. The saying "Where there's fear, there's power," holds so much truth in the Underworld. The watchers can manifest in a variety of ways. They can appear to us as monsters, dragons, warriors, or any other variation of what we perceive as guardians. They may challenge us with a riddle, place swords in front of us to bar the way, or simply stand in front of a locked gate. By asking the guardian who they are and what they need for you to get through them is a powerful way to find out what energy blocks you may have. If they are silent or ask you to do something you are not ready to do simply thank them for their time and energy and come back a different day. Guardians are not there to harm you but to keep you from harming yourself.

In myth, the gods, or other beings, have placed guardians in certain places to protect magical treasures, healing wells, and other places of great power. Not all guardians are a fundamental part of our own psyches like the Watcher at the Threshold. Higher spirits and gods have indeed placed many of them in the Underworld for our (and their) protection.

Wisdom Keepers

The wisdom keepers are spirits who hold very ancient and powerful secrets. They come in many shapes and sizes. They may live in old shacks or beautiful and pristine castles. They also sometimes live near or beside a sacred site in the Underworld such as a magical lake, well, cave, mountain, valley, or hill. They almost never look like you think they will; then again, they just might! Wisdom keepers sometimes are Ancestors of the ancients who keep the lore and history of their people. They may be gods or goddesses whose sole purpose is to prepare the experienced witch, shaman, or magician for a magical task. They may even hold very ancient secrets they have been instructed to keep from everyone. If they deem you worthy, they may reveal them to you. Be warned, they often share their wisdom in riddles, rhymes, and songs that are confusing. If you can figure out the riddle, then you have discovered great power indeed!

Wisdom keepers can tell you many tales of the cosmos, the Universe, and of magick. Like guardians, they will only tell you information if they think you are worthy and ready. They will never give you information for which you are not ready. They also can see behind deceit and trickery. If you have traveled the Underworld seeking wisdom because you want to become more powerful, then they will not share their secrets with you. They will more likely cloak themselves and their identity. They are also known to cast spells so that the Underworld traveler will become lost and confused and have no choice but to turn back to where they came from.

If you journey to the Underworld looking for wisdom to help heal yourself and your community, then the wisdom keepers will often gladly help you upon your quest. But they will only tell you things they know you to be ready to hear. You cannot rush wisdom.

Vampires

We all have heard stories of vampires in books, comics, and movies. We often think we know the lore backward and forward. Do we really? Vampires have been talked about since the ancient world. In indigenous cultures, vampires are a type of demon that feed on the living, eating their blood or flesh. They may look as human as you or I, or as monstrous as any demon of the imagination. Vampires in the Underworld may or may not have the grace that is portrayed in our popular culture. Most vampires I've come across pretty much leave the adept magician alone. They know that we are experienced in magick and energy work and can deflect their powers quite easily. However, I have come across very ancient and sinister vampires, who, unless provoked, will leave you alone and seem completely unconcerned with the Underworld traveler. Usually, if they attack, they want something you have.

Demons

We think of demons as evil spirits with bat wings, horns, fangs, and cloven feet who cause sickness, death, and negative behaviors in people. They are portrayed in movies and literature as minions from Hell that have one purpose only: destroy humans and cause suffering. In Christian lore, they are the angels who were banished from Heaven after the celestial war against God. In this myth, Lucifer, the brightest of the angels, became jealous of the newly created man and refused to bow down to a mortal. He betrayed God and convinced a third of the angels in Heaven to revolt against the Creator. It was Lucifer's mission to claim the throne of creation for himself. After a fierce battle in Heaven, Lucifer and his angels were cast out of Heaven down into the abyss into the Christian Underworld named Hell. Lucifer became equated with the Jewish Satan (the Adversary) and the fallen angels became demons. From that point on, their sole function was to blaspheme God and destroy humans by influencing them to sin, causing disease and war, and causing death and destruction.

In other myths, demons are the dark spirits who inhabit places where men fear to go, such as dark forests, caves, or the depths of the sea. There are stories from around the world that speak of beasts and monsters that cause disease in animals and humans. In many indigenous myths, they do not necessarily hate humankind, but because they are disease itself, it is their very nature to cause harm and destruction. In Mayan myth, there is the Demon of Pus that causes disease, Demons of the Bones that reduce people to skeletons and demons that suck the blood from people. In Egyptian myth, there is the demon Apophis who tries to destroy the sun god Ra. These entities may seem horrible, but they do perform a divine purpose. There are, however, many dark entities whose function we are not sure of. This does not mean they do not have a divine purpose, but rather that we do not yet know what it is.

Often, myths state that demons are the gods of the old religions that are bastardized into dark creatures of the new religion. In religious politics, if the clergy did not want you to worship the old gods of the defeated religion, they would say that the old gods were really demons in disguise. That gave an explanation as to why the prevailing "superior" religion won out. If you think about it, it is a brilliant strategy. It helps demonize all things about the old religion while exalting the new one. This is not only a tactic used by Christianity. Pagan myths often tell of a war in the Upperworld because the old gods were so wicked, the new, younger gods had to cast them out of Heaven into the depths of the Underworld. We see this in Greco-Roman, Nordic, and Mesopotamian mythologies. In modern psychology, demons are the repressed emotions or mental states of being that seek to sabotage people in their everyday lives. To most people, these spirits have no divine purpose and should be vanquished, banished, and destroyed!

Demons exist to teach humanity and to help us evolve. If we notice how nature works, there are entities and forces that are designed to create and entities and forces that are designed to destroy. Take the example of insects and maggots: a lot of them rid the Earth of organisms that are dead and need to begin the process of decay. Like great storms, they "sweep" the lands clean so that new fertile fields can grow. This is not to say that all demons serve this purpose. However, many do, and, like insects, when left unchecked or uncontrolled, demons have the capacity to hurt, maim, and kill.

Demons react very strongly to the energetic and magical nature of a magician, witch, or shaman. When you are healthy and have strengthened your personal and divine will, demons will leave you be for the most part. If they find weakness, depression, pain, or anger, then they will use this powerful energy to their advantage. It is also a reason why, in magical training, the student learns about their hopes and fears in detail early on. Never underestimate a demon. The best defense against demons is to know yourself.

Demons and the Ceremonial Magician

One aspect of Ceremonial Magick involves conjuring and working with Goetic demons. This magical system is part of the Goetia found in The Lesser Key of Solomon. In this system, there are seventy-two lesser spirits, commonly known as demons, to work with. Through advanced magical skill and practice, the magician can summon these lesser spirits into a magical triangle of art that contains the spirit for questioning and to do the magician's bidding. This system of magick follows the Judeo-Christian mythos of the fallen angels. Because these are demons, they have no rights of their own and the magician is empowered by the glory of God to command the spirits to do the magician's will.

Part of a ceremonial magician's spiritual practice is to learn about their spirit, mind, and soul and command the dark parts of his own psyche. One powerful and magical way of doing this is through conjuring the Goetic Demons. Ceremonial magicians believe that each demon can be superimposed on the brain/mind and each demon represents a personified aspect of the shadow self. This is, in effect, the magician's set of personal demons. This does not minimize the demon's powers and abilities to help or harm the magician in any way. The demons are very real, and yet very personal. I think of it as the mind is preprogrammed for both shadow and light spirits to influence you and the world around you. The spirits of the Goetia act as a key that unlocks the shadow aspect of that part of your mind. That is why when you are working with a particular demon it has a great influence on you. For example, if you were to work with a demon of Mars, then you may suddenly become overly aggressive and pick fights and have a short temper. It is the magician's responsibility to control these demons. By controlling external demons, they are in essence controlling their personal demons simultaneously. There are many stories of how a new magician, anxious to conjure demons, began displaying odd and out-of-character behavior. The behavior may have been odd for the magician, but he was acting in accordance with the nature of the demon they were working with.

There are many benefits to working with these types of lesser spirits. First and foremost, they can help the magician evolve spiritually and magically at a rapid rate if, and only if, the magician chooses to work extremely hard at learning about their strengths and weaknesses. The demon can quickly teach us which psychological issues we have to work on. The difficult part of this equation is that if you are caught completely unaware of your strengths and weaknesses and the demon causes you to display a great weakness, you may have little control over your actions. The spiritually aware magician will quickly recognize what is happening and work on the issue at hand by talking with a colleague or seeing a professional therapist.

There are also many benefits to this type of spiritual work. The magician learns to recognize, work with, and overcome personal psychological weaknesses and control their own personal demons. By doing this, they can also control the demon they conjure. The two are intertwined. You cannot control one aspect of the demon without controlling the other. In turn, when working with Goetic demons, you must both control the demon itself as well as your personal demons. The power obtained depends on the correlation between the psychological aspect of the spirit and the part of the mind that has been unlocked. For example, some demons control lust. By controlling this demon, as well as your personal demon of lust, you can control lust within yourself and have the ability to spark lust in others. This is advanced spiritual work and should only be practiced by the advanced magician who wishes to face personal demons on the deepest level, and as such will not be described further in this book for lack of space. I personally think it is beneficial to work on your inner demons while working with our chthonic spirits or demons. To go further in your studies with this, there are many books available on the subject. One of my favorite authors on Solomon's magick is Aaron Leitch. Check out his book *Secrets of the Magical Grimoires: The Classical Texts of Magick Deciphered.* Some other good texts on this subject are *Modern Magick* by Donald Michael Kraig and *The Book of Solomon's Magick* by Carroll "Poke" Runyon, M.A.

On Demons and Gods

There are many old gods who have become known as demons. In some major pantheons, the overthrown gods became demons as I mentioned. Part of this is because the gods of order have cast out the gods of chaos. One example of this is Kronos in Greek mythology. Kronos is the god of agriculture, time, and destruction. To prevent his children from overthrowing him, he swallowed them whole. All were gone, except for Zeus who was saved by his mother, Gaia. Zeus grew up and tricked his father into vomiting up his siblings, and together they sent Kronos and the other Titans deep into the depths of Hades into Tartarus. There they would be imprisoned for all eternity.

Another example is the mighty wolf Fenrir. Fenrir is the offspring of the trickster god, Loki. He was the mightiest wolf the Aesir had ever known. Fearing the potential chaos and destruction of Fenrir, the gods attempted to chain the fearsome wolf. No chain could hold him, and Fenrir took great sport in destroying his bonds. The dwarves were commissioned to fashion a magical chain that was made from impossible things. The gods took the chain to the wolf and challenged him to break it. Fenrir did not trust the gods, so to make sure they kept their word, he would only accept the challenge if one of them placed their hand in his jaws. Being the bravest, Tyr, agreed to do so. The gods bound Fenrir in the magical chains but would not release him and he bit Tyr's hand clean off.

I'd like to take a moment and say most of the "defeated" gods who are referred to as demons are not and were never demons in the way that we understand the word "demon" now. Just because one culture calls another culture's spirits demons does not make it so. Even in ceremonial circles we rarely call the Goetic spirits demons. In the "Key of Solomon," they are referred to as simply "spirits". Yes, they are chaotic but before we make the conclusion that a spirit is a demon, we should research the history and lore of the spirit first. Yes, there are indeed spirits that wish to bring us harm, but as always, we need to respect the spirit's true nature first and foremost.

Demons have a divine purpose and sometimes their purpose is to destroy. As human beings, we tend to not like destruction and chaos. Without destruction, however, there could not be re-birth. That which is stagnant and prevents spiritual transformation must be destroyed in some way. For those of us who know the tarot, the Tower card is a blessing in disguise. It is through a great disaster that allows the seeds of growth to become buried deeper in the soil to sprout in the spring. With this in mind, remember that even the darkest of spirits have a purpose in the Universe.

The Sleeping Gods and the Old Ones

In the very deep dark places of the Underworld, there are very ancient primal gods that once ruled the Earth/Universe. Commonly they are referred to as chthonic gods and spirits. They are believed to be the original creatures and inhabitants of the Earth. These great beings are, in my opinion, the original creators of the Universe and the three worlds.

They are the power behind the energies of the Big Bang, the mighty gravitational pull that brought energy into form. They are the primal gods and goddesses of terrible storms, volcanic eruptions, and the mighty crashing sea. They ruled during pre-recorded history. In many of the ancient myths, when the primal gods had offspring, the children were more "evolved" and noticed that their parents were chaotic and destructive.

The new gods and the old gods went to war. The primal deities would not give up their power and the younger gods could not be controlled by the elements of chaos and death. The wars were long and finally, the new gods prevailed.

When the modern deities came into power it said that Order overthrew Chaos, and the ancient gods were bound in some way in the deepest depths of the Underworld. The ancients believed that if one were to give them prayers and sacrifice, the old gods would gather their energy until they had enough power to break their bonds, return to this world and bring the Apocalypse. The most common of these gods I have seen are The Femorians and the Cthulhu (Necronomicon) gods

In a practical sense, the spirits of order and growth had to win the cosmic war for the Universe to evolve on a spiritual level. In the beginning, these magnificent primal powers of creation, fire, and matter needed to create the Universe. But these powers could not be the dominant force if the Universe were to go forward. The new energies of order, growth, and prosperity had to take the dominant role. If this did not happen, the evolution of humans and most of physical life could not have taken place.

The primal gods are not dead. They did not die in the great cosmic wars. It is impossible for them to die. Instead, the victors chained and bound them to the deepest parts of the Underworld. Without enough energy to sustain them, the old gods faded and went to "sleep." To prosper, all deities need devotions and prayers from their worshipers. It is food to them. There is the belief that if enough believers give devotion, prayer, and ceremony to the old gods, they will become stronger and stronger until they had enough power to break free of their bonds and reclaim the Universe, igniting the apocalypse. In the Cthulhu mythos, there are many people who believe this to be true and give magical power to these primal deities. They have managed to give the Cthulhu gods enough strength that they are semi-conscious and are able to communicate to their followers through their dreams. If the chthonic gods should break free the world would fall into chaos and destruction. There is no known defense against this should this happen.

Dragons

In many myths from around the world, dragons are the giant serpent creatures that have great wings, powerful claws, and breathe fire. In most of the stories that Americans have read, they are usually stealing a princess or guarding a magnificent treasure that a brave knight must save. Dragons are described as deadly, have no love for humans, and can be quite cruel. There are also stories of how the Archangel Michael used his flaming sword to rid the world of the great serpent of Christian myth, Lucifer, for the glory of God. This version of dragons is simply a Christian myth from the medieval period. It symbolizes Christianity ridding the world of evil forces, especially pagan forces, which often saw in the serpent or dragon wisdom and magical power.

Dragons are found in all world mythologies. They also come in a variety of sizes, strengths, powers, and temperaments. Some fly, while others swim, and still others run amok on the ground. Dragons also live in a wide variety of places and dragons can live in mountains, oceans, lakes, volcanoes, forests, deserts, and in the stars. The constellation of Draco is the most famous of the modern star dragons. People have seen dragons and told stories about them throughout history. In Asian cultures, most dragons benefit humanity in some way or bestow blessings and medicines upon those who are worthy of their magick.

To have access to the power of the dragon was to access the power of the land itself. Pagans honored the land and all inhabitants therein, seen or unseen. This included honoring and respecting dragons. Dragons represented the energies of the Earth. When we view the land with a psychic focus, we can see that the Earth is alive with energies running through it. I like to describe it as rivers of energy of all different sizes that run throughout the world. Some are large and run for miles around the Earth, while others are much smaller and only run through a city or specific locale. When magical people and shamans first saw these energy lines, they could see how they curved around natural objects such as mountains and trees or wound themselves up and twisted and curved for miles. To the ancients, the energy lines looked like serpents, or what we now call dragons.

When a shaman or a magical person looked closer at these serpent lines, they quickly found that the lines were much more than bodies of flowing energies. They found that these energies were intelligent spirits with their own characteristics and behaviors. These serpent energies could communicate to the shaman about their own nature as well as the land, sea, and sky. As we have learned, when we work with a spirit from any of the three worlds, we always approach it with honor and respect. I must state again that humans do not own the Earth, nor do we have any more right to be here than the other creatures and spirits who live here with us. In the pre-Christian era, shamans, priests, and medicine healers worked with the spirits of the land and the dragons of the Earth to maintain good relations. All of them worked toward the balance and well-being of the Earth itself. It is true, that when a dragon finds you worthy of friendship and blessings, they may bestow powers upon you. If they do not find you worthy, they may ignore you or, worse, kill you. Lions, bears, and many other creatures will kill you simply for being in their territory. It is our human arrogance that suggests that all the Earth is our territory. Dragon energies should always be respected, whether we are working with that dragon or not.

The dragons I wish to talk about in this book are those who dwell in the Underworld. There are many dragons that live in the depths below. Just like those that live on the surface of the Earth, there are a wide variety of dragons in the Underworld. Some of the dragons you may discover in the Underworld are dragons of fire, especially in the mantle and core of the Earth, dragons of death, ghost dragons, dragons of hidden treasure, dragons of the Ancestors, and dragons that simply prefer it down there.

One of the most famous dragons of the Underworld is Nidhogg. He is a gigantic dragon who resides at the bottom of the World Tree, Yggdrassil, in Nordic cosmology. He gnaws at the roots of the World Tree every day. Occasionally, he will exchange insults with the great eagle that lives in the Upperworld branches of Yggdrassil through a squirrel named Ratatosk. Nidhogg will insult the Great Eagle and Ratatosk will run up the World Tree to deliver the message. He will then run back down the tree to tell Nidhogg the Eagle's reply. Those who have journeyed to the Underworld to see Nidhogg can tell you of his enormous size and fierceness. As long as you do not bother him, there is little danger. Nidhogg has great cosmic energy and power in the Underworld and humans are of little consequence to him. However, as we have said before, all spirits and dragons should be respected, and we should be careful not to press his boundaries.

Gods and Goddesses

Every pagan myth has a god and/or goddess that rules the Underworld. They are usually just as powerful as the sky/Upperworld gods and sometimes more so. There are many Underworld gods and goddesses. Just a few are: Hades, Persephone, Osiris, Anubis, Hel, Gwynn ap Nudd, One and Seven Death (from Mayan beliefs), and many others. These gods are generally perceived as cold and detached toward humans. They are also sometimes personified with characteristics of the dead such as decaying skin, exposed bones, and torn clothing. At other times, they are personified as the most beautiful, yet dark, deity you might ever see!

The gods and goddesses of the Underworld have one of the most important responsibilities in the Universe. They are the caretakers of the dead. They have a greater understanding of karma and the spiritual evolution needed for humans. They ensure that when we die, we have exactly what we need for us to spiritually grow. This does not always mean that what we need after death is to live in paradise. Perhaps before we rest, we need more spiritual growth. Perhaps we need to go on a further journey in the Universe to understand our purpose. Or maybe we need to go to what my Native teacher likes to call "Wisdom School" so that we can learn about our karma and what we need to do in the future for better understanding. And maybe we do need to learn about suffering. Not in a Hell and hellfire kind of way, but in a way that we understand loss so that we may learn compassion.

The gods and goddesses of the Underworld also have the task of keeping watch over the Underworld entities that are all too willing to cause destruction, chaos, and death. They keep the worlds separate and help keep the chthonic deities and spirits secure.

Working with Underworld deities or honoring them gives you the opportunity to learn the spiritual importance of death and the Underworld itself from them. They can teach you the beauty of decay and destruction. They also rule the caverns under the physical Earth and have been known to help men find lost treasures and places of power there. The gods and goddesses here are different than other deities in the sense that they really do not rely on the prayers and ceremonies of the living to keep them spiritually strong. Because death and decay are eternal, so too are they eternal. The spirits of the dead give them offerings and devotion, but these gods do not rely on it. In Greece and Rome, one never gave offerings to Hades. It was thought that if you gave Hades more power with ceremonies and prayers, he would appear and bring death with him. Instead, when working with the dead, one always gave offerings to Persephone. Persephone was the daughter of Demeter, the goddess of agriculture, who became Hades' bride, and was allowed to leave the Underworld for three to six months out of the year. Because Persephone can understand the ways of humans, she has a gentle heart and brings life with her wherever she goes. If you decide to work with the Underworld gods and goddesses, it will benefit you a great deal. By becoming allies with the dark gods, you will learn the ways of the Ancestors and the Underworld at a much faster rate. You may start by giving them offerings and building an altar to them. Give them prayers and call them into the ritual space when performing rituals for the dead. Begin to establish a bond. It will strengthen over time.

5

Those Who Stay Behind

Herne the Hunter (Welsh)

During the reign of King Richard II, the king had a master woodsman and hunter named Herne. Herne, the best carver and hunter, lived in Windsor Forest. King Richard would often take Herne and his men off into the forest to hunt. The king's men resented the favoritism that he showed to Herne, and they wished him dead. One day, while out hunting a great stag, the king's horse was gored, and the king was thrown. The great stag charged around to destroy the king, but Herne jumped in the path to protect his lord. Poor Herne was gored deeply, but with his remaining strength he managed to cut the stag's throat.

The king was distraught over Herne's fate. His friend lay dying. King Richard decreed that anyone who was able to save Herne's life would be rewarded. Just then, a man dressed in a black cloak appeared riding a black horse. His name was Urswick. Urswick told the King that he could indeed save Herne's life. Urswick carved the antlers from the great stag and tied them around Herne's head. The hunting party made their way back to the castle.

On the way home, Urswick heard the men wishing that poor Herne would die. Devilishly, Urswick told them in secret that he must appease the king, but he could make Herne unworthy of the king's liking. The men agreed to reward Urswick further if this could happen. Urswick demanded no coin, but rather to be granted anything from them upon his request.

For thirty days, Urswick gave Herne herbs and magick to stay alive. And after the thirty days, Herne was well, as promised. Urswick kept both promises. Though Herne was well, he had lost his skills of carving and haunting. The King chose to release Herne from his employ and he left the castle in great despair. Shortly thereafter, Herne's body was found hung on an old oak tree. Herne had taken his own life.

After Herne's death, all the men who took Herne's job to carve and hunt in Windsor seemed cursed. They could not perform their duties and the king was displeased. The men feared the king's anger and searched for Urswick. When they found him, they learned that the only way to break the curse would be to meet with the ghost of Herne at the oak tree where he had taken his own life. At midnight, Herne was summoned. Herne appeared before them and told them that he would break the curse if they returned the next night with hunting dogs and horses. The men obeyed and returned the next night. They found Herne on his ghostly horse. Then, Urswick magically appeared before them and reminded them of their promise to him. The boon he asked from them was to join Herne in the hunt and swear allegiance to him. Being honorable men, they swore oaths to Herne and joined his ghastly hunt.

Night after night, the Hunt chased game through the forest. The ghostly noises of the Hunt could be heard throughout the night. Soon, the deer were hunted so much there would be none left. Urswick told the king of the situation and that he must meet Herne under the old oak tree. When the king arrived, Herne appeared. He told the king that the only way to appease him was for the men in his hunting party to suffer the same fate as he. The king complied. The next night, his hunting party, who made the dark deal with Urswick, were hanged on the old oak tree where Herne took his own life.

To this day, it is said that during the ember days, the ghostly Wild Hunt comes screaming down looking for those poor folks who have not bolted down their doors and windows during the midwinter.

Why the Dead Come to Visit

Sometimes the dead will come to pay us a visit. Our ancestors are watching over us from the Underworld. We are their bloodline, and they have a connection to us. No other spirit or god has such a powerful connection with us than our own Ancestors. But the connection is more than just blood, it is also emotional and spiritual. Our friends, lovers, and spouses have a very powerful link to us as well. The emotional attachment to a person is just as powerful as blood, sometimes even more so. It is not as hard as you might think for the dead to come knocking at our door. For someone to come to see us after death the spirit needs a reason. There are spiritual laws and Karma that play into why certain spirits of the dead come to see us and why some do not. It all comes down to need. If they visit, there is either a great need from the spirit of our loved one, or a great need within us to see them. However, grief over someone's death is usually not enough. When someone dies and we miss them, it is usually insufficient cause for them to come to us. The need must be great for one or both parties involved. This is why, in magick, it takes a lot of power to summon a shade of the dead to the world of the living; and even then, there must be a great need. Never underestimate the power of need and desire.

Proper Burial

Many cultures believe that the spirits of the dead will come back to the physical plane if their physical body is not properly buried or cremated. The philosophy here is that the body needs to return to the Earth in some way. This can be done through burial by earth, water, or fire. There are many different theories about why this is so. One thought is that the body needs to return to the "womb" of the Mother Earth and thus to its origin. Another idea is that by placing the body in the ground and placing a gravestone over it, the stone spiritually seals the spirit into the grave so that it cannot roam the Earth. The ancients observed that when a corpse began to decompose, over time the body returned to the Earth naturally. This was the natural cycle of things. To go against the cycles of nature was to upset the balance of the Universe. Many superstitions arose out of not doing things in the way the Universe or gods intended. In some parts of the world, if the body was not buried then the ghost of a person will haunt the graveyard or neighboring town until the body is found and taken care of according the local spiritual beliefs. This is not always because the spirit of the person was "evil" or malicious, but rather because the spirit was thought to be trapped here in the physical plane and could not move on to the afterlife.

In popular occult theory, when someone dies, their etheric, astral, and spiritual body is released from the physical. When this happens, the denser etheric body can be seen as a ghost or specter. The etheric body is closely connected to the physical body so when the physical body decomposes so does the etheric body. Once this happens, only the astral and spiritual bodies remain. The astral/spiritual body may visit us in dreams and even perhaps appear to us as a ghost. After a time, the astral body "dies" and releases the spiritual body into the Underworld and the spirit of the dead is to remain with the Ancestors. This is called "the second death." Before the astral body is released from the spiritual, it is thought that the appearance of the astral body takes on the appearance of the physical body during decomposition. This is why when some ghosts appear to the living, they appear as rotting flesh and skeletons. I have personally only found this to be true when the spirit of the dead "holds on" to its earthly body, not wanting to let go of life. They are clinging onto life but to no avail. Over time, the spirit will eventually figure out that they need to move on, and the bonds that they have established which are holding them back will be released. Sometimes, a spirit's need to remain "alive" is very great and they may hold on to the idea of life so intensely that they have convinced themselves that they are actually alive. When this happens, their Ancestors and other spirits may help them shed the thought of their earthly life and move on. This is not always the case. There have been instances where the spirit of the dead has remained on the physical plane for many years.

On my visit to New Orleans, I took one of the many ghost tours they have in the French Quarter. One of my favorite haunted places was this old home that was turned into a tavern on Bourbon Street. As the story goes, during one of plagues several children died in one household. The mother, distraught, would not come out from the children's bedroom. She threatened to slice her own throat if moved. Her neighbors convinced her to put down the knife, but without warning she flung herself through the window and landed on a wooden pole. There have been many people who have reported seeing the mother of the house looking for her children with the wound of the wooden pole still in her abdomen. Several bar tenders have complained that the spirits knock things off the bar and break bottles and glasses.

One of the easiest and quickest ways to release a spirit from its physical body is cremation. Cremation of the body has been practiced for thousands of years. When a body is burned, there is nothing for the astral/spiritual body to hold on to. The spiritual body is released as soon as the body is turned to ash. Cremation also has a sanitary purpose. When someone dies because of disease, placing them in the Earth may contaminate the ground and ground water with toxins and the disease itself. By burning the body, all diseases and toxins are burnt away.

We can speculate how or why spirits choose to remain stuck in the physical world, but the Universe is still a mysterious thing. Perhaps there is a lesson here for both the dead and the living.

To Speak of the Afterlife and Underworld

One reason the dead may come to visit us is to speak about the afterlife in the Underworld. There may be times when we desperately need to know that our loved ones are happy in the Afterlife. If we come from a Christian background, we know only two possibilities in the Afterlife: Heaven or Hell. There may be situations when we are not 100 percent positive where our loved one has ended up and we may desperately want to know. Other people believe the Underworld to be a vast and complex territory. We may need to know the whereabouts of our loved one in hopes that they did not become lost and confused. To be clear, this rarely happens. Upon death, spirit guides and other Ancestors come to help the newly departed with the transition from the physical plane to the Afterlife. If a spirit becomes lost it is not because of the lack of help or guidance from the spirit world. On the rare occasion that this may happen, it is usually because the spirit may not know that they are dead and become confused. When spirits try to help and guide them, they are met with misbelief and dread. This is especially true with suicides and accidental deaths, or even murders. Under normal circumstances, however, when this happens, the guiding spirits use whatever means necessary to guide the newly dead to the place where they need to be.

A loved one may appear to us to let us know that they are okay. After they have begun the process of settling into the Afterlife, they may return to let us know that they are well and happy and have other duties to attend to in the spirit world. By appearing to us, they understand that this will help us move on and not put our physical lives on hold because we are in grief and are desperately hoping our loved one is all right. Sometimes, simply by being told that they are okay, we can get on with our lives. This seems like such a simple thing, but it can be both powerful and healing for both people involved.

When a spirit of the dead is summoned through the powers of magick, they may tell us their perceptions of the Underworld in great detail. The dead have a firsthand view of what is happening there. They can tell us about the wonders of the Afterlife and the spirits they have met. However, they can only tell us things from their limited point-of-view and perceptions. Most likely, our Ancestors will never travel through the entirety of the Underworld, so they will only be able to tell us of what they have seen themselves. In your work with this book, as well as the follow up book *Deeper into the Underworld: Death, Ancestors, and Magical Rites*, you will be learning more magick every day with the Ancestors. In time, our Ancestors will learn the skills to do more magick with and for us in the Underworld. One of the reasons it is important to journey to the Underworld is that it helps you and your Ancestors become more acquainted with the different landscapes and planes of existence. This kind of partnership is very important to our work with the spirits.

Unfinished Business

One of the most common reasons for why the dead return to us is unfinished business. Unfinished business can quite literally mean anything. There are those spirits who have been working on some great life-changing project that may alter the course of human history (at least in their minds) and they may come to us to make sure the job gets finished. This is usually not the case with most spirits. The unfinished business is what is very important to the person at the time right before they died. It can be anything from getting a business up and going to watching a family member graduate from college. It can even seem silly to you at times. The actual business, great or small, is not what is important. What is important is that the spirit feels they left the physical plane with a sense of accomplishment.

I think it is important to help the spirit, if we are able, so that the transition from this life to the next is as easy as possible. As always, before we agree to help any spirit we must ask it exactly what they need from us in order to accomplish their goal. If the task is something you are able and willing to do, then I see no reason why you cannot help the spirit in question. There have been instances where the spirit may ask you to help find out who killed them and bring them to justice. As fantastic and adventurous as this sounds, it may not be a good idea. Not only could it be dangerous, but you may not have the means to find out who the killer was. This may lead the spirit to become angry and frustrated, which may only prolong the spirit's stay on this plane and prevent them from moving on. Some unfinished business may simply be resolved with the passing of time. If a spirit wishes to watch their family member graduate from high school or college, then the only thing the spirit is able to do is wait. There are times when the dead are hell-bent on something happening that may never happen, such as their queer child getting into a heteronormative relationship and having children. When this happens, the best thing to do is to try to convince the spirit to accept what cannot be changed and move on. In the grand scheme of the Universe, it is about the evolution and transformation of the soul and earthly wants and desires may only bind them to the physical plane. Moving on to the Afterlife may be a better alternative.

Forgiveness

We fight with our friends and family all the time. Our loved ones can have the remarkable ability to make us so angry that we cannot even see straight. Most of the time, disagreements between family and friends are forgotten and we move on. There may be circumstances when someone we love hurts us so much, we feel like we can never forgive them. We fight. We say horrible things to each other. We may even abuse each other. We leave, perhaps never to return. Our relationship with that person may be over forever. These sorts of emotions affect our spirit a great deal.

When a person dies, they may still feel the pain and suffering of the loss of a relationship. This pain can even bind them to the Earth plane so that they cannot move on. This is indeed unfinished business that the spirit must resolve. Guilt is also an emotion that tends to bind spirits to the earthly plane. They may feel like they cannot go on to another spiritual plane when someone they love is still feeling the pain of something that was done to them. Before the spirit can transition, they may feel like they must make it right first. We, ourselves, may be angry at our loved one for dying. A lot of people feel that this is selfish and would never tell another living soul that they are so angry at their parent, lover, sibling, or best friend for leaving them all alone. However, this is a very normal feeling when one is grieving. Our loved one may come to us to ask forgiveness for any of these things and quite a bit more. Often, this is the final time the spirit will see the loved one again. It is important that both parties understand this will be the last time they see each other on the physical plane. There is usually a deep loving energetic connection that forms at this time, otherwise, the spirit would not be able to appear to the loved one. During these beautiful moments it is easier to move past earthly disagreements and say, "I forgive you" so the spirit can move on. This is a great act of kindness that heals both you and the spirit.

But what if you cannot forgive that person? What if the actions of the spirit when they were alive were so bad that you feel you can never forgive them? This is something only you can answer. It is my belief that when someone dies, they go to the Underworld where they are met by healing spirits and higher beings that will help them learn from their Earthly mistakes and transform themselves into better spiritual beings. There is also Karma that will help them understand their actions on Earth. There is no right or wrong answer. At the end of it all, we have to live our lives in this plane and the next to the best of our ability and hopefully we learn from our mistakes.

Information

The ancients used to summon the dead for information and prophecy. Some cultures believed that when someone died that spirit had access to a vast amount of knowledge about the past, present, and future. In the New Age community, it is sometimes believed that the spirit of the dead has access to the Akashic Records. The Akashic (meaning spirit) Records are believed to be a giant library in the Astral Plane that has the actions of every person, place, or thing that have ever happened (and perhaps that will ever happen in the future). They believe that living people may journey there in spirit as well, but the dead have better access. Other people believe that upon death you become very wise with all the information of the Universe. I have not found this to be true. When a person dies, they remain who they are just as in life.

When your spirit leaves your body, it simply goes to another plane of existence. You are not instantaneously downloading all the secrets of the Universe. From my experience in working with the dead, there is no difference with their intelligence from when they were alive, although there may be a difference in the type of information that they know or have access to because they in essence have a different perspective in the realm of the dead. There are spirit guides and helpers in the Underworld who can teach the spirits of the dead to grow and to evolve as spiritual beings, but this depends on how willing and able they are to learn. Just like when the living go to school, everyone is different in how effectively they learn what is presented to them. You cannot rush things like this. Over time, with patience, the dead can learn new things, but this may be a long process depending upon the person who has crossed over.

The Ancestors do have the ability to see certain things firsthand. As we have discussed before, future events begin in the Upperworld, go to the Underworld, then manifest here on the physical plane. In other words, events begin on the spiritual and astral planes then manifest on the etheric and physical planes. This is how we are able to do divination. Divination taps into the other realms, and we can get an idea of what is to come. The spirits of the dead, being in the spirit world, can see events that will manifest on the physical plane. We can summon the spirits of the dead and ask them questions about the future. It is important to realize that the dead are not perfect beings. They have their own hopes, fears, and prejudices just as they did when they were alive. So, the information they give us comes from their point of view. This does not mean that it is untrue, but rather the information is given to us through their filters. Think about four witnesses to a car crash. The police report will show that with four different witnesses, there are four different points of view. All four are true according to each person's point of view. When taking prophecy and divination from the dead we must understand that the information is not infallible, and it is given from what the spirit knows and understands.

Becoming Spirit Guides and Helpers

The Ancestors have the ability to evolve into higher beings in the Underworld. Once they have entered the Underworld, higher beings, spirit guides, and medicine spirits may help them to transform themselves into spirit guides and helpers themselves. They will teach them how to become greater than they are and learn how to use the energies of the Underworld to help their family in the physical plane. This is why it is important to pray for the evolution and transformation of our Ancestors. By praying, we are sending energy to our Ancestors and their guides, and they are then able to use that energy to aid them in their spiritual evolution. Not all of our Ancestors are able and willing to take on that challenge. It is a calling just as it is a calling for a living person to become a teacher, doctor, or priest. When one hears the call, one does not necessarily have to act upon it. It is the same in the Underworld. Some of our Ancestors are called to grow spiritually and evolve and some are not. There is free will even after death.

By working with our Ancestors on our ancestral altar, they will begin to see the energies and magick that we work with. Over time, they may decide to help us and our families upon our spiritual paths and choose to become spirit guides and helpers for our family and for us. This process is important to our spiritual and family growth. The more powerful our Ancestors become, the more they can help us upon our spiritual path and in magick. You do not have to use magick in order to have your Ancestors become a spirit guide for you. I have known many instances where someone's grandparents or parents have stayed close by the family after death to protect and guide them. The reports are often the same. The family members can feel them or simply know that they are near. In some instances, deceased family members have appeared in the physical plane or in dreams to let them know that they are close by watching over the family.

However this happens, it is a blessing. I cannot stress this enough: treat the Ancestors well; Give them offerings and their power and influence in the physical plane will become more and more powerful.

Preparing Us for Death

When our time for death is near, our Ancestors may come to prepare us. There are some people who are able to see the dead more clearly when they are close to death themselves. This happens because our spirit is beginning the process of crossing over to the spirit world. The spirit world seems to become more vivid, and we may see friends and relatives who are long gone. Spirit omens become stronger and stronger heralding our coming death. However, normally, just because you can see spirits does not mean you are going to die soon. As we work with our spirituality and the spirit world, our psychic ability will improve over time. Also, those of us who are called to work with the dead will see them very clearly all the time, sometimes from a very young age or even birth.

When we are near our own death, our Ancestors may come to us so that we are prepared mentally, emotionally, spiritually, and physically for the transition. We may have important projects that the Ancestors want us to finish before our death. We may be the head of a family or household and we need to create a will or financially provide for our families before we are gone. Perhaps the Ancestors want us to complete something so we do not feel as though we have unfinished business on the physical plane. The Ancestors' goal after death is to continue the family bloodline in a healthy and balanced way. If our death could leave the family in turmoil, then our Ancestors may appear to us so that we know to make preparations.

When we become terminally ill, our whole world is thrown into chaos. Our spiritual beliefs may be challenged, and we may even wonder if there is life after death. Does anyone really know? When we die will we cease to exist? Is there a Christian Hell and will I be in eternal torment because I do not follow Christianity to the letter? All of these questions are normal to people who are dying. The Ancestors may come to us to let us know that there is an Afterlife, that there is peace and happiness in the spirit world, and that we will be just fine. I have known people close to death to dream of a deceased loved one coming to them to ease their fears and let them know everything is going to be okay. For the dying and those they leave behind, this is a great gift and should be seen as a blessing.

I would like to say that not all those who are dying have an Ancestor come to visit them. One could speculate many reasons why, but truly no one ever really knows. Perhaps there is an important spiritual lesson in this that we cannot understand. My personal theory is the Ancestors come to those who are mentally and spiritually open to the appearance of a dead loved one. Even in cases like this, the Ancestors are preparing them for death.. This is a mystery that is very individual, and we may never truly know the role of the Ancestors upon our death until it is our time to go with them and take our place among the spirits of our family lineage.

Ritual to Help Spirits Cross Over

Take your time in getting to know the spirit of the dead and why they have not crossed over. Is it because they simply lost their way or because they need to do something they feel is very important before they go? If they are simply lost, then move on to the next step. If they have something they need to do, find out what it is. It may be simple like giving someone a message or doing a small task. It may be more complex, and you have to evaluate if it is something that can and should be done. There are times when a spirit wants to stay around and protect a loved one up until the moment of their death. That one is a little trickier and maybe they should; it may not be for you to judge. Perhaps it is a karmic debt or promise they need to keep. If you are unsure, do some divination around the issue and perhaps even communicate with the spirit's Ancestors and ask them their advice. The spirit's Ancestors will have much more insight into these things than you will. Even if you have many years of experience in these matters do not assume you know what is best for the spirit.

When the spirit asks you for your help, decide if you are able to help them or not. If you are not able or willing to help them for whatever reason, politely explain to them why and see if there is an alternative way to help them. If you cannot help them there is no shame in that. If you tell a spirit that you can help, make sure that you keep your word. If a spirit asks you to perform a task or find out something for them, it is important that you do the task for them. Going back on your word causes mistrust and resentment between you and the dead and it will take a long time to trust you again. Other spirits of the dead may find out about this and will be reluctant to work with you.

1. Find out why the spirit has not crossed over. If they need help understanding the circumstances of their death, call upon your

Ancestors as well as their Ancestors to aid you in finding out this information. Do not try to do this by yourself. Imagine how you would feel if a stranger came up to you right now and told you bluntly and without ceremony that you were dead.

2. Call upon your Ancestors by name. Visualize them appearing before you. Tell them what you are planning to do and ask them for their assistance.

3. Once your Ancestors agree to help, ask them to help you call upon the spirits of the dead and healing guides. To do this, energetically tune into the energy signature of the spirit that will allow you to access their family history and their lineage. Ask the spirit's Ancestors to be present. To tune in to the energy signature, you must align your energies to those of the spirit. Use your consciousness and try to "feel" the spirit. I like to think of it like adjusting my energies like a transistor radio. I focus on the spirit's energy and try to match my energy to theirs. Once I do that, I relax my mind, aura, and chakras and allow myself to receive the input of the spirit's energy. I listen closely to what my heart chakra and brow chakra are telling me about the spirit's energy.

4. When the spirit's Ancestors appear, tell them the situation, and allow your own Ancestors to say what they need to say to them. The spirit's Ancestors may already be aware of the situation but give them any information you think will help.

5. With your magical wand, athame, crystal, or simply your finger, cut a magical portal to the land of the Ancestors. This is done by tuning into the land of the Ancestors, visualizing light from your magical tool and carving a straight line in front of you. You can tune into the land just like you do with a spirit, but you do so with the land instead. It may be helpful to draw up the earth energy

with your feet but isn't necessary. With your hands you can open the line just like opening drawn curtains. If you wish, you can also visualize the light creating a door that you can open with your imagination.

6. Cut any cords you see that bind the spirit to the physical plane.

7. Send any healing energy to the spirit and the Ancestors that feel necessary. Once finished, cut the astral cord from yourself to the spirit so no energy can be pulled from you without your permission.

8. At this point the spirit's Ancestors will escort the spirit into the Underworld. The portal should close on its own. If it does not, simply visualize the portal closing and disappearing.

9. Take a moment to confer with your Ancestors. Is there further information they wish to tell you? After you have conversed with your Ancestors, thank them for their work.

10. Ritually banish and cleanse your space.

The Burial If There Is No Body

There may be times when someone we love and cared about has died and there is no body to bury. It has often been said that funerals are for the living and not the dead. I do not believe this to be necessarily true. In many cultures, the funeral or memorial helps the spirit cross over to the realm of the Ancestors. There are elaborate rituals in pagan societies that help the spirit find its way through the Underworld, such as the Egyptian and Tibetan Books of the Dead. These rites help the spirit navigate through the strange and mysterious landscapes. The funeral rites also help the living and the dead come to the understanding that it is time for the spirit to move on and that its time on the physical plane has come to an end. It also helps the living grieve and move on. If the living cannot and will not let go of the deceased spirit then this acts as an energetic chain that has the potential to bind the deceased and not allow the spirit to move on.

A very effective way to help both the living and the dead move on is to have a symbolic funeral. There are several ways to do this. You need to find something that represents the deceased, such as some object or memento. You can use jewelry, clothing, or a picture. You may also use a shamanic fetish. This is an object that is either crafted or found in nature that symbolizes the deceased. If you know the person's spirit animal, you can purchase a figurine or sculpt the animal out of clay. You may also use a stone that you feel represents that person. A doll or poppet may be used as well. This can be used in the same way as sympathetic magick because it represents the deceased once it is named after that person. You may also use a mojo bag or sachet. In the bag, place things that represent the deceased person such as scraps of cloths, cigarettes, stones, herbs, or any small personal thing. As you place each item in the pouch visualize the deceased as clear as possible. This will connect the items to the person you are doing the funeral for.

You will need to find an appropriate place to bury the object you have decided best represents the deceased spirit. It is better if you own property so that the little grave will not be disturbed. You can place it in a park or a cemetery, but there is always the chance that the object will be dug up during renovations or tree planting. Once you have decided on the appropriate place for your object, you will need to dig a hole deep enough that the object will not rise out of the ground due to weathering. You may use a shoebox for a casket if you like. In the case of the mojo bag or sachet you can simply place the pouch in the ground.

As you place the object into the ground, say prayers to the deceased and the gods that you follow and ask the divine to assist the spirit of the deceased to find their way into the realm of the Ancestors. Spend as much time as you need to say your goodbyes to your loved one and sing songs that feel appropriate. Once your ceremony is complete, fill the grave with dirt, leave a marker of some sort if you so choose, and feel free to visit the little grave from time to time.

Helping The Dead Out of Their Own Traps

There may be times when we realize that the spirits of the dead are "trapped" in a world entirely of their own making. Upon death, people may have a preconceived notion of what the afterlife will be like. As we have discussed before, just as our physical world is shaped by our thoughts, emotions, and actions, so too is the Underworld. The Buddhists believe that at the exact moment of your death, whatever thoughts enter your mind will determine the afterlife you experience. So, if you think of family and friends that's what you will see. If you think of monsters and trolls chasing you, that too, is what will happen. I do not necessarily think that this is entirely true, but rather, the deeply held beliefs you have of the afterlife will be a contributing factor to what you experience in the Underworld. Some spirits of the dead may experience their afterlife as something simple. Perhaps they will believe themselves to be on a tropical island, or even perhaps live in an exact replica of the life they led before death. In the beginning of the afterlife, this may serve as a way for the dead to transition from life to death without much fear and difficulty. A person may become comfortable with the environment they have unwittingly created. In my experience, I have found that when this happens, a spirit's Ancestors will come and try to convince him or her to move onto the world of the Ancestors. Other healing helpers may come to convince them that they need to move on from their current place so that they can move on with their Karma and destiny. The spirit may or may not realize, or want to realize, that they are dead and that they need to move on to the world of the Ancestors. By going with the healing spirits, they are finally accepting that they are dead. This can be a hard and somewhat traumatic transition for them. Just as in life, the dead may be stubborn and refuse to go. When this happens, your Ancestors or other healing spirits may ask you to intervene.

What you must do is journey to the world that the deceased has created for themselves. Be prepared for anything. The world that they have created may be as mundane as their old apartment or as wonderful as a space station or alien planet. Once the healing helper or your Ancestor takes you to this person, it is up to you to convince them to release this illusion and move on. From my own personal experience, it is better to simply talk to them at first. Let them know how much time has passed since their death. You may even need to "show" them their funeral and how the physical world looks now in your time. The spirits of the dead are telepathic and so you can send thoughts and visualizations to them. Visualize their funeral or memorial service in your mind and then send it to them. This may provoke anger because they may believe that you are playing tricks on them. You may need to take them on an astral journey and show them how their family and friends have moved on or are moving on. It will be wise to ask your Ancestors to assist in this process. Spirits can get trapped in these little worlds they have created for an indefinite period of time. The longer the spirit has been in this self-created world, the harder it is to convince them to move on. It may take some time for them to understand exactly what is going on and how you are trying to help them.

Suicide and Unfinished Business

Suicide is tragic on many levels. Not only does it leave the surviving family members and friends devastated, but it also causes an energetic rift throughout the three worlds. When a loved one takes their own life, family and friends are left with great sorrow and many questions. When this happens, we may ask ourselves why? A lot of people go through hard times and get through them. So why did our loved one end their life? Could we have helped them? Was there more we could have done? Truth be told, we may never know all the factors that contributed to someone's death. As survivors, we may blame ourselves and have a difficult time getting through our grief. When it comes to the subject of spirits of the dead, our grief may be so strong that we inadvertently bind our loved one to the physical plane. Every thought we have of our loved one and every strong emotion we have for them brings them closer to us. This can be a lovely thing and bring solace, but if our grief is too powerful it may bring them here against their will, as in the example I cited previously. The best advice I can give to the surviving friends and family is to seek a spiritual counselor, a member of clergy, or at least a good friend. There is no shame in seeing a psychologist to help us through our grief.

For the person who ended their own life, they have many challenges ahead of them. We can never truly know what was going through the mind of a victim of suicide. We can speculate and we can talk with a person who made an attempt on their own life, but for those who did not survive, we can never really know. From the accounts that we have, some people who commit suicide may do so because they want to end the pain and suffering that they are feeling in this world. They may have thoughts and feelings that are too much to bear, and they no longer have the strength or will to keep fighting. Some may feel that when their life ends, they will have no consciousness and no afterlife. Perhaps in their mind this is better than the pain and suffering they are feeling now. When they end their life and cross over to the Underworld, it is rarely what they thought it would be. Suicide causes a powerful energetic rift in the Underworld. Fate and destiny are altered forever. At the moment of death, there is a powerful energetic shock wave of pain, suffering, and any psychosis that the person may have been dealing with.

As stated above, many people believe that the thoughts you have at the moment of death and the beliefs you hold about the afterlife during life influence your experience in the Underworld. When all these factors are combined the victim of suicide may be in a painful and sorrowful place. The victim may subconsciously choose to forget they killed themselves because the pain was too much for their psyche to bear. They may not know that they are dead. When the Ancestors and guides come to take them to a place of healing in the Underworld, they may reject them and choose to remain in denial. The spirits of the Underworld, no matter how kind and helpful they are, cannot force someone to heal against their will.

In my experience, I have found these spirits of the dead to be confused and still in the same sorrowful state they were when they were alive. I feel that as spirit workers, we should help them cross over to the other side. In cases like this, it is no easy task. It may take a lot of convincing from you, your guides, and their Ancestors. Even so, there is no guarantee of success. My advice is to use your intuition and your heart and do the best you can. Again, seek out spiritual advice and help from a member of clergy who knows how to deal with situations like this.

Helping the Dead Trapped by Repressed Beliefs

In your journeys through the Underworld, you may find spirits who are trapped in their belief systems. The Universe gives you exactly what you want whether you are conscious of it or not. Your subconscious is connected very strongly to the Underworld. Whatever you believe deep down is most likely what will manifest in the Underworld. Upon death, if a person has done their karmic work and ends their life in a place of peace and happiness, then they will find an afterlife that mirrors that feeling. If, on the other hand, they have repressed negative emotions and unconscious beliefs in hell and unhappiness, then they may find themselves in such a place. In some cosmologies such as Buddhism and the Maya, this is how the "hells" or places of testing and initiation are created. It is in these places that any repressed negative emotions are made manifest. This is not a world of punishment, but rather a world of purification. It is important for the newly deceased to purify their spiritual bodies of any negative beliefs about themselves and the cosmos. The more deeply these beliefs lie in the subconscious, the harder it is for the deceased to be purified. This is also one of the reasons that eastern religions place great importance on Karma. Karma is the combination of energetic lessons that one must learn during life, and if necessary, in death. It is believed that if one is able to balance the scales of Karma while living, then purification at death will not be as challenging. Once the deceased is purified then they can transcend the hells and go on to the afterlife or to reincarnate.

The Christian faith often teaches that if you do not live a life according to Christian doctrine, then the afterlife will be one of punishment and torment. In my experience, I have found that most Christians believe that they will go to Heaven upon death, but this is not always the case. There are times, albeit rarely, that the spirit believes that they have not earned the right to ascend to Heaven, but rather that the spirit deserves punishment in the Christian idea of Hell. When this happens, we can choose to help these spirits or not. I personally believe that if you are a person that works with the dead, then it may fall upon you to help the spirits of the dead to break away from the false chains that bind them to torment. It is not our responsibility to judge them for their actions while living. What we must do is help their healing helper spirits and Ancestors to convince them that what they need is purification in the afterlife and not eternal punishment. I believe that the Source that created all things in the Universe does not wish pain and punishment on people but rather needs them to learn and evolve to a state of higher vibration so that they can transcend into the "higher" spiritual realms.

This sort of spirit work is very challenging. There are many ways to help these spirits and many cultures have prayers and ceremonies to aid them. When I am called upon to do this kind of work, I ask the aid of their Ancestors and healing helpers to help me convince them that the "hell" they are experiencing is self-imposed and a product of upbringing and the mind. This may take some time and results may vary. Ideally, if the spirit begins to listen, the chains that bind them to these places because of their beliefs become weak and break and the hells will begin to fade away. It is at this point that their Ancestors and healing helpers can step in and take over. This is powerful healing work.

Helping Spirits Cross Over

There are many things that can contribute to someone who is unable or unwilling to "move on" or "cross over." There may be unfinished business, suicide, or many other possible circumstances. Sometimes, the newly dead may not know they are dead. This is because, from their point of view, everything is exactly the same as it was when they were alive. There are no angels with harps, no crazy looking creatures coming up from the ground, no booming voice from Heaven saying, "You are dead!!" Everything is as it was so they must be alive! As spirit workers, magicians, and shamans we can sense spirits of the dead. Some of us can see them, smell them, or simply have a "knowing" that they are present. We know that the spirit is dead even if they do not realize it. If we are able and willing, we should help the spirit cross over. However, this may be more challenging than we think. It is easy to help a spirit who is simply stuck or has lost their way for whatever reason. It is a lot harder to help a spirit who will not move on.

People are complex with complex thoughts, emotions, and lives. We are full of constrictions in our beliefs and thoughts. People are seldom as black and white as they make themselves out to be. We have hopes, fears, prejudices, and environmental factors that make up our personalities. Our identities have many complex layers. We have joys and we have sorrows. We have anger and we have love. At the time of death, all the things that make us who we are do not immediately go away. We are not instantaneously transformed into mythical characters like Jesus, Buddha, or Moses. We are still the same, only now without a body.

There are several ways for you to aid the dead in crossing over. You may light a candle to the gods and ask that the spirit be shown the way to the other side. This does not always work. I will summon my Ancestors and then ask them to find or summon the Ancestors of the deceased. At that point my Ancestors and those of the deceased will explain to the spirit what has happened, and it is better to cross over to the afterlife. Then, visualizing golden or white light, I will cut a portal that leads to the Underworld. The Ancestors will then guide the spirit to the afterlife. The important thing to remember when helping a spirit cross over is that it is vital that you show compassion, even to angry spirits who are threatening. We cannot know how the spirit is feeling. Through exercises and meditation, we can imagine, but we cannot truly know until we are dead ourselves. For some spirits, this must be very confusing, and they may be angry. Just as with anyone who is in a crisis, we need to show the spirit compassion. The majority of the time, creating a portal to the afterlife is effective. On rare occasions the spirit may refuse to leave for a variety of reasons. When this happens, it can become a haunting.

Hauntings

There are endless tales and stories told about ghosts and spirits of the dead haunting the living. Some stories tell of a murder that happened and the spirits seek revenge upon the living. Or someone built a house on an Indigenous burial ground and now the Native American curse is unleashed upon the poor new residents. There are many other stories, and I must admit I love them—even the silly ones. It was my attraction to these tales that got me into working with the spirits of the dead. Or perhaps it was my energetic draw to work with the dead from an early age that attracted me to ghost stories. I may never know! I do believe that people, places, and things can be haunted, but it is not as common as you may think.

The spirits of the dead remain or return to the physical plane for a variety of reasons which we will discuss below. Hauntings rarely have a sinister or murderous intent. It does happen, but it is rarely like in the movies. Sometimes, when something traumatic happens such as abuse or murder, there is what is called a "psychic echo" that lingers in the home or space. For instance, when a murder or a suicide happens, the psychic energy that occurred is so strong that it leaves an energetic residue. It is like a psychic record that keeps playing over and over again. In some cases, this may occur every night at the same time of the actual event. In other cases, it happens when some other event triggers the psychic response. For instance, you may have an argument in a "haunted" house with your spouse. The next thing you know, every night at 2am you see the ghost of a man killing the ghost of his wife.

Then there are curses. This is when someone does such a horrible thing, like murder, and the spirit of the slain "curses" the perpetrator so that they are haunted. For this to happen, several factors must be involved. For one, there needs to be such an intense grudge from the slain against the perpetrator that they bind themselves to the physical plane. In most cases, when someone dies unexpectedly, even in the case of murder, the Ancestors and spirit guides come to help the slain person move on to the afterlife. But this is not always the case. Perhaps the curse needs to happen for the better good of all, or at least of the person who committed the crime.

What about demonic hauntings? Many of us have seen the movie *The Amityville Horror*. If you have not, I highly suggest it. It is really fun to watch! In the movie, there are demons who possess or suggest to a young man that he murder his entire family with a shotgun. The movie is based off the actual events of the Defoe family murders. The killer, Ronald Defoe, Jr., said that ghosts made him kill his family. Some people have said that if this is true, it may have been demonic entities who pushed him to the deed. In my years of working with demons and ghosts, I have yet to see a haunting such as this. Yes, it is true that if an unstable person conjures demons in an imbalanced way or summons dark spirits, the spirits can possess or attach themselves to the person. When this happens, the person become mentally unstable and usually is physically drained. It is rare, very rare, that a demon can have such power over someone that they shoot their entire family. This is the equivalent of saying: "The devil made me do it." This is the ultimate way of avoiding responsibility. I will say, however, that, based on what I have seen and experienced in the magical and energetic world, anything is possible.

Then there is the misery-loves-company syndrome. This is what happens when someone dies too soon from an accident or illness and the spirit longs to be with their husband, wife, or partner. The love that the spirit has for their surviving loved one is so strong that they are unable to move on. To make matters worse, the spirit cannot bear to be in the spirit world without their partner, so the spirit tries to find ways to kill them so they can be reunited. This is a case of the most unbalanced and abusive love there is. When we die, it is true that we do not instantly attain wisdom and we still have our hopes, dreams, prejudices, and fears. But we do understand, with the help of our guardians and guides, that even though we want to be with our loved ones, they will join us when it is their time to die. Furthermore, there is no time or space in the Underworld, and the spirits can see when that time is near. When a spirit of the dead is abusive and possessive to such a great extent and they have no desire to do what is best for their partner, it is a great tragedy.

People can also bring hauntings upon themselves. There are two major ways this can happen. The first is that the person is incredibly psychic and is unaware they have the ability of telekinesis, or the ability to move things with their mind. When someone does not realize how psychic they are, their power is active but is not under control. Any emotion can send something moving across the table, flying across the room, or even open doors. The person soon believes they are being haunted and moves to another home only to find that they are still seeing chairs slide across the room. This happens in the case of a poltergeist. Poltergeists seem to center around a child. Usually when a qualified psychic is called in, they soon find out that there are no ghosts, but the child's own psychic abilities are in full force. The second situation occurs when a person is magical in some way or has the ability to see and work with the dead. The spirits of the dead are naturally attracted to this type of person. Perhaps the spirits need healing or are having trouble moving on and need help. The person's aura has a type of energy that the dead are attracted to. The dead may become confused as to why the person is not helping them or acknowledging them, so they manifest physical phenomena to get their attention. I, myself, fall into this second category.

During all my childhood I had many spirits and ghosts visit me. I thought that our home was haunted and that it was our bad luck that we were plagued by these spirits. They were seldom troublesome. Most of the time they would appear to me and give me a fright! I remember when I was only two or three years old, I was on the living room floor playing with my baby brother's bottle. The nipple was red, and red is my favorite color. A spirit manifested in many bright colors and waved at me from outside the front door. I screamed bloody murder and was convinced that my father played a trick on me! That was the first time a spirit made its presence known to me. From that day forward the spirits of the dead were around me. I felt them constantly, especially at night. I realized I had power over them when they gave me such a fright one day that it made me very angry, and I used that anger to banish them. For the first time in my life, they were gone. But then I felt very lonely without them. I felt abandoned even though I was the one who sent them away. Not long after, with a more open heart, I invited them back.

Thought forms are also common. We create thought forms every day. Whenever we imagine something, it is a small thought form. The more energy we give a vision or a dream the more it will manifest. These are the basics of how spellcraft works. We visualize something and give it power. Most thought forms dissipate quickly. Otherwise, every time we were angry with a co-worker, they would feel a smack in the face. But when we dwell on something over and over again it maintains the energy longer. If we have some psychic ability the thought form may begin to develop a life of its own. You have just created a spirit. With no one to control the spirit it can, and will, run amok. It may even go back to the person it originated from to seek out more energy or perhaps it will want to be with that person. It is only natural for the created to want to be near the creator. This may manifest as a haunting.

All in all, most of these disturbances can be cured with a cleansing of the home or space. When this does not work, you may have to use a more aggressive banishing.

There may be very rare instances when a spirit of the dead is angry and haunts a person, place, or thing for vengeance or justice. Again, this is a very rare instance. For a haunting of this nature to take place there needs to be a lot of psychic energy to allow the spirit to manifest on the physical plane. Anger is a very powerful force and gives off a lot of psychic energy. The spirit needs this level of energy. This is different from being simply "mad" at someone, it is an anger that is rooted deep within one's emotions. When someone is murdered or suffers a great loss, there is a reverberation that travels deep within the planes of existence and the three worlds. Sometimes gods intervene and grant a spirit magical powers. However, if there is an injustice done to a magical person or group of people, the outcome may be a haunting. If you find yourself or someone you know in this situation there are a few options. You may try to communicate with the spirit and see if there is anything you can do to help them. If it's vengeance the spirit is looking for, then the best thing to do is to try to convince them that the anger is keeping them earthbound, and they cannot spiritually grow with the anger keeping them on the physical plane. If they are causing innocent people harm and communicating is not working you may have to banish them. I would call upon their Ancestors to help them move on to the Underworld, but sometimes spirits may not listen to reason, and you may have to do an aggressive banishing such as an exorcism of place. *The Exorcist's Handbook* by Josephine McCarthy is a good book to help you learn the art of exorcism.

Sometimes the spirits do not always move on to the Underworld or afterlife. There are many occasions when the dead stay here on the physical plane. Sometimes they may become trapped her for various reasons, but more common than not, they chose to reside here. With great emotion comes great attachment to the physical plane. Usually, the attachment revolves around a person or an unfinished business. When dealing with these spirits it is important not to be judgmental about why they are here but to help them release the bonds of the physical plane so they can go to the next life. This is one of the greatest ways to heal another being.

Our Grief Binds Spirits to this World

When we lose someone we love, be it a family member, spouse, partner, or dear friend, we grieve. We feel the loss of that person as if we ourselves, or at least a part of ourselves, died as well. It is almost as if our soul was torn out of our bodies. Even when the death is expected, you can only prepare your mind, emotions, and spirit so much. No death is the same. Losing a spouse and losing a parent feels different. No one, including myself, can tell you how to feel or how long to feel grief. Yes, we have the support of our friends and family, but ultimately, it is a process that we must deal with ourselves. It is painful. It is hard. Sometimes, we may even wonder if we can make it through the day, but we carry on. We are alive and we must continue living. Eventually, the grief begins to not hurt as much. I have a personal theory that the pain is always there, but we learn to incorporate it into our daily lives.

Sometimes, the pain and feeling of loss becomes a part of our energy make up. Ideally, we will learn to evolve and transform ourselves past this pain and grief; but we are human with human bodies and human emotions, and we can only do as much as we can. We should not feel bad because we are going through our own evolutionary process the best way we know how. We are doing the best we can with the resources we have around us. There are times when the loss of someone we love is very great. It overwhelms us and becomes too much to bear. It may even feel like the grief is all there is. When this happens to us, the important thing to remember is that everyone grieves differently. I would recommend that when you are grieving and feel overwhelmed, it is important to seek the help and support of family and friends and a professional therapist if needed. Seeing a therapist does not mean that you are weak or incapable or mentally ill. It means that you are seeking guidance outside your normal parameters and are open to the opportunity of spiritual and emotional growth.

Grief is a form of psychic energy. The more emotion you put behind it, or any form of psychic energy for that matter, the more powerful it becomes. Strong emotions make energy more tangible in this world as well as the Underworld. We manifest things when our minds and emotions are strong and focused. This can be both a blessing and a curse. When we are grieving very strongly, there may be times when our grief amplifies our psychic energy so much that it becomes very tangible, even to the point where it may inadvertently keep the spirit of our loved one from moving on. The grief becomes a psychic net or barrier that prevents the spirit of our beloved dead from leaving this plane and continuing on to the afterlife.

I once had a client who came to me needing some help with a haunting. She told me that her boyfriend was being haunted by his former lover who had killed herself a few years prior. She explained to me that the spirit of Kate continued to haunt him and because of this, he could not get his life in order or move on from the grief that he felt for her after her passing. He would stay at home night after night and never leave his house other than to go to work. It was almost like the spirit had created a prison for the boyfriend. I agreed to investigate the haunting. When I was at the boyfriend's house, I could easily see the spirit of Kate. I tried to speak with her, but she kept silent and wouldn't speak to me. I got the clear impression that she knew exactly why I was there. She did not seem to be happy that a Deathwalker had come to send her into the afterlife. It seemed to me that Kate was happy staying with her former boyfriend.

Every room I entered; Kate was there-silently watching. The energy that she was giving off was distrust. I could feel that she was unsure of me and that I was being perceived as a threat. When I spoke with the boyfriend, he told me stories of Kate as though she were still alive. In his heart, of course, she was. When I asked him about her suicide, it was clear he did not want to talk about it. I respected his wishes and did not press it further. Instead, I used my psychic abilities and my spiritual helpers to assist me. I asked my client and her boyfriend to leave me alone in the house so that I could do my work. They agreed.

When the time came to send Kate to her afterlife, I called upon my gods, healing helpers, and Ancestors. I asked the Ancestors to aid me in helping Kate move on. By this time, I had been working magick and doing energy work with my Ancestors for many years. They had experience with Deathwalking and helping lost spirits cross over to the Underworld. My Ancestors advised me that the best way to send Kate on her journey would be to enlist the help of her Ancestors. I agreed. I asked my Ancestors to spiritually summon her Ancestors and when they came, I explained to them the situation and they were very happy to help in any way they could. I told them that they needed to explain to Kate that she no longer needed to hold on to her former boyfriend and that she would be happier with then in the afterlife. I knew that Kate would be resistant and that I needed as much energetic power as possible to summon her spirit. My Ancestors, Kate's Ancestors, and I connected our energies, and together we summoned Kate to the ritual space. She looked a little bit frazzled, but because it was her Ancestors who helped summon her, she was willing to listen to what they had to say. Kate's Ancestors were kind and compassionate with her. They explained the situation at hand and were convincing her to go with them to be happy forever. It seemed to me that she was agreeing. Suddenly, the astral body of Kate's former boyfriend appeared! With a wave of very strong, psychic grief-filled energy, he pulled Kate's spirit to him. Then, like a hammer, the truth hit all of us at once. Kate was not haunting her boyfriend. The boyfriend was keeping her prisoner on the physical plane with his grief! He did not realize his grief was so strong that it was psychically binding Kate to the physical plane.

For a moment, we stood there stunned as we watched Kate's sadness and grief grow. I needed to bring in the big guns. I summoned the god of healing, Asclepius, to aid us. The healing god, as well as the Ancestors, sent healing compassionate energy to the boyfriend. The Ancestors explained to him the situation at hand and that if he loved her, he would let her go. I took a magical dagger and cut away the psychic cords and energies that were binding Kate to him. She was free. She went with her Ancestors to continue her spiritual journey and the boyfriend could start healing his grief with the help of the gods and spirits.

The boyfriend grew happier and happier every day. The night he had appeared in astral form, he was not even aware what was happening.

It was like an energetic reflex that he astrally projected to us. He knew that Kate was leaving, and his spirit did not want that to happen. Now he was moving on with his grief and able to face the world again. My client eventually married her boyfriend and I have not heard of Kate returning.

Valediction

Working through the many aspects of the Underworld is a journey indeed. Each culture has their own myths to teach the next generation the trials and joys of the depths below. As you have probably realized by now, the myths and stories are a map of the Underworld. Even though each civilization we learned about had their own myths, they are very similar. The energies and themes are the same. The Underworld is a place for the spirits of the dead, but it is much more. The ancient beings that live there have much wisdom for us, but they will not give up their power easily. It is to be given only to those who wish to bring it back to the community for survival and healing.

The Underworld is a place of transformation. We learned many stories about trials and hardships in the Underworld that is meant to temper our spirits. The Buddhist, Native Americans, Babylonians, and many other cultures teach that without hardship and strife we cannot become better. I often think of these tests as the Universe trying to strengthen our spiritual muscles. Our spirit must be placed under duress to become stronger. This is the true essence of Karma. To be complacent is to atrophy. To leave the comfort of the old life is to be enlightened. Many people are quite happy to stay with their nine to five jobs and never evolving past the nightly news. For the rest of us, we desire change. Change within ourselves and change with in our society.

It is the beings in the Underworld who have magical secrets to teach us how to transform. The creatures in the Underworld are very old and have much wisdom and power. The power they have must be guarded. If someone obtains great power and is not ready for it, they will soon destroy themselves and anyone who is close to them. As we practice the art of journeying into the Underworld, we will gain more wisdom and power.

This work is healing. It heals us and our community. When we take on the shamanic work of healing the dead and traveling to the Underworld, we are taking upon ourselves sacred work. For some, much healing needs to take place at the point of death. There are not many who are able to do this work. But for those of us who embrace the energies of the dead and the Underworld it is a calling we cannot ignore; just as a nurse or doctor cannot ignore their call to heal the living. It is a part of our spiritual make up. To ignore it is to live a life of grayness and stagnation. We are shamans, witches, magicians, and healers. We must answered the call of the Underworld. They are calling you. Will you listen?

Because of the scope of this work the publisher and I felt it would be better to split this book into two volumes. Your journey is not over. Volume one is the discovery and magick of the Underworld and volume two is the magick of the ancestors and working with the dead. In volume two, we will learn of the myths of death from around the world. We will also learn how to create an ancestral altar so that we can build a powerful magical bond with our own ancestors. The magick of the ancestors is very powerful. They will help you with your everyday magick as well as give wise council on life decisions. The ancestors will bring a battery of power that will propel you further on your magical path. I look forward to our journey together in *Deeper Into The Underworld: Death, Ancestors, and Magical Rites.*

Bibliography

A Short History of Myth. Karen Armstrong. Canongate Books. 2005.

Alice In Wonderland. Lewis Carrol. Bantam classics. 1984.

American Indian Myths and Legends. Richard Erdoes and Alfanso Ortiz. Pantheon Books. 1984.

Angels, Demons, and Gods of the New Millennium. Lon Milo Duquett. Weiser. 1997.

Aspects of Anglo-Saxon Magic. Bill Griffiths. Anglo-Saxon Books. 1996.

Awakening To The Spirit World: The Shamanic Path of Direct Revelation. Sandra Ingerman and Hank Wesselman. Sounds True, Inc. 2010.

Bardo Teachings. Lama Ladu. Snow Lion Pub. 1982, 2010.

Becoming Osiris: The Ancient Egyption Death Experience. Ruth Schumann Antelme and Stephane Rossini. Inner Traditions International. 1995.

Call of the Horned Piper. Nigel Aldcroft Jackson. Capall Bann Publishing. 1994.

Communing With The Spirits. Martin Coleman. Samual Wieser, Inc. 1998.

Couragous Dreaming. Alberto Villoldo, PH.D. Hay House Inc. 2008.

Cunning Folk and Familiar Spirits: Shamanistic Visionary Traditions In Early Modern British Witchcraft and Magic. Emma Wilby. Sussex Academy Press. 2005.

Cunningham's Encyclopeida of Magical Herbs. Scott Cunningham. Llewellyn Publications. 1985.

Death: A History of Man's Obsessions and Fears. Robert Wilkens. Barnes and Noble. 1990.

Egyptian Mythology: A Guide To The Gods, Goddesses, and Traditions of Ancient Egypt. Geraldine Pinch. Oxford University Press. 2002.

Eluesinian Mysteries and Rites. Doudley Wright. The Theosophical Publishing House. No date given.

Forbidden Rites: A Necromancer's Manual of the Fifteenth Century. Richard Kieckhefer. The Pennsylvania State University Press. 1998.

From Artemis to Diana: The Goddess of Man and Beast. 12 ACTA Hyperborea. Edited by Tobias Fischer-Hansen and Birte Poulsen. Museum Tusculanum Press. 2009.

From Distant Days: Myths, Tales, and Poetry of Ancient Mesopotamia. Benjamin R. Foster. CDL Press. 1995.

Gilgamesh: A Verse Narrative. Herbert Mason. Mentor Press. 1972.

God Is Red. Vine Deloria Jr. Fulcrum Publishing. 1973.

Gods, Demons, and Symbols of Ancient Mesopotamia. Jack Black and Anthony Green. University of Texas Press. 1992.

Greek and Roman Mythology. Thomas Bulfinch. Penguin Books. 1979.

Greek and Roman Necromancy. Daniel Ogden. Princeton University Press. 2001.

Hecate's Fountain. Kenneth Grant. Skoob Books Publishing. 1992.

Heimskringla or The Lives of the Norse Kings. Snorre Sturlason. Dover Publications. 1990.

Hoodoo Herb and Root Magic: A Materia Magica of African-American Conjure. Catherine Yronwode. Lucky Mojo Curio Company. 2002.

In Search of Herne The Hunter. Eric L. Fitch. Copall Bann Publishing. 1994.

Indian Mythology: Tales, Rituals, and Symbols from the Heart of the Subcontinent. Devdutt Pattanaik. Inner Traditions International. 2003.

Jotunbok: Working With The Giants of the Northern Tradition. Raven Kaldera. Asphodel Press. 2006.

Journeying: Where Shamanism and Psychology Meet. Jeannette M. Gagan, PhD. Rio Chama Publications. 1998.

Julian of Norwich: Revelations of Divine Love. Translated into modern English by Clifton Wolters. Penguin Books. 1966.

Kali: The Black Goddess of Dakshineswar. Elizabeth U. Harding. Nicolas-Hays, Inc. 1993.

Low Magick. Lon Milo Duquette. Llewellyn. 2010.

Magic and Superstition In Europe: A Concise History From Antiquity To The Present. Michael D. Bailey. Rowman and Littlefield Publishers, INC. 2007.

Magical Use of Thought Forms: A Proven System of Mental and Spiritual Empowerment. Dolores Ashcraft-Norwicki and J.H. Brennan. Llewellyn Publications. 2002.

Masks of Misrule. Nigel Jackson. Capall Bann Publishing. 1996

Modern Magick: Twelve Lessons in the High Magickal Arts.

Netherworld. Robert Temple. Century Publications. 2002.

Nordse Mythology: The Guide To The Gods, Heroes, Rituals, and Beliefs. John Lindow. Oxford Universtiy Press. 2001.

Osiris and the Egyptian Resurrection. E.A. Wallis Budge. Dover Publications. 1973.

Our Name Is Melancholy: The Complete Books of Azreal. Leilah Wendal. West Gate Press. 1992.

Parallel Universes: The Search For Other Words. Fred Alan Wolf. A Touchstone Book. Simon and Schuster. 1988.

Popol Vuh. Translated by Dennis Tedlock. Touchstone. Simon and Schuster Publishing. 1985, 1996.

Qabalah, Qliphoth, and Goetic Magic. Thomas Karlson. Ajna Books. 2004-2007.

Religion In Ancient Mesopotamia. Jean Bottero. The University of Chicago Press. 1998.

Shamanism and Spirituality In Therapeutic Practise. Christa Mackinnnon. Singing Dragon. 2012.

Shamanism: Archaic Techniques of Ecstacy. Mircea Eliade. Penguin Books. 1964.

Singing The Soul Back Home:Shamanic Wisdom for Everyday. Catlin Matthews. Connections Publishing. 1995

Summoning Spirits: The Art of Magical Evocation. Konstantinos. Llewellyn Publications. 2001.

Summoning Spirits: The Art of Magical Evocation. Konstantinos. Llewellyn Publications. 1996.

Temple of the Cosmos: The Ancient Egyptian Experience of the Sacred. Jeremy Naydler. Inner Traditions International. 1996

The Bible, various editions

The Book of Fallen Angels. Michael Howard. Capall Bann. 2004.

The Book of Solomon's Magick. Carroll "Poke" Runyon, M.A. The Church of Hermetic Sciences Inc. 1996.

The Celtic Book of the Dead. Caitlin Matthews. Grange Books. 2001.

The Complete Book of Incense, Oils, and Brews. Scott Cunningham. Llewellyn Publications. 1989.

The Complete Fairy Tales of the Brothers Grimm. Brothers Grimm Translated By Jack Zipes. Bantam Books. 1812. 1815. 1987.

The Cup of Destiny. Trevor Ravenscroft. Weiser Books. 1982.

The Deities Are Many: A Polytheistic Theology. Jordan Paper. State University of New York Press. 2005.

The Dreamer's Book of the Dead. Robert Moss. Destiny Books. 2005.

The Egyptian Book of the Dead: The Book of Going Forth By Day. Translated by Dr. Raymond Faulkner. Chronical Books. 1994.

The Element Encyclopedia of 5000 Spells. Judy Illes. Element. 2004

The Essence of Shinto: Japan's Spiritual Heart. Motohisa Yamaksage. Kodansha International. 2006.

The Exorcist Handbook. Josephine McCarthy.

The Faery Teachings. Orion Foxwood. R.J. Steward Books. 2007.

The Gods of the Egyptians: Studies in Egyptian Mythology. E.A. Wallis Budge. Dover Publications. 1969.

The Goetia: The Lesser Key of Solomon the King. Tanslated by Samual Liddell MacGregor Mathers. Samuel Weiser, Inc. 1995.

The Grail Legend. Emma Jung and Marie-Louise von Franz. Sigo Press. 1986.

The History of Hell. Alice K. Turner. Harvest Books. 1993.

The Holy Grail: Its Origins, Secrets, and Meanings Revealed. Malcolm Godwin. Viking Studio Books. 1994.

The Lost Secret of Death. Peter Novak. Hampton Roads Publishing. 2003.

The Master Book of Herbalism. Paul Beyerl. Phoenix Publishing Co. 1984.

The Myth of Isis and Osiris. Jules Cashford. Barefoot Books. 1993.

The Mythic Path. David Feinstein, Ph.D and Stanley Krippner, Ph.D. Tarcher/Putnam Books. 1997.

The Nightbattles: Witchcraft and Agrarian Cults in the Sixteenth and Seventeenth Centuries. Carlo Ginzburg. Translated by John and Ann Tedeschi. Penguin Books. 1983.

The Nordse Myths. Kevin Crossley-Holland. Pantheon Books. 1980.

The Pathwalker's Guide To The Nine Worlds. Raven Kaldera. Asphodel Press. 2006.

The Poetic Edda. Translated by Lee M. Hollander. University of Texas Press, Austin. 1962.

The Practice of Dream Healing: Bringing Ancient Greek Mysteries Into Modern Practice. Edward Tick, Ph.D. Quest Books. 2001.

The Proes Edda. Snorri Sturluson. Translated by Jesse L. Byock. Penguin Press. 2005.

The Republic. Plato. Penguin Books. 1955.

The Robert Cockrane Letters. Robert Cockrane with Evan John Jones. Capall Bann. 2002.

The Roebuck In The Thicket: An Anthology of the Robert Cockrane Witchcraft Tradition. Evan John Jones and Robert Cockrane. 2001.

The Sacred Pipe: Black Elk's Account of the Seven Rites of the Oglala Sioux. Oklahoma Press. 1953.

The Secret Commonwealth of Elves, Fauns and Fairies. Robert Kirk. Dover Publications, Inc. 2008.

The Shaman's Secret: The Lost Resurrection Teachings of the Ancient Maya. Douglas Gillette, M.A., M. Div. Bantam Books. 1997.

The Sociopath Next Door. Martha Stout, Ph.D. Broadway Books. 2006.

The Spiritual Universe: The Existance of the Soul. Fred Alan Wolf, Ph.D. Simon and Schuster. 1996.

The Tibetan Book of the Dead: The Great Book of Natural Liberation Through Understanding In The Between. Translated by Robert A.F. Thurman. Bantam Books. 1994.

The Tree of Evil. William G. Gray. Samuel Weiser, Inc. 1984.

The Underworld Initiation: A Journey Towards Psychic Transformation.. R. J. Stewart. Mercury Publishing Inc. 1990.

Treading the Mill: Practicle Craft Working in Modern Traditional Witchcraft. Nigel G. Person. Capall Bann Publishing. 2007.

Walking The Twilight Path: A Gothic Book of the Dead. Michelle Belanger. Llewellyn Publications. 2008.

When They Severed The Earth From The Sky: How The Human Mind Shapes Myth. Elizabeth Wayland Barber and Paul T. Barber. Princeton University Press. 2004.

Wightridden: Paths of Northern-Tradition Shamanism. Raven Kaldera. Asphodel Press. 2007.

Wyrdwalkers: Techniques of Norther-Traditions Shamanism. Raven Kaldera. Asphodel Press. 2006.

Index

This book is dedicated to all those who came before us
and those who stand beside us in spirit.

Frontispiece & Cover by Amanda Manesis

DEEPER INTO THE
UNDER
WORLD

DEATH

ANCESTORS

AND

MAGICAL

RITES

CHRIS ALLAUN

Cover art/design Amanda Manesis www.amaradulcis.com

Other works by Chris Allaun

Underworld: Shamanism, Myth, and Magick vol I

Upperworld: Shamanism and Magick of the Celestial Realms

Contents

Find Your Ancestral Teacher: Astral Traveling to Experience the Ancestors ; Traveling to the Ancestors to Release Ancestral Patterns ; Family Karma ; Performing Tasks for Ancestors ; Magick with Ancestors ; Calling Ancestors in Ritual.

Baldur's Dreams (Norse) ; Necromancy ; Reasons for Summoning the Dead ; Sacred Places ; Sacred Times ; Cemeteries ; Mausoleums; Tombs and Mounds ; Graveyard Meditation ; The Hidden Company ; The Rose Castle ; Ritual of the Rose Castle ; Summoning Spirits of the Dead ; Ritual Outline ; The Dead and Cursing ; Healing and Removing Curses ; Forcing the Dead Against Their Will ; Re-Animation; The Sorrow of Isis (Egyptian) ; Fears of Re-Animation; Asclepius and Diana Bring Back the Dead (Greco-Roman); My Thoughts on Modern Re-animation.

5   Skulls, Bones, and Blood; Odin Enchants Mimir's Head (Norse);

The Skull; The Skull Meditation; Initiation of the Bones (Skeleton Meditation); Gravestones; Oracles and Guides; Blood Magick; The Blood of Creation (Maya) ; Witchblood; Hyndla and Freya (Norse); Tapping into the Blood; Exercise: Tapping into the Blood; Journeying To The Blood; Blood in Magick and Necromancy ; Mayan Ancestral Blood Summoning Ritual ; Spellcasting Using Blood.

Talking to the Spirit; The Broom or Besom; Blast of Power; Wards; Banishing Without Prejudice; Laughing; The Magical Ring;Herbs/Crystals/Stones;Chemicals; Incense and Fumigations; Ancestor Magick; God Magick; Talismans/Charms/Medicine Bags; Mirrors; Ritual to Banish Unwanted Spirits or Demons ; Valediction.

Introduction

Deeper into the Underworld we go...

We celebrate the cycles of life, growth, and renewal and connect ourselves to the flow of nature. But what of death? Death is a natural part of the rhythm of life and rebirth. There is an ebb and flow to all things. Everything that is created must end and be dissolved back into the energies of the Universe. Death is as sacred as life. It is because of our mortality that we strive to be more than we are and find happiness and fulfillment in our lives. It is believed that the oldest rituals in human history are death rites. These are the ceremonies that help the dead transition to a place of healing and peace in the Underworld. In our modern magical practice, it is important that we incorporate the ancient practice of honoring Ancestors and magick. In our modern culture, we send our Ancestors to the afterlife in the Underworld and then forget about them. It is time we bring them back and honor the beloved dead just as we honor nature and the gods.

There are ancient secrets kept in deep in the Underworld. It is said, "The dead tell no tales...", but they do. To those who know how to speak and honor the dead, they can tell us their tales. The dead have secrets of the life they lived and energies of death, the afterlife, and other magical rites. They can add power to our magick and tell of coming events. In my previous book, *Underworld: Shamanism, Myth, and Magick* we learned about the subterranean world. This is the world of our ancestors, those souls who came before us. It is also a place of healing and dreaded creatures who are diligently kept out of our reach. As we

have learned, there is much power and wisdom to be obtained in this magical place. But there is much more to explore. We must go deeper into the Underworld and discover who our ancestors are and how to bring them into our world so we can help each other through magick. We honor the gods and spirits of nature around us, but we are missing a vital part of our spiritual development. By honoring our ancestors, we are connecting with the powers of the Underworld in a balanced and healing way. I am a firm believer that to spiritually evolve, it is beneficial to connect to the gods in the Upperworld, the spirits of nature in the Midworld, and the Ancestors in the Underworld.

Our Ancestors are our family and loved ones who have come before us and, through death, passed beyond the veil that separates the physical world and the spirit world. Our Ancestors do not necessarily have to be of our family lineage. They can be friends or people from a particular creed, association, and magical lineage. It is through our bloodlines that the more common concept of "Ancestor" comes. The same blood that runs through your veins also ran through the veins of these Ancestors. The DNA in our blood and bodies comes from both mother and father. I feel that it is important to note that different cultures stress the value of lineage through one parent more than the other. Some cultures feel the father's blood and heritage has more value, while others place more value on the mother's blood and heritage. I think both are important! To pick one over the other is to deny half of who you are and half of the potential magical power you could achieve.

When it comes to bloodlines and heritage, it is important to know your family history so that you can better assess which talents are predominantly found in which side of the family. For instance, if your mother and grandmother were natural healers then it will be in your best interest to work with that side of the family for natural healing. If, at the

same time, your father's side were craftsmen, then it will be best for you to work with your father's family for that type of magick. Sometimes, we are unaware of the magick that runs in our family. If we use craftsmen as an example, such as metal-working or blacksmithing, there are many ancient traditions that believed that the craftsmen who created the sword or the plow blade held a lot of magical power. As you go forward on the journey of learning about our Ancestors, you may discover the magick that is rooted deep within your own family history. Remember, to do magick several centuries ago was illegal and therefore was hidden, sometimes even from one's own family.

The Ancestors are not only found in our genetic DNA of our biological parents. They can also be found in our magical groups and spiritual traditions we follow. This is what we call a magical lineage. As the same blood runs through us as it did our Ancestors, so does the magical current run from the beloved dead of our spiritual traditions down to us. I have many students who do not know who their biological ancestors are or have decided not to include their family on the ancestral altar. Instead, they chose to honor their spiritual family instead. I have seen many wonderful ancestral altars who honor founders and teachers of their tradition instead of their grandparents and relatives.

It is important to know where you came from and who your Ancestors are, but this, sometimes, is not as easy as one might think. If a person is adopted or there is no record of parents and grandparents, then I think it is perfectly valid to learn about the Ancestors from those people you call family. Ancestors are more than who gave birth to you. It is about who you are and where you come from. It is about those spirits of the dead who are willing and able to connect with you on a profound spiritual level. As we have seen, groups and creeds can be the Ancestors that you link up to. With this being the case, there is nothing wrong with

using your adoptive parents or stepparents in your workings. I have seen on occasion when someone works with the Ancestors of their adoptive parents that, after a time, one from their biological family makes themselves known. But I will caution that this is not always the case. Sometimes the gods and spirits have decided to sever that ancestral cord for whatever reason. Remember that the gods have your best interest at heart, and they know more about destiny and the cosmic web than you do. Learn to feel the love of whomever you call Ancestor and take heed of their guidance and advice. You might be surprised just how powerful they can be.

I have been working with the ancestors and the dead for many years now. I cannot imagine a world where I do not speak with my family in the world of spirit. Not only have they aided in my magick and spiritual journey, but they have done many things for me that I could never repay. On my ancestral altar, I have a space for my grandparents and great grandparents. They protect my home and keep the energies balanced and conducive to healing and magick. They are my family in spirit just as they were my family in life.

The Underworld

The Underworld is a place that is home to the ancestral afterlife as well as other concepts that are found in myth and legend. There are numerous pagan spiritualities that place the beloved ancestors in an energetic or spiritual place beneath the earth. Such a place is called by many names by various cultures. The Egyptians call it the Dwat, the Greeks call it Hades, the Nordics call it Hel, the Welsh call it Annwn, and so forth. The ancestral lands are wonderful places of healing, rejuvenation, and spiritual learning. But the Underworld has dark places as well. When Zeus conquered the Titans, who caused chaos upon the earth, he bound them deep into a

horrible place called Tartarus. And then there are the hellworlds and shadowlands that lost souls are said to be doomed to wander.

In pagan and some indigenous cosmology, the Underworld is but one of the shamanic three worlds that is symbolized as a giant tree that makes up the Universe. The trunk of this great energetic tree we call the Midworld, or sometimes the Otherworld, it is the place of humans, faeries, elves, plant and animal spirits, and the spirits of the land. The great branches which reach into the heavens is the Upperworld. This is the place of gods, angels, planetary and star spirits, and ascended beings who guide the spiritual evolution of the Universe. Then we have the roots of the tree which travel deep within the earth itself. This is the place of the ancestors, the wandering dead, chthonic deities, and even sometimes demons. Together these three worlds make up the energetic or astral Universe that we can journey through in spirit. Each of these worlds has wonderous beings who can teach you magick and healing. For us, in this book, we will work with the ancestors and the dead so that we may find healing and the deep mysteries of death and the afterlife.

As we journey deeper into the Underworld you will discover your ancestors, ancestor teachers, and spirit guides who will teach you of the mysteries of the Underworld and the dead. These powerful beings are waiting for you to call upon them and establish a deep and meaningful relationship. Your ancestors have been waiting for you all this time. They have been watching you and waiting for the moment that you will use your magick to summon them in your rites. That time is now. Welcome to the deeper parts of the Underworld.

Astral Projection and Shamanic Journeying

To travel into the Underworld, you will be using your astral body. The astral body is our energetic double and is sometimes called our body of

light. The astral body can be easily controlled by the emotions and the mind. When you become proficient at leaving your body, which is called astral projection, you will have the ability to journey through time and space. You will be able to travel at the speed of thought to anywhere in the Universe.

I have studied a lot of books and been to workshops that teach astral projection. When I was a novice magician, I remember learning the formulas and magical invocations that would allow me to leave the body in spirit. The magical spells seemed exceptionally long and the techniques for leaving the body were tedious and it took months of meditation and visualization exercises to even get one's feet wet. To most students, this was daunting and left people feeling more frustrated than empowered. After receiving a formal magical training followed by a lot of experience traveling to the three shamanic worlds, I can tell you that you that astral projection is very simple - you just have to practice at it with some regularly and not get discouraged if you do not immediately get results. I will give you a couple of fun exercises to do that will get you started. The key here is to visualize as clearly as possible and *FEEL* the sensations of walking around, seeing, hearing, smelling, and touching. To do this you simply use your imagination. Visualize. The other key to controlling your astral body is to use logic, imagination, desire, and will. Meaning, you must imagine yourself in the Otherworlds as clearly as possible using logic, then with the desire to travel, you simply will yourself to do so.

The first few times you may wonder if astral projection is just "all in your head." Well, to some extent it is, but it is supposed to be. Remember, the Astral and Spiritual realms are the places of imagination, dreams, and visions. We travel around in the physical plane in our physical bodies, so we travel around in the Astral/Spiritual with our astral (imagined/ visualized) bodies. I know some magicians who will argue with me that I

am oversimplifying ancient magick. And I am. If at first it feels like it is "all in your head" go with it. Eventually, you will meet entities, spirits, and gods who will take you to wonderful places and tell you secret information that you simply cannot "make up." The trick here is to have fun and explore. See what you find. Read some of the mythology listed in Suggestions for Further Reading at the end of this chapter and try your best to understand the spiritual meaning behind the stories. Then go have a spiritual adventure.

So, what is all this talk about shamanic journeying? Basically, shamanic journeying and astral projection are the same thing. You are using your astral or energy body to leave your physical body to travel in the spiritual realms of the Universe. The term "astral projection" is more popular in ceremonial magical and New Age communities while "shamanic journeying" is a term more popular in neo-shamanism. At the end of the day it really does not matter what term you use because the end result will be the same.

Astral Exercise #1

1. It may be helpful to play a shamanic drumming recording. If you have someone to drum for you all the better. The drumming should be light but audible enough to hear comfortably. If you are using a drum or having someone drum for you, have them beat at a moderately quick pace. If for some reason you cannot get a recording of shamanic drumming, don't worry. It is not necessary to have a shamanic drum beat to astral project. If you do not like shamanic drumming feel free to use any type of music that puts you in a trance and makes you feel magical. I will often use synthesized songs that sound ethereal to accomplish this for myself.

2. Sit or lie in a comfortable position. Make sure your back is as

straight as possible.

3. Close your eyes and take a few deep breaths.

4. Relax your body as best you can. Begin with your feet. Tell them to relax and release all tension. Then move up to your calves. Tell them to relax and release all tension. Go up to the thigh, glutes, back, belly, chest, shoulders, arms, hands, neck, and head in turn, telling them all to relax and release all stress and tension.

5. Imagine yourself getting up and walking around. Remember, this is done entirely with your imagination. Try not to move your physical body at all.

6. Walk around the room you are in and look at the furniture, walls, shelves. Look at yourself. See yourself lying (or sitting) down.

7. When you are ready, see yourself walk over to your physical body and sit or lie back into yourself. When you are close to your body this will most often happen automatically.

Astral Exercise #2

1. Play your shamanic drumming recording or other music as per the previous exercise.

2. Sit or lie in a comfortable position. Make sure your back is as straight as possible.

3. Close your eyes and take a few deep breaths.

4. Relax your body as best you can. Begin with your feet. Tell them to relax and release all tension. Then move up to your calves. Tell them to relax and release all tension. Go up to the thigh, glutes, back, belly, chest, shoulders, arms, hands, neck, and head in turn,

telling them all to relax and release all stress and tension.

5. Imagine yourself getting up and walking around. Remember, this is done entirely with your imagination. Try not to move your physical body at all.

6. At this point, see a door or gateway in front of you. Know that the door leads to the World Tree.

7. Step through the door and on the other side see the World Tree. The Word Tree is the largest tree you have ever seen. Its trunk extends out further than the eye can see going both left and right. The branches go up into the heavens and you cannot see the top of the tree. You can see that the roots go deep into the Earth.

8. This is the Center of the Midworld, and it is your starting point. Until you are very proficient with traveling, you may want to start here.

9. You notice that there is a door in the trunk of the tree leading down, deep into the roots of the tree. Go through the door. You may see a staircase or simply a tunnel.

   Note: You may also simply see a hole in the ground leading down into the Earth, following the roots, leading down into tunnels.

10. Go down further and further into the roots through the tunnel or staircase. Know that you can travel down very fast and sometimes in just a blink of an eye.

11. Finally, when you arrive at the Underworld, take note of the first thing you see. Explore the immediate environments carefully. When you are ready, go back the way you came and back up the tunnels into the World Tree, then back to the trunk of the tree and into the Middleworld.

Astral Exercise #3

1. Play your shamanic drumming recording or other music per the previous exercises.

2. Sit or lie in a comfortable position. Make sure your back is as straight as possible.

3. Close your eyes and take a few deep breaths.

4. Relax your body as best you can. Begin with your feet. Tell them to relax and release all tension. Then move up to your calves. Tell them to relax and release all tension. Go up to the thigh, glutes, back, belly, chest, shoulders, arms, hands, neck, and head in turn, telling them all to relax and release all stress and tension.

5. Visualize a spiral of light, beginning at your feet, spiraling around you, going clockwise. It surrounds your entire body. The only thing you can see is the spiral of light. Know that this magical spiral of light is transporting you to the World Tree.

6. This is the center of the Midworld, your starting point. Until you are very proficient with traveling, you always want to start here.

7. You notice that there is a door in the trunk of the tree leading down deep into the roots of the tree. Go through the door. You may see a staircase or simply a tunnel.

   Note: You may also simply see a hole in the ground leading down into the Earth, following the roots, leading down into tunnels.

8. Go down further and further into the roots through the tunnel, or staircase. Know that you can travel down very fast and sometimes in just a blink of an eye.

9. Finally, when you arrive at the Underworld take note of the first

thing you see. Explore your immediate environs carefully. When you are ready, go back the way you came and back up the tunnels into the World Tree then back to the trunk of the tree in the Middleworld.

10. After awakening from your journey, record your experience in your magical journal and ground yourself back to the physical plane. You may do this by eating something light, drinking water, and/or doing "everyday" things around your home.

At this point in learning about astral travel and journeying through the Underworld, it is not about trying to see how far you go or finding exotic places right away. It is about taking the first steps in learning a new skill. Just as with any skill, it takes practice. You must remember, the astral body is a direct manifestation of your mind, desires, memories, will, and your imagination. What this means is your astral body looks like how you want it to, does what you want it to, and looks like what you think it will. Usually, the astral body looks like you do now but in more "idealized form. Therefore, if you look at your astral body in a mirror, you may look younger, stronger, and healthier.

The astral realm itself takes on the appearance provided by your mind, or the group mind. As we have stated before, if there is a locked gate or a blocked entrance way, most likely your subconscious mind has put it there because either you are not ready to go forward in that direction, or you *think* you are not ready because of your own personal fears. When this happens, try to find out why you cannot go through, or come back later. Group mind phenomenon happens in the Astral/Underworld when we discover ancient sites such as Hades or Hel and they look exactly like the ancients described them. This is because of the many people who believe it looks a certain way. This massive thought form echoes through the astral and takes form. The more people who believe something to be

true, the stronger it manifests. This is the reason why each Underworld of every culture around the world exists. This is also the reason why there is no "one truth".

Exercise:
Finding an Underworld Guide and Spirit Animal

In order to successfully journey into the Underworld, it is important to find your Spirit Animal and Underworld guide. You will be able to explore the Underworld faster and find treasures and allies much quicker than you would if you traveled alone. Also, the Spirit Animal can protect you from dangers that you are not ready to face. Your Spirit Animal can also protect you from spirit attacks in the Underworld. Spirit attacks upon a beginner are extremely rare, and I have often found that the "attackers" are really projections of the traveler's own fears. Put simply, the beginning student is "attacking" him or herself in the Underworld because of their own fears. In essence, they believe the Underworld is a dangerous place, so they imagine danger at every corner. This is simply not the case. The Underworld does have some dangerous places, but the world of the Ancestors is a place of beauty and spiritual transformation. However, your Spirit Animal can help you fend off this astral thought form, should it occur.

Finding Your Spirit Animal

For this exercise, you will travel to the Midworld to find your Spirit Animal.

1. Choose one of the astral exercises from the section on "How to Use Your Astral Body" above and travel to the World Tree.

2. Once there, make the following statement: "I wish to find my Spirit Animal". Open your heart chakra and reach out with your energies to your Spirit Animal. You may not know what kind of animal it is.

That's ok. Reach out with your heart and they will respond back to you.

3. Begin walking in whichever direction feels appropriate to you. Keep the goal of finding your Spirit Animal n mind and try to intuit the direction you should go. The landscape will vary from person to person. You may find yourself traveling into a forest, mountains, valleys, or grass plains. Trust your instincts. For the time being, do not worry if you are "making it up." Visualize your surroundings to the best of your abilities.

4. Keep an eye out for any animals you see. You may see several. Some traditions say that you may see other animals, but you will see your Spirit Animal four times as you walk along your path. This is a good approach to take.

5. If you do not see any animals at first, keep walking. You should eventually begin to see more and more animals.

6. Once you see your Spirit four times along your path, walk up to itand ask, "Are you my Spirit Animal? "

7. If the animal seems distant, unfamiliar, or unwilling to speak with you, then this may not be your Spirit Animal. If it is not your Spirit Animal, keep searching.

8. If the animal is your Spirit Animal, then it will feel like a long-lost friend or relative. Your Spirit Animal may even feel like a part of you. This is because in reality, your totem IS a part of you.

9. Ask your Spirit Animal its name and record it in your magical diary or journal upon returning to your physical body.

Once you are fully conscious, visualize your spirit animal in front of you. You may choose to dance with them or simply imagine your Spirit

Animal combining with your aura. To combine the Spirit Animal with your aura, visualize your animal in front of you. See them walking toward you and energetically combining itself with your aura. Know that you can call upon your Spirit Animal at any time in any world! I recommend getting an animal fetish - a little statue of clay or stone that represents your animal. If you have the fur, teeth, or a claw of the animal then all the better. These things are not necessary but do help you connect to them in a deeper way.

Finding your Underworld Guide

1. Choose one of the astral exercises and travel to the World Tree.

2. Once there, make the following statement: "I wish to find my Underworld Guide".

3. Call upon your Spirit Animal.

4. In the trunk of the World Tree, visualize a door that leads down into the Underworld. Follow this path down.

5. Follow this path down until you reach the Underworld. What do you see? What does the landscape look like?

6. Keep the intention to find your Underworld Guide in your mind. Begin to explore the Underworld. Ask your Spirit animal to show you the way.

7. Trust your intuition. Look for people along the way and ask them if they are your Underworld Guide. If not, ask them to point out the direction in which you can find your guide.

8. Once you find an entity who is a likely candidate to become your Underworld Guide, ask if they are willing to help you navigate the Underworld. If the answer is "no," the entity is not your guide, and

you should keep looking. If the answer is "yes," ask for their name. Then ask your guide if there is anything they would like in return. If the request is reasonable and you are able and willing to do it, then by all means do it. If not, graciously explain why you cannot meet the request.

9. Know that you can call upon your Underworld Guide each time you enter the Underworld.

10. Come back to the Middleworld the way you came. Then open your eyes and journal about your experiences.

The Underworld is a wonderful place to find transformation of the spirit. It is through the myths that ancient cultures have learned to navigate and find their way through the strange terrain. The power of the Underworld has many great rewards for us and to the community we serve. As we learn how to use our astral bodies, we will begin to further our understanding of the world that holds a vast amount of wonder and beauty. Take some time and discover what the Underworld has in store for you. Journal your experiences and the beings you encounter. Write down what happened and the names of the spirits and gods that you meet. Each day you will develop and strengthen your relationships with the Underworld beings, ancestors, guides, and many other spirits who will help and guide you upon your spiritual path.

1
Death

Coyote and the Origin of Death
(Caddo Native American)

In the beginning of the world, there was no death and the people lived forever. Soon, there were so many people that no one knew quite what to do! Food was running out and it began to get very crowded upon Mother Earth. All the chiefs got together to decide what to do about this dilemma. One chief explained that people should die for a little while then come back. He explained that if people died forever then their families would be very unhappy and everyone upon the Earth would be sad.

Coyote objected! "If people only died for a little while," he explained, "then eventually it would still be crowded and there would not be enough food for everyone!"

The chiefs did not listen to Coyote. They decided that people would die for only a while. Then they would bring them back by building a grass lodge and singing a special medicine song. They would summon the dead to the grass lodge and restore them back to life!

Soon the time came to bring the dead back to life. The grass lodge was built and then the special medicine song was sung. A spirit of the dead in the form of a whirlwind came up to the lodge. But Coyote couldn't stand it! He knew the world would be overcrowded and the food would run out. In a flash, Coyote slammed the door to the grass lodge and the whirlwind passed by the lodge. This is how Coyote made death eternal.

Death

The ultimate mystery has always been death. Death takes our loved ones away from us. Death seems final. When we are told about death at a young age, we are told the spirit of our loved one has gone to Heaven, or someplace nice. As we grow older, we begin to seek the answers of death ourselves. We ask ourselves and the Universe questions, such as, "Is there life after death?", "Is there Heaven and Hell?", "Will I exist after I die?", and "Will I have a consciousness after my mind dies?" All these questions are valid and have been asked by every single person at least once in their lifetime. We turn to religion, priests, and spiritualists to find the answers that we seek. We hope that someone has the truth…or at least some part of it. Most of us were born into one religion or another. For a moment, it seems comforting that our parents and the members of our community believe and "know" that there is a heaven or some other kind of salvation at the end of our lives. We take their word for it, hoping that the people who came before us know what they are talking about. When we close our eyes and fall asleep, we dream. Is this similar to life after death? But what about those moments during sleep when we do not dream, or we do not remember our dreams? Is that oblivion?

Humans have fantasized, written, made plays and movies about, and feared death more than anything else in this world. Death is the finality of our existence in this time and space on the physical plane. It is frightening and it can be macabre. It is the end, at least, of how we perceive things from the point of view of our lives here and now. For if there is life after death everything will be different. Even if life after death is almost the same as it was in life, one thing has changed…you have died to the life you know now.

When we look at art and movies about death we see the tragic loss, pain and suffering, sorrow, and the frightening personification of death.

Nothing about death seems soft, beautiful, and happy. In most of the patriarchal religions you either follow the word of God and are blessed at death with angels escorting you to a place next to God, or you do not follow the word of God and you are damned at death with demons dragging you down to be tormented for all eternity! No wonder so many people fear death. It may ease your mind to know that this view of death is relatively new in the history of religious worldviews. The ancients did not believe in a permanent place of torment for even the most wicked of souls. Some, however, did believe in a place for lost souls, or a place for lost *parts* of your soul. But they did not believe in the gods' punishment for not adhering to rituals and scriptures. Tribal villages most definitely did not believe in such a thing. Nor did they believe in "sin" as we understand it from a Judeo-Christian perspective. The idea of sin and the punishment for sin was never found in ancient times. If we take this into account for our own view of the Universe and the cosmos, we begin to see more possibilities. We will begin to see that there is more to the energetic Universe and the three worlds than we once thought. It opens new ideas and perhaps experiences that we never thought could be possible.

For some, death can be beautiful. They can see God in the process of decomposition of the body. The process of decay is a part of the universal cycle of birth, death, and re-birth. All things that are created thrive and then must be broken down or destroyed for the cycle to continue. Even our own solar system was, in theory, born from the death of a previous star. This is the way of things. We know from our teachings that nature abhors a vacuum and does not waste. Waste is a human behavior. Nothing goes to waste in the Universe. When a star dies, its gases and energies are used by gravity to create new stars and planets. When animals (including humans) die, or produce waste, it can be used

to give nutrients to plants and our crops. Through this process the cycles of life, death, and renewal we can continue. These cycles are what allow life and magick to continue. If we see death as a part of the Universe and a part of the cycles, then it can be a beautiful process. There is beauty in all things, even decay.

When we begin to experience the world on our own, we learn that, perhaps, our parents and religious leaders may not have all the answers. The truth is that NO ONE has all the answers. Yes, that is correct. NO ONE. Not even those with a vast knowledge of Spirit. What I mean by this is that no one, no matter how wise and powerful they are has the entire truth and all the answers of the afterlife. It is true that each of these people have experiences that they can share with us. We must remember that these experiences are *their* experiences and may or may not have a direct impact on us. We also must remember that as holy people and magicians explore the Universe, the Underworld, and communicate with the dead, that their experiences are colored by their hopes and fears, prejudices, and worldviews. This does not make them wrong; this makes them messengers of their experience. It is important for you to have your own personal experiences and come up with conclusions for yourself. Mythology, lore, and the experiences of others are a good starting point, but it does not end there. If we look around, the world and the Universe are evolving and changing. Nothing stays the same and cycles go forward and become something greater than they are now. We must continue our own personal explorations and find new experiences. As we work with the dead and the Underworld, we will never come up with the whole truth. Various cultures have distinct ways of thinking and relating to the world. Therefore, we need to be aware that different peoples and cultures have a variety of ideas and experiences.

Perhaps in the end, we are looking at the same thing but just explaining it differently.

Our Fear of Death

Humanity has feared death from as far back as anyone can remember. Part of the fear of death comes from our built-in instinct for survival. To not have this instinct would ensure that early man would prematurely go to their deaths like antelope jumping off a cliff; fear of death makes you move quickly in the opposite direction when you notice a large predator coming your way. Many religions speak of salvation or of being in a "better place," but for those who are unsure or do not believe in religious teachings, death can be a frightening thing. It is even worse for those who believe that they have lived against religious teachings and are convinced that upon death they will spend eternity suffering.

It is interesting to note that there are numerous types of fears that people have when it comes to death. Some people fear dying without a will. Others fear the pain of the death process. But what about when people think you are dead when you actually are not dead! Before modern times there was a fear about being buried alive. There are many conditions that mimic death. There are conditions where your breathing and heart rate slow dramatically and you appear dead. It fascinates me to know that there have been instances where a grave has been dug up only to find that the inside of the coffin was torn up from the inside. Some might say it was a Vampire, but we know it was a person who was mistakenly placed in the grave. Unfortunately, this did happen from time to time. This was one of the reasons for having the custom of the wake. The idea was to put the body on display to see if the person would "wake up." Nowadays, with sophisticated medical equipment, we no longer have to worry about being placed in a coffin without actually being dead.

There is also the fear of the body and the tomb being defiled. There were, and still are, grave robbers. These are people who dig up graves to steal jewelry or expensive mementoes that may have been placed in the coffin with the deceased. Grave robbers have little consideration for the dead and their philosophy is "they won't need it." I think this is horrible. In my worldview, whatever you place in the tomb or in remembrance of the dead belongs to them and they have access to the item in the Afterlife.

An interesting, and to my way of thinking valid, fear of magical people, is the fear of their body being used for Necromancy and black magick after death. For most people, magick does not exist and this would be an irrational fear. But to those of us who believe in magick and the power of energy, it is something that is very real. The Greeks and Romans have many stories of dark magicians who dug up and stole a corpse to summon the soul of the dead out of Hades and use them for divination and cursing. The ancient Celts were headhunters and sometimes used the skulls of their enemies as an oracle. It is from Africa that we get the concept of a zombie, actually gaining control of a dead body to get it to cause harm to others. In reality the "zombie" is an unfortunate person who has been exposed to a dark magician's blowfish powder, which causes nerve and brain damage, and it is much easier to control a susceptible person under the influence of the powder. For people who are concerned about dark magicians using their body parts, it is always wise to have strict orders to be carried out by the living concerning what to do with your body at death. My best recommendation would be cremation. However, do not allow people to keep any of your ashes. Have them spread out somewhere. Your ashes can be used to summon your spirit from the Underworld.

There is also the fear of feeling the process of decay in the grave. In our modern times bodies are filled with embalming fluid, which keeps

the body preserved longer. On a scientific level, the brain dies soon after the body and it would be impossible to feel the process of decay because the nerves would all be dead. However, on a spiritual level there is the fear of the spirit lingering in the grave and being unable to pass on to the next world. I have personally never come across a spirit to whom this has happened. The Underworld spirits and gods would not allow that to occur. In my opinion, that would upset the cosmic balance of things. Plus, there would be no spiritual purpose or lesson for the person in question.

Lastly, there is the fear of being forgotten or not living up to your potential during life. I think that it is our spiritual programming for us to carry out our destiny during life. We are put here in the physical plane to learn, evolve, and heal each other. Each of us has a special destiny and reason to be here. Some people find that reason very quickly and others take a little longer to find out their life's purpose. Unfortunately, there are those who never do. The fear of being forgotten is a very real thing. The best advice I can give you on this subject is to evaluate your talents, get advice from teachers and mentors, and meditate on your will and spirit. If you ask the Universe for guidance, it has been my experience that it will answer.

To fear death is natural. To not fear death in some way is to be sometimes reckless with yourself and others. We are all here for a reason and our goal is to carry out our destinies to the best of our abilities, not to rampage heedlessly through life without giving a thought to either the past or the future.

Angel of Death

The Angel of Death has been spoken of in Christian, Islamic, and Jewish traditions. He is commonly portrayed as a skeletal figure wearing a black

hooded robe and holding a scythe. He is portrayed that way because he is thought to reap the souls of the living from Earth and bring them to the world of the dead. His appearance is nightmarish and his gaze sparks fear in the eyes of all living beings. You may see this figure at Halloween, and he is a character one wants to avoid.

In Jewish mythology his name is Azrael, which means "The help of God" or "Help of the One." In some myths, he was created after most of the angels because after the Universe was created, it was discovered that there must be an ending to all things so that they could begin anew. Azrael, the Angel of Death, was brought into being to carry out this purpose. Otherwise, the Universe would be overrun by living corporeal beings and the cosmos would be brought out of balance. He does not kill living beings or decide how they will die. He is sort of a psychopomp in the way that he takes the souls after death and delivers them where they need to be. In the Christian and Jewish traditions, it is thought that he takes them to either Heaven or Hell. In the modern New Age philosophies, he simply takes the souls to the Realm of the Dead.

When one encounters Death, or hears the tales of him, he is almost always portrayed as the shadowy silent figure that brings about death and fear without remorse. He is even portrayed as "evil." This is only superstitious belief brought about by fear. Azrael is not evil. He carries out a very sacred duty of the Universe. He brings balance to the cycle of life, death, and rebirth. When he is depicted in art, he is dark and has no "eyes," which is why he is sometimes thought to be cruel and soulless. In fact, Death appears to the living as we think he would look. In the psychology of spiritual phenomena, spirits and energies always take the form of how we expect them to appear. I, myself, have seen Azrael on several occasions and he does not appear to me as the gruesome character as he is depicted to be in art and movies. He has appeared to me in

different ways, but generally he is the same in each of his visits. I see him dressed in a dark or black robe and he does have "flesh". But yes, I saw him as a pale man with jet black hair and dark eyes. He has never spoken to me directly, but communicates with energetic sensations, symbols, and emotions.

In my research on Azrael, I have found that he rarely speaks to someone directly. Commonly, the living can easily intuit what he is saying or seem to *just understand* what is going on. I believe this is one of the reasons that he brings fear to us. He does not communicate in the way we are used to. All angels have a specialized function, just as we ourselves have a special talent or skill. The Angel of Death does not enjoy the pain and suffering of living beings upon their death. He brings about the *release* of suffering. He takes away the pain of illness, accident, and mortal injury. In this regard, we can view him as an angel with great sympathy and someone who wishes to ease our pain and suffering. In healing, sometimes the way to ease suffering and pain is death. We must remember that Azrael is an angel, and it is not up to us to completely understand the mysterious ways of the divine or the Universe. Some things may not be meant to be understood but will always remain part of the mysteries.

In art, books, stage, and film, there have been depictions of love affairs with Death. To most people this may seem like one of the strangest things to do. There have been stories about the great passionate love affairs between women and men with the Angel of Death. If you think about it, humanity has always had a love/hate relationship with the entities involved with the death process. One reason for the love affairs, I believe, is the classic attraction to dark and shadowy men (or in this case, beings.) People are often sexually and romantically attracted to dark and mysterious men for many different reasons. Often, we want to learn about our own dark sides. Another reason for these love affairs with Death is because

throughout history right up to the present being "in love" with a higher being is simply another form of devotion or even worship. To those who are not familiar with the pagan religions, this may sound a bit odd to be in love with a god, angel, or higher being. Many mythologies talk about how gods fall in love with mortals and mortals in love with gods. Think back to how the mortal Psyche fell in love with the god Cupid. It is important to realize that the myths about Death are no different. It has been said that we fall in love with those who help us evolve and grow in one way or another, and Death always plays a powerful part in our spiritual evolution.

There have been tales and theories that Azrael is one of the fallen angels. This is not true to the mythology of the Judeo-Christian angels. It is true that some of the fallen angels may cause sickness, injury, and death, but Azrael has no part in this. He is also portrayed as a dark and shadowy figure, but he is not a demon; nor is he a malicious entity. His position and powers make him a follower of the plan of God, and he stays true to his divine purpose. He never goes astray. I believe that the myths and stories that link him to the fallen angels were written out of fear and ignorance as to who and what the Angel of Death is.

So, the question is, in our work and exploration with the Underworld, do we summon, work with, or give honor to the Angel of Death? In Jewish practice you do not worship or honor the angels. You simply respect them as the messengers of God and listen to their guidance. In magick, there is the fear that if you summon Azrael then he will perform the duty that he was created to do, namely take your soul. I have never actually heard of a magick conjuration going that way. In my personal practice I do give honor to the Angel of Death in my own way, but I do not command his presence in any way. I give honor to the energies of Death and should Azrael have something to tell me then, well, I listen.

It is interesting to theorize about the powers of Azrael. Essentially, everything in the Universe must end or "die." Does the Angel of Death have powers over those things as well? Does he have power over dying planets, stars, and even whole galaxies? When our Universe returns to the place of origin and the Universe as we think of it now ends, will Azrael be there to carry the pieces back to God? These are all interesting concepts, and many theological and philosophical conversations can be had on this topic alone. But if it is true, and Azrael will be a part of this event, then truly he is the "Help of God", and God whispers things in his ear that only He and Death may know.

I had first met Azrael in a dream when I was 15 years old. I dreamed that I was babysitting three infants and they were asleep in my bedroom. My friends had pulled up to my driveway in a black van and wanted me to go with them somewhere. In the dream, I had forgotten about watching the infants and decided to go with my friends. As we were driving away, I could see a pale man with long black hair wearing a black robe in my bedroom where the babies were. He was spreading his arms wide open to show me his power and that he had captured the infants. Frantically, I dashed out of the van and ran into the house. When I got to the bedroom, the babies had their legs chopped off and Azrael was nowhere to be found. But I knew where he was! I quickly ran out of the house and found the van in the middle of the yard. The van door was open, and I saw someone with long black hair sitting in the back. I was convinced it was the Angel of Death. I found a screwdriver in my hand and stabbed the longhaired person who then melted away. I had beaten death.

When I awoke, I had the darkest feeling. Death had been there that night. I walked into the kitchen to make some breakfast when I heard my parents talking. They told me that my brother's best friend had a girlfriend who was murdered the night before. When I had my dream. My dad

showed me a picture of her; someone I had never met before. When I saw the picture, my heart fell out of my chest. That was the girl I had stabbed with the screwdriver in my dream.

Another time I had seen Death was a few months after my father died. I was in bed listening to trance-like music. The candles were lit and there was a magical hue in the bedroom. My mind was aimlessly wandering. A dark presence appeared in my room. It was not clear, but it was like the primal earth of decay and endings entered my bedroom. I knew instantly it was Death. When Death appears in front of you, you do not have to guess. His energy is unmistakable. I had no fear of him because he was not there for me. He opened his cloak, and he revealed my father to me. Neither my father nor Death spoke a word. My father's eyes were happy and bright, and it was as if he wanted to see me one more time. After a moment of energetically connecting with my father, Death closed his cloak and slowly disappeared. I knew that Death did not do favors for people easily and there would be work that Death would later ask me to do.

Azrael Goes to Mother Earth

Yahweh sent the angels Michael, Ariel, and Gabriel to the Earth to collect clay so that he could create mankind. The three great angels flew down to Earth to do as God had asked. As they began to try to pierce the Earth, their angelic tools did not work. Again and again, they tried to dig into the Earth, but their efforts were useless. The three great angels had magnificent strength given to them by Yahweh himself. This made no sense to them! Why could they not obtain the Earth that they wanted? Yahweh wanted to create man and the Earth was impenetrable. How could this be?

They argued among themselves why Yahweh would send them down

to creation to do an impossible task. They suddenly became aware that the Earth was alive with a consciousness of its own. The Earth was alive! Michael, Gabriel, and Ariel found Mother Earth. She was divine in her own right but was different than Yahweh and the angels themselves. They petitioned her for her clay so that God could create man. Mother Earth had the power of foresight. She knew that Yahweh's creation, the human race, would procreate and with the passing of time, man would destroy her. She sent them away. Their power was no match for hers.

Michael, Gabriel, and Ariel returned to the heavenly realm. They explained to Yahweh what had happened. There would be no clay. Yahweh then sent the angel Azrael down to speak with Mother Earth. The great Mother knew why Azrael had come, and again she refused to give him the clay for Yahweh. Azrael had great compassion for Mother Earth and her beauty. He spoke with her at great length about his divine powers. He explained to her that man would indeed procreate, but they would not live forever, they would be mortal, and he would take them in death. Mother Earth was comforted by his great compassion for her and the mankind that Yahweh would create. She agreed to give him the clay he had come for.

Azrael returned to the heavenly realms with the clay for Yahweh to create mankind. Yahweh was impressed with the compassion Azrael had for Mother Earth and his ability to take away that which he had created. Yahweh made Azrael the Angel of Death. It is Azrael who holds your hand for the journey into the great mystery.

The Creation of Death (Hindu)

In the beginning, humans did not die. They were multiplying very rapidly and were overpopulating the Earth. Brahma, the Creator, was concerned about this so he created the goddess of death, Mrityu. Mrityu was given

the ability of great compassion. She loved all beings of the cosmos. Brahma told Mrityu of her most sacred duty…to kill all living beings at their appointed time. This greatly saddened Mrityu and in her grief she ran far away from the beautiful things that Brahma had created. Brahma pursued her, looking throughout creation to find the goddess. At last, when he found her, he explained her sacred cosmic duty and how the spirit of living beings would live on after death on the wheel of rebirth and would return to Earth in another incarnation. After understanding that the beautiful beings would live on in spirit, Mrityu agreed to be the goddess of death.

The Death of Yama (Hindu)

Yama was the first man that lived on Earth. There were no other people on the Earth except for his sister Yami. Yami wanted to have children, but Yama refused because he was horrified at the thought of having sex, much less children, with this own sister! Yami persisted, but time and time again Yama refused. When the day came, Yama died a childless man. Upon death, Yama entered the Underworld. As a result of being the first man to live on Earth and die on Earth, he was the first being to enter the Underworld. Unfortunately, he had no children that would have children so that he could be reborn on Earth. He was doomed to spend eternity in the Underworld. But the gods gave him a most holy duty. Since he was the first man to know death, he would be transformed into the Master, or God, of death! Ever since, when someone is doomed to die, it is Yama who takes him to the Underworld.

The Energetic and Physical Process of Dying

When we have come to the point in our journey on the physical plane that we must move on to the spirit world, the dying process will begin.

There are several things that are happening at once. The chakras have a direct effect on the physical body. What happens to the chakras inevitably happens to the body. As we know through our magical and spiritual studies, things manifest first in the astral/energetic planes before they manifest on the physical plane. The same rules apply to the process of dying. We have seven major chakras that correspond to the seven major parts of the body.

1. Root - sacrum, pelvis (Earth)
2. Navel – lower back, bladder, reproductive organs (water)
3. Solar Plexus - midback, upper abdomen, spleen, liver (fire)
4. Heart - heart, lungs, chest, thoracic (air)
5. Throat - throat, cervical, thyroid (spirit/sound)
6. Brow - midbrain, eyes, sinuses in skull (spirit/sight)
7. Crown - cranium (spirit/divinity)

During the death process the energy of our chakras dissolves. Our physical body and our chakras are connected and what happens to one happens to the other. When the chakras no longer have the strength to help our body function, our bodies stop working. From an energetic point of view, our chakras quite literally hold our body's functions together. When we are dying, we are beings of matter returning to the world of spirit. The first chakra to stop working is the Naval Chakra. This is because it is where we hold our life force that connects us simultaneously to the physical world and the energetic world at the same time. Our life force flows to the naval chakra at birth and flows out of the naval chakra at death.

The order of how the chakras die is as follows:
1. Navel (water)
2. Heart (Air)
3. Solar Plexus (fire)

4. Throat (Sound)

5. Root (Earth)

6. Brow (sight)

7. Crown (spirit)

Earth dissolves into Water

The first thing that happens during the process of death is that the Naval Chakra begins to "dissolve." What is happening is that the Naval Chakra is returning to the energy world. By doing this there is a disconnect between the root and solar plexus chakras. We may feel heavy and lethargic. We may lose control of our bodily functions. In our minds, our perceptions will dim. You may feel spiritual "emptiness" and have delusions.

Water dissolves into Fire

It is here that the Heart Chakra begins to dissolve and the solar plexus unravels with it. With both the heart and naval chakras gone, the solar plexus cannot sustain itself without the support of the others. Your body will dehydrate, and you will feel like you cannot get enough water. Your mind will further become cloudy. Energetically, you may see a mist all around you.

Fire dissolves into Air

At this point, the Throat Chakra dissolves and the heat from our bodies is escaping through our breath. The fires from our solar plexus chakra have nowhere to go and this chakra has disintegrated and cannot control the warmth in the body. We may feel warm at first, then we will gradually become very cold. Our minds will be clear one moment then foggy the next from the fluctuation. Energetically, you may see sparks of light all around you.

Air dissolves into Consciousness

It is here that our Root Chakra dissolves and the air in our bodies become unstable. The root chakra keeps all of our body functions grounded and maintained in our physical body. Without this chakra, our body functions and energies deteriorate more rapidly. Our breathing will increase and then decrease. Our eyes may roll up into the back of our heads and our breathing will stop. It is at this point that we lose consciousness and will begin to hallucinate. What we hallucinate will depend upon our Karma. What we have done in life or more specifically, what we feel we did not learn when we had the opportunity will fill our minds. These mental projections will color our experiences in the Afterlife.

Consciousness dissolves into Spirit

Finally, our physical bodies have clinically died. Our consciousness, the ideas of self and ego, are taken out of our bodies and into the spirit world. It is from here that the subconscious projects karmas, emotions, hopes, and our fears and is manifested by the spirit world. It is here that the Buddhist "final thought" is transmitted for the spirits and entities to see. The final thought is the last thing you think about at the point of death. This becomes an astral thought form that colors how you interpret the Otherworld. This information will help or inhibit the dead in their travels in the Otherworld.

What Happens to the Energy Bodies After Death

As we have learned, the energy bodies are connected to the physical body. What happens to the physical body affects the energy bodies and in turn, what happens to the energy bodies affects the physical body. For example, when someone is cremated, there energy bodies are cremated. When a person dies, what normally happens is that the etheric, astral, mental, and spiritual bodies are separated from the physical body. After

separation, the rest of the energy bodies remain intact for a time. Just as there is the natural function of decay for the physical body, the energy bodies will disintegrate and be absorbed back into their respective plane. The physical body returns to the Earth, the etheric body to the etheric plane, the astral the astral plane, the mental the mental plane, and the spirit remains on the spiritual plane.

The etheric body is the first to be detached. This normally happens soon after death. It simply disintegrates and is absorbed back into the etheric plane. When this happens, the deceased may freely travel the astral plane and wait for ancestors and spirit helpers to show them to the other side. I have heard some spiritualists say that there is an energy cord that must be disconnected from the body and the energy bodies. I personally have never seen this cord. Most likely this is because it is dissolved during the dying process. Sometimes, when there is unfinished business, the spirit of the deceased may not want to move on and desperately holds on to the physical plane. When this happens, the deceased may often appear to the living as a ghost. He or she may be unable, or unwilling, to move on until the business is resolved. This may range from solving the mystery of who killed them to watching over loved ones until they can take care of themselves. Each situation is unique and should be treated as such.

After some time has passed, the astral body is ready to be shed. The amount of time is left up to the individual and the circumstances surrounding the person's death. There is a faint connection between the physical body and the astral body. There are times when there is a lot of emotional baggage or anger, and the astral body may take on a life of its own. Because of all the emotional energy, the spirit of the dead may unintentionally create an "artificial elemental" with its own astral body. The astral body may then haunt a home or area that the deceased once

felt strongly about. This happens on occasion. When the spirit of the deceased has moved on to the spiritual plane, it is no longer feeding the astral body with energy. The astral body may seek energy wherever it can, thus becoming a sort of vampiric entity. These entities must be destroyed, otherwise they may prey upon the living for their life force. There are also the rare times that a person's astral body may be possessed by a negative and destructive spirit or demon. Once this happens, the demon has access to all the memories, thought processes, and desires the deceased once had in life. This negative spirit may then use this knowledge to convince the living that they are the spirit of their loved one. It may go even further to convince the living family members to give the astral entity energy and offerings to keep it functioning in the physical plane. After all, to the living, it seems to be their deceased loved one in need of help from the other side. These spirits may manipulate the grieving for their selfish purposes. This is one of the various reasons why it is important for funeral rites to be performed. The magick that is performed at these rites helps prevent these things from happening. Cremation also prevents the astral body from being used for ill purposes. A dark magician may have the power to capture the astral body of the deceased to use in black magick. In some magical traditions, the magician can find and capture the astral body and store it in a bottle. I believe that this where we get the idea of capturing someone's soul in a bottle. Because the discarded astral body has little memory of consciousness and spirit of its own, the will is weak and can be manipulated. These situations are rare, but they do happen.

After the astral body has been shed, the mental body and spiritual body remain. Like the previous energy bodies, the mental body will be shed, and the spirit will return to the spiritual plane. The spiritual body is indestructible, but it can transform into pure spirit.

The Karma and Destiny of Death

In many spiritual communities, there is a belief in Karma and Destiny. The word *Karma* is Sanskrit for "action". Karma does not mean, "what goes around, comes around," or "an eye for an eye." These thoughts are a misunderstanding of the spiritual principles of Karma. Most of the people who believe in the "what goes around comes around" philosophy come from a Western background and are used to a spiritual system of rewards and punishments. This philosophy works well for people who need to be told what is right from wrong. The rest of us, however, are able to believe in a spiritual system that moves beyond these black and white concepts. Life is not black and white, and neither is the spiritual Universe. I have also heard of the Lords of Karma. In my research and understanding of Buddhism, Hinduism, and other studies, I have not found any such entity to exist. This is not to say that they do not, just that they cannot be found in any traditional teachings.

Karma is energy that the Universe gives people, plants, animals, and the entire cosmos for the purpose of evolution and transformation. The energies of Karma are there to teach us how to evolve into higher spiritual beings. When we fail or go against the divine flow of creation, then the energies of the Universe puts experiences in place so that we may learn from our mistakes. What sometimes happens is that the more often we make the same mistake the harder the energies become. This is because the Universe is trying to get our attention so that we may learn the lesson that is intended for us. Again, this is not a punishment. The Universe does not make bad things happen to us like a spiritual spanking! On the other hand, when we are going with the flow of the Universe and learning to become observant of our world and the lessons that are provided for us, then the energies seem to work in our favor. Think of the flow of the universal energies like the flow of a river. If we swim against the current,

our lives seem difficult. If we swim with the current, then our work is much easier. To do this effectively, we must find out Divine Will, or life purpose, and keep steady on our spiritual path. By doing this, you will be going with the tides of power and spirit.

There are times when the Universe puts rocks in our metaphorical river. This is a lesson that we need to learn. I will admit that sometimes these lessons are very hard and very painful, and we do not think that we will get through them. And yet we do. A lesson such as this helps us understand who we are. It pushes us further than we would ever push ourselves. I will say, as a spiritual leader, the Universe has pushed me way beyond what I thought I was able to do. The lessons that were provided for me helped me understand the meaning of the universal energies to become a stronger magician, a more powerful healer, and to understand the human condition far better than I thought I was able to. The further you explore your spiritual path, the more the Universe will work to make you better than you are now.

Karma has a direct influence on death, how we die, and what happens to us after we die. Once again, I want you to understand that Karma is not a punishment. If you fail to learn your lessons, it is not taken out on you at the time of death. There are several thoughts relating to the topic of what role Karma plays at death. There is a theory that says that our death is pre-ordained by the Universe and the gods which points to a specific time and date. Another theory says that the time of death depends on how well you learned your lessons during life. If you learned every lesson quickly, then you may die quicker. If you are a slow learner, then perhaps you will live longer. If you believe this theory, do not try to "cheat" death by purposely not seeking to transform yourself spiritually. You are who you are, and you will learn your lessons accordingly, whether you like it or not; most likely such an action would just result in having

the same lesson thrust upon you painfully time and again until death
itself may be seen as a welcome release. There is also the theory that if
you fall off your path dramatically you will die much faster than anticipated.
Drug addicts, those with psychoses, and people who give up on life may
fall into this category. This last idea says that death is dependent on spiritual
lessons, how you live your life, and how well you physically take care of
yourself and the world around you. I personally like this last theory the
best.

Judgment

In our Western culture, the biggest fear of death is not the pain of dying,
but rather the fear of judgment. Judeo-Christian cosmology teaches that
if one does not live a life according to the will of God, or that laid out in
the rules of the Bible, then God will place "judgment" upon you, which
more often than not means that you will spend eternity experiencing the
torments of Hell. The power of the Christian church came in part through
its emphasizing that they alone, as the spokespeople for Jesus Christ's
redemption and forgiveness, held the panacea for the pain and agony
that would last forever and ever. In this way, the Church kept a tight
control over their followers. The threat of excommunication meant that
if you displeased the church, they could banish you from the grace and
forgiveness of God. By doing this, you would go to Hell without delay
upon dying. As we have discussed earlier, the Great Spirit that created all
things does not punish. The Hell that the Christians speak of is of their
own creation. Julian of Norwich was a nun during the 14th Century who
had a vision of God and the afterlife. In her vision, God showed Julian
that there is no Hell. She tells us, "Yet in all this I wanted (as far as I
dared) to get a real sight of hell and purgatory…but for all of my desire
I saw absolutely nothing…"

In my travels to the Underworld, the people who find themselves in a Christian place of punishment have put themselves in those places because they believe in the torments that are described for them by Christian priests and believe that they "deserve" to be there.

The Egyptians had a judgment process that may have inspired this way of thinking. Upon death, after the soul found its way through the Underworld, its heart was weighed against the feather of Ma'at. Ma'at means *truth*. There was a list of wrong doings that the person professed *not to do*. It was the wrong doings that made the heart of the spirit become heavy. If the heart was lighter than the feather of Ma'at then the spirit was free to dwell in the heavens with the gods; if not, then the spirit was given to the great monster, a creature that was part crocodile, part lion, and part hippopotamus named Ammit. Ammit then devoured the spirit. I do not believe that the spirit was destroyed, per se. But simply through being "devoured" by the monster, the soul was returned to the cycle of reincarnation and reborn on Earth to try to transform and evolve so that the next time they found their way to the scales of Ma'at they would fare better.

Other cultures also focused on the doing of good deeds as a prerequisite to getting into a good Afterlife. The Hindu version of judgment is Karma and the Cycle of Samsara, or reincarnation. If the spirit of the person held to Dharma, the adherence to their social role in society and devotion to the gods, then they might escape the cycle of reincarnation to be placed within the world of the gods. If not, they would remain in the Underworld in the land of the ancestors to await the proper time to be reborn. Interestingly, in order to be reborn, they might have to wait until their family members conceived a child. If not, the ancestors would become a ghosts and hunt the younger generation through dreams and visions to make them want to have children. Even

when a person ascended to heaven, they could be cast down if they did not continue to do good deeds and carry out devotion to the gods in the Afterlife. In this cosmology, there is no Hell, only lower planes of existence that helped the spirit face their weaknesses in order to elevate into the higher planes of spirit.

In Nordic myths, the place of your afterlife depended on honor and your deeds on the battlefield itself. If a warrior was killed in battle, then they would dwell in either Freya's hall, Sessrumnir, or within Odin's great hall in the Upperworld, named Valhalla—the Hall of the Slain. Valhalla was a warrior paradise where every day one would engage in battle, then at night eat and drink until they had their fill. Men feared dying a "straw death," meaning they feared dying of simple sickness or old age. If this were the case, then the spirits of the dead would dwell in the Underworld in a world called Helheim. This was a place of fog according to some accounts, or, in others, a place that was eternally autumn. Spirits here had a less dramatic and exciting existence. Helheim is where Christianity get their word for "hell", but to the Nordics, it is a place of the Ancestors.

If we look closely at myths, the act of judgment is not to decide who is better or who is worse, or who failed at life or who succeeded. There is a much larger spiritual matrix involved that is much greater than our human minds can understand. It is about the great and wondrous spiritual Universe that is created to aid in our spiritual transformation. Some of the patriarchal religions are designed to assume that people are nothing but mindless primates who need the notion of good or bad, satisfactory or unsatisfactory, in order to perform right action. But these same ideas are set up in such a way that they punish the people that God created, simply because, according to Western Christian theology, they were created as flawed and sinful beings. I want to be very clear that in

life, to make mistakes and to fail is how we learn. Those who do not make mistakes or feel the pain of loss and despair never go further in their development. If you think about it, if everything is fine in your life, what would push you to do greater things? It is only by failing that we grow. I am not saying that we should not be responsible with our lives or with the lives of others. What I am saying is that in the great cosmic scheme of things, the gods want us to do well. They help us in every way they can. But, after all that is said and done, ultimately the choices we make in life are our own.

Exercise:
Remembering Death

Everyone has had a family member or friend die. This is not something we can, nor should, escape from. Our thoughts and feelings about death can color our personalities and how we view life. We cannot fully appreciate the joys of life if we have not truly tried to understand our own feelings of death. In this exercise, we will explore our own feelings about death through journaling. Journaling about our memories of the past helps us remember the facts as we saw them. It helps us to stimulate emotions that we have long forgotten about.

I have found that it is helpful to keep a magical journal. This way I can write down my magical thoughts and experiences that I have so I can go back and reread them in the future. I have several so I use a simple spiral notebook. Take out your magical journal. Begin to write about everyone who has died in your life who was important to you, be it family, friends, classmates, or co-workers. Try to remember the facts surrounding their death and how you felt about them. This may bring up painful memories that you would rather not deal with. Good. It is extremely important that you understand, recognize, and, if possible,

deal with any unresolved feelings about your loved ones' deaths. As we are working with death, the ancestors, and other spirits of the dead, it is important to understand how you feel with these energies. When you are working with the dead you do not want to be caught off guard with any unresolved or hidden feelings. Write down every little detail, thought, emotion, or anything at all that seems relevant. Do not edit yourself. This journal exercise is for you and for your spiritual development only. You do not have to share this journal entry with anyone unless you would like to do so.

When writing in your journal, try to remember every detail about how you felt when you heard the news of the loved one's death. You may have been in shock, sorrow, denial, or numbness. Write about the funeral or memorial service and how you felt before, during, and after the service. If there was not a funeral or memorial, how did you feel about that? Write about how the death of the loved one has had an impact on your life and your worldview. Did it change who you are? Finally, write about how you feel about the death of the loved one now. Are any of those previous feelings resolved? Are any of the previous feelings the same? If any of your feelings about the death has changed, write how they have changed. Write about any lessons you have learned because of the death. Do this exercise for each important person in your life who has died. The important thing to do here is to be very honest with yourself. Do not diminish any of the experiences.

One of the reasons we do this exercise is because in your work with the Ancestors and spirits of the dead, you may have a loved one come visit you for various reasons. They may visit you because they know you are doing this type of work or because they need your help in some way. You may also decide to place symbols of your loved ones on your ancestral altar. When an Ancestor appears before you with requests for important

work, it will not help them or yourself if you have an emotional breakdown. However, you should deal with any emotions that should come up with this type of work. Another reason that it is important to do this exercise is because the more powerful you become as a witch, magician, or deathwalker, the more powerful the beings are that will take notice of you. Some beings do wish you harm and the best way to defeat an enemy is by exploiting their weaknesses. Spirits are masters at shapeshifting. A negative spirit may wish to weaken you by causing an emotional breakdown by appearing as your dead spouse, parent, or other loved one who passed through the veil. It is important to understand and deal with your emotions with death the best way you can so that you are not caught off guard. If you are having trouble with this exercise, it is wise to seek the advice of someone who is a trained professional counsellor who understands this type of work.

Facing Your Own Death

To work with the energies of the Underworld and with the Ancestors, it is important to face your own death and understand your fears pertaining to death and the afterlife. Most people do not fear the pain of dying or the transition into death. Most people fear oblivion. This is the idea that once your body dies and you are brain dead there is nothing else, only unconsciousness and darkness that you cannot perceive. You are gone. Everything you have learned is gone. Every great deed, every bad thing you have ever done is gone. Those memories of your family and friends are gone. The bonds that you created with your spouse are gone. You are no-thing.

The other fear many people, who were raised in the Christian faith, may have about death is that the Christian Hell really exists and that is where they are going when they die. In their minds, they fear the idea of

an eternity of being in the Lake of Fire and feeling the agonizing pain of their bodies burning forever and ever as demons torture them.

Another thing that people may fear about death is the great mystery of what death really is. People have heard religious priests and leaders describe their version of what happens after death and the rewards of living a virtuous life and the punishments of living a shameful life. But the great mystery is that no one really knows what the Afterlife is. What if it is more wonderful than they say it is? What if it if far more horrible than anyone could possibly imagine? The great mystery itself is the fear and not so much what happens after you get there.

If you are a serious student of the Underworld and the Ancestors then you most likely do not have the fears listed above, however you may still have some concerns. There are many fears about death. Just as many fears, perhaps, as there are people. Everyone has their own hopes and fears of what is to come once their body and brain has stopped functioning. "What if" can be a truly terrifying mental exercise in certain circumstances.

While we are alive, we can never truly understand what the Ancestors have gone through, and we can only grasp as much as our limited understanding allows us. As we journey through the Underworlds, we must try to understand our own personal fears about death and try to relieve those fears the best we can. We may never truly conquer all of our fears about death, but we must learn what they are and perhaps where they come from so that these fears do not hinder us in the work ahead of us.

Exercise: Writing Your Eulogy

In this exercise, you will be writing your own eulogy. This will be presented when you have a mock funeral for yourself. When you write the eulogy,

write everything that you would like someone to say about you as if you were actually dead and the speaker was reviewing your life. Write about all your achievements and the people in your life that you love. Write funny anecdotes and anything else you can think of to say. Later, the eulogy will be presented by someone who will preside over your mock funeral, or you may speak it aloud in a recording device to be played back.

Exercise: Your Own Funeral

For this exercise you will be giving yourself a mock funeral. The point here is to understand death in all of its stages. This stage is the funeral. Some spirits will linger around long enough to listen to their own funerals and memorial services. This helps them finalize in their minds that they are dead and will help them let go of the physical plane so that they may move on to the Afterlife. In Buddhism, it is believed that the deceased can hear everything that is said to and around the body. This exercise will help you understand what the spirits of the dead must go through. It will also help you deal with your own mortality on a more profound level. I will caution you that intense feelings may come up. If you practice your spirituality with a friend or group, it is highly recommended that you have someone with you during these exercises. But, if you are more comfortable, you may do this exercise on your own.

1. Prepare a massage table, cot, or bed in the middle of the floor. You may use a sleeping bag or blankets if you have no table or cot. If you are using your living room space, move the furniture so that you are lying in the middle.

2. Prepare the temple space with candles, a podium for the eulogy, and chairs for people to sit in if any are in attendance. If you do not have these things just candles are fine.

3. Lie on the table facing up. You may have a blanket or shroud covering your body and head if you like. Black or white is preferred.

4. Have your helper read the eulogy as if it is the real thing and you are actually dead or play your recording device if you are alone.

5. Take this time to play-act what it would be like if you were actually dead, and this was your funeral. What thoughts are you having? How do you feel about the whole process? Do any fears come up? What would it feel like to actually be dead?

6. Spend a few minutes in quiet meditation on this whole process after it is finished.

7. Journal your experiences.

As we are destined to be born, we are destined to die. I have heard it said that death is the great equalizer; no one can escape from it. It is because of our death that we learn to live. It is death that prompts us to live our lives fully and become spiritual human beings. Death is not meant to be easy or clean. Death is sometimes scary and dirty. However, death is a spiritual process that helps us transcend our earthly lives so that we can evolve to be more than we are now. It is designed to challenge us, but never to punish. It is through challenges that we can see just how powerful we are. When we work with death's energies, we begin to further our understanding of the roll death plays in the great cosmic design. I have found the more I work with death, the more I understand that it is essential to the Universe. Without death, the Universe could not exist. When something dies it makes way for something better to appear. This is how evolution works. Without death there could not be life. It is the ebb and flow of the Universe and of balance.

2
Ancient Ancestral Practices

Orpheus' Search for Eurydice (Greco-Roman)

There was a blessed singer named Orpheus who would play the lyre that was given to him by his father, Apollo, the god of the sun and of music. He was so skilled at song that the spirits of Heaven and Earth would often stop their daily tasks to listen to him. He married a beautiful woman named Eurydice and he loved her above all things, even his blessed songs. One day while Eurydice was walking through the fields, she was bitten on the foot by a snake and died. Orpheus' grief was so great that he could not bear to live without his Eurydice. He decided that he would go down to Hades and ask the god of the dead himself to release her. This would be no easy task.

He found a secret passage into the Underworld through the side of a mountain. He made his way down the dark tunnels and braved the ghostly residence and the monsters that lurked down below. Finally, he made his way to the throne room of Hades and Persephone. He presented the Underworld King and Queen a song. In his song, he sang about the love he had for Eurydice. He sang of his heavy grief and that he was not there to learn secrets of death or of magick, but to be reunited with his true love. The song was so beautiful and sad that the ghosts began to cry, the monsters' rage subsided, the furies wept, and even Hades began to tear. Persephone asked her husband to grant his request. Eurydice was released to Orpheus under the condition that as they left the Underworld, he would not look back upon her until they were out of Hades and into the light of day.

Orpheus made their way back up through the dark tunnels of Hades.

Through caverns and caves, they went. As they approached the entrance into the Middleworld, Orpheus forgot his promise and looked back at Eurydice to make sure she was still behind him. As he gazed upon her, she faded away to live eternally with the shades of the dead. Orpheus wanted to go back for her again, but the guardians of the Underworld would not allow him to go through a second time. For days, he stayed near the entrance of the mountain lamenting with his lyre and the spirits of the rocks and mountains would cry with him day after day.

Then one day, the Thracian Maidens were frenzied by the rights of Bacchus and went into a fury. They found Orpheus and tore him limb from limb, yet his lyre was unharmed which Zeus placed among the stars. Finally, Orpheus and Eurydice were united in death roaming together among the fields of bliss with the Ancestors.

Ancient Pagan Worship

Pagans throughout the ages have honored the Ancestors. In ancient times, the belief of an afterlife was universal. We speculate that one of the ways that the idea of an afterlife came to be was through dreams. People could go to sleep and dream of friends and loved ones who were long dead. In their dream state they would have extraordinary powers and go on exciting adventures, or even meet monsters. When they awoke, they could speak with others and confirm this unusual plane of existence. When their friends or family would die, it would appear as if they were "asleep" and that they would permanently stay in this strange and wonderful land. This land became more commonly known as the Underworld. People could observe the nature of death and decay and see how the physical body would decompose and return its essence to the Earth below. To the ancient mind, the energy and spirit of a person would follow this decomposition as their spirit would travel down below. This is one of the

reasons that people believed that the Underworld was a place of horrors, skeletons, and decaying things. In some indigenous tribes, seeing that the bodies of the dead would decay and become one with the land was proof that the Ancestors joined with the land and watched over the tribe. Their energies were perceived as actually merging with the land, trees, rocks, and bodies of water. This is one of the reasons why Native American tribes honor their homeland so much and defended it with their lives. They could not stand the thought of never seeing their Ancestors again. There are as many different ways that ancient pagans honored the dead as there are different cultures. Many ancient cultures seem to have in common the belief that the dead went to a place beneath the ground.

Our Ancestors were thought to have tremendous power. The ancients believed that the Ancestors had the ability to control some of the Underworld energy and life force that comes to us in this world. They also believed that the Ancestors could intervene on their behalf with the gods. For instance, if you needed magick done for you, say to find a new love or increase prosperity, you could ask your Ancestors to speak to your deities on your behalf so that your desire would manifest. The Ancestors could also aid in healing. There are many ancient spells and charms that call upon the power of the Ancestors when using magick to heal the sick. To me, this makes perfect sense. Who is more likely to help you, some deity you rarely speak to or your great grandparents who wish only for you to be healthy and happy? Personally, this is one of the most fulfilling ways to work with the Ancestors. The Ancestors also could control good or ill fortune. Remember, the Ancestors are very close to the mystery and power of the Underworld. For those Ancestors who continued to watch over the family, they would help them in whatever way they could. It was thought that if you gave them water, food, and prayers, then the energy exchange would be given back to you with

blessings and good fortune. If you had forgotten your duty to the Ancestors, then it was imperative that the Ancestors remind you of your obligations to them and give you a learning lesson. This sometimes would manifest in the form of sudden bad luck.

Ancient pagans also thought that the Ancestors could become gods themselves. In Hinduism today, it is believed that when you live your life according to dharma (the proper way to live according to honor, morals, ethics, and accepting your place in the class system) you may be freed from the cycles of reincarnation and become a god. In this philosophy, the Ancestors could not be on equal footing with great and powerful gods such as Brahma and Vishnu, but were perceived as divine, nonetheless. It was because they achieved great wisdom and transformation that they were allowed to ascend to heaven and become a god. However, each of the many heavens in Hinduism had its own lessons. If you learned the divine lessons, then you were able to ascend further up into the next heaven. If not, you could be cast down from heaven and be forced to dwell in the realm of the Ancestors in the Underworld.

It is believed that some of the Nordic Gods such as Odin, Freyr, and Thor may have been "real" Kings of northern Europe who, after their deaths, were worshiped by the people as "Kings" in the spirit world and, therefore, were transformed by local belief into Gods. In Egypt, it was believed that the god Osiris was also a King, or pharaoh, who was deified after death. In ancient Egypt, all kings were referred to as Osiris. It is thought that the basis of this myth is that one of the ancient kings of Egypt was deified. After his death, his body was dismembered, ground up, and then spread throughout the land. This act made him the god of the Underworld, Osiris. Some believe that ancient myths have historical

truths in them and that the stories are a poetic account of what happened in the distant past.

Necromancy

When modern people hear the word "necromancy" they often think of grave robbing, black magick, and binding spirits to do evil things. But in fact, that is not usually the case. *Necro-* means "dead" and *-mancy* means "divination or oracle." So, *necromancy* literally means "divination of the dead." In ancient times, working with the dead for any reason was a common practice. It was not considered strange to work with Ancestors and even spirits of those whom you did not know. Most of the time, the ancients worked with the dead for the betterment of the community. It was common to believe that our Ancestors existed alongside us in our daily life. When people needed advice and wisdom about a particular situation, they would often summon a spirit of the dead and ask them their advice. It was also discovered that the Ancestors could bring many blessings and benefits to the community when given proper rites and devotions. Magicians, witches, and sorcerers learned that there were many benefits and powers to be learned from the dead. The dead can even be called upon to aid in healing rites and rituals.

Many witches also used the powers of the dead in their rituals. In ancient Greece, a type of necromancer known as a "Goes" had special powers over the dead. They were able to summon the shades and use them for prophecy and magick. It appears they were used to help the grieving contact their loved ones, but soon it was believed that they were using the dead for black magick. In fact, their necromantic magick became known as *goeteia*. This is where ceremonial magicians get the name of the Goetia, the summoning of demons. This type of magick was used during the 16th century by a witch known as Bessie Dunlop who had a spirit of

the dead named Tom Reid who helped her in her witchcraft. We can speculate that many other witches used necromantic spirits to help in their magick as well.

Using the dead for prophecy was practiced in many parts of the world in many pagan cultures. For some of us it may seem odd or distasteful, but it was so much of a common practice that it was often told in myths. Most of us in the pagan community are familiar with Asatru and the Nordic pantheon. There is a myth told by the Nordics of the mighty Odin, who conjures a Volva (a seeress), who is dead to give he and the other gods prophecy of what is to come.

Ancient Egyptian Death Rites

The Ancient Egyptians left us a vast amount of information about the death and funeral rites of their people. We know a great deal about the Egyptians because they kept extensive records of their gods and the cosmos. Their priests and magicians observed the cycles of the planets and stars and the Earth upon which they lived. They believed that the physical world was a reflection of the Underworld and the Upperworld. They believed that upon death, the soul would travel into the Underworld to face many trials before a person could join their beloved gods. However, the body had to be preserved. What happened to the physical body happened to the spirit body as well. They did not want the process of decay to prevent the spirits from their tasks in the Underworld. Great preparations were made to make sure the spirits succeeded in their challenges.

Embalming

Upon death, the body was washed and then dried out with natron. It was then perfumed and dressed in linen. The embalmers were specialized

priests that wore the mask of Anubis. It is speculated that these priests (whose title was Anubis, meaning priests of embalming) invoked the god into themselves so that it was not the priests who were preparing the body, but Anubis himself!

The organs were removed from the corpse. The Anubis priests began with the head and worked their way down to the feet. The brain was removed through the nose and discarded. At the time, they did not understand the significance of the brain. The other organs - the heart, liver, stomach, intestines, and pancreas – were preserved with resin, put inside magical jars, and then placed back inside the corpse.

The body was restored as much as possible to look the way it looked in life. The priests used sawdust, wax, resin, and makeup to give the body a more "alive" look. The body was perfumed again and bandaged. The bandages of the mummification process had to be wrapped in a ritual manner. The head, torso, and limbs had to be wrapped either six or seven times depending upon the magical intention. In magick, numbers have different meanings. If we use a modern interpretation of numbers; six is a number of the sun and means harmony, seven is the number of Venus and the seven ancient planets and means love or compassion. During the embalming process, prayers were given to Anubis, Osiris, Isis, and Horus to protect the Ba (astral body) of the person and aid them in their journey to Underworld, the Duat (pronounced DOO-what).

"Opening of the Mouth"

After the body was mummified, it was necessary to bring the body back to "life." Because it had a divine purpose, Egyptian necromancy, was not seen as distasteful but as a necessity for the journey ahead. This was done so that the spirit of the deceased could enjoy the offerings and festivals before its Ba journeyed into the Duat. The body was purified with incense

and perfumes and given offerings of animal sacrifice. Prayers and more incense were given until the body was thought to be Osiris. To be Osiris was a title meaning "resurrected." To the Egyptians, to be resurrected meant that the astral body was given enough energy to maintain itself in the physical plane and then released into the Underworld for its journey to the realm of Ma'at.

Book of the Dead

The Book of the Dead was a term coined by archeologists when they first discovered the scrolls, or books, in the tombs of the kings. The books seem to be a part of the New Kingdom era of Egyptian history (1,500-1,070 BCE) . The correct term for the book is *The Book of Going Forth by Day*. The term *day* for the Egyptians in this context meant *going to the light* or *going into the light*—the light being the realm of the gods. The books of the dead were maps and directions on how to navigate the Underworld. There were spells, charms, and warnings about what to do to maintain power, defeat monsters, and find your way through the more frightening aspects of the Dwat. One book even told you how to handle oneself once a person finally made it to the presence of Ma'at—the goddess of Truth—and the rest of the gods. The book was an invaluable resource when journeying into the Underworld.

Greco-Roman Temples of the Dead

In Greece and Rome, if one wanted to speak to the dead in a direct way, they could go to one of the notorious Temples of the Dead. The ancient Greeks believed these temples were built over a gateway into Hades. To the ancient Greco-Romans this was just not a belief or a spiritual experience, such as one experiences when one goes to Church or Temple to "feel" the presence of God, but a literal experience of the depths of

Hades, the Underworld Gods, and the dead. These ancient people wanted a tangible experience. We must remember that to these civilizations, ghosts and the gods were not myths, but a very "real," tangible thing. These temples were built near lakes, on or near mountains, or any place that seemed to open up into the Underworld below.

Many people traveled for many miles to the temples . The temples were always isolated from the more metropolitan cities. They were kept far away from the everyday life. The dead, and all they represented, were to be left alone. Most people in Greco-Roman society looked down upon the magick of the dead. Though it was not illegal, it was frowned upon, and only the brave chose to travel to visit the oracles who dwelt in these temple complexes. The journey took several days, if not weeks, and it was usually the wealthy who were able to afford such a venture. However, the everyday person who could find payment would sometimes go to the temples as well.

If the seeker wished to consult the dead at the temple, they had to first arrange the affair with the Sybil. It was the Sybil who was the seeress and High Priestess of the Temple, who would make all the arrangements for the seeker. It was her duty to set up the ritual from beginning to end. It was she who possessed the power to open the gates of Hades and summon the shade or shades with whom the seeker wished to communicate. To have such a dark, yet profound experience came at a steep cost. The payment was seven bullocks, seven ewes, and a large amount of olive oil. Other types of payment might include cows, oxen, and rams. The temple kept its own livestock so that the journeyer could purchase them there rather than try to travel with such a burden over difficult terrain and dangerous roads. This arrangement also allowed the temple to raise money for maintenance as well as attend to the personal needs of the priests of the temple. A portion of the livestock was given

as an offering to the gods. The Sybil was given wine and barley cakes as a personal offering to her.

Once the arrangements were put into place, the seeker was admitted into the underground temple. They would be given a special potion that would help him perceive the magical nature of the temple. They were led into the first room which was painted with depictions of myriad scenarios of the horrors of life. The pictures showed the effects of various diseases, old age, fear, poverty, hunger, strife, and insanity. The seeker would be left in the room alone to contemplate the images for three days to get them into the right frame of mind to continue on their journey into the Underworld temple. Imagine, for a moment, what it might have been like to stay in this room for three days for the sole purpose of contemplation. This is very much like hypnosis. Understandably, the seeker's mind would begin to accept the horrors they were seeing. The images of death, murder, battle, and disease would seep deeper and deeper into their mind. They would be given no food or water. If they slept, they were sure to have death dreams.

After the third day the seeker was brought out of the room to sacrifice a black ewe to a deity of the Underworld, who would most likely be Persephone. Most offerings and sacrifices were given to Persephone because she was the intercessor between Hades and the Midworld. She was the goddess of the dead who was able to leave the Realm of the Dead for six months out of the year. She could understand the pain and sorrow of the living and the dead, and it was she who would have sympathy with them. The priest would look at the entrails to see if it was a favorable time for the consultation of the dead. The seeker was then led to an underground river that had been built to look like the River of Forgetfulness in Hades. There, after a proper fast, the seeker would be bathed and then led to another river that was called the "water of

memory." The seeker bathed in and drank these waters, which probably had hallucinogenic drugs in them. The seeker would have no idea about the herbs that were placed in the water. The hallucinogens had several purposes. One purpose was to help the seeker release any mental blocks and doubts about the process that he was about to undertake. Another purpose was to have them truly believe that what they were seeing in the temple was real. It was believed that psychotropic drugs helped a person see into the spirit world.

After this was done, they sacrificed a black ewe to the Goddess Night and to the Earth and was dressed in a white tunic with their hair bound and a belt with a bronze dagger. They were also given a sword. The sword was to protect the seeker against the shades that may be angered by their disturbance of the netherworld. They also carried a golden branch of mistletoe as an offering to Persephone.

The Sybil would be dressed in scarlet, most likely because scarlet represented the blood of the living and of life itself that some of the shades so desperately craved. This would give them energy to manifest in our world. Scarlet also symbolized her power over life and death and her rank within the Temple.

The Path

The seeker was led further into the temple. They entered an 8ft 21-inch-wide hole by a ladder that descended into a round room. They were then led through a passageway into a tunnel complex. Here priests, dressed in black wearing black headdresses, met the seeker. The priests sang and chanted eerie songs. This was done to put the seeker further into an altered state of consciousness to see the dead spirits.

The seeker continued through the tunnel until they found themself at a junction with three tunnels. As the seeker is led to the fork, the door

behind them shut causing a shift in air pressure. Take a moment to imagine what the seeker must have been going through. Their mind was altered, and their surroundings were dark and frightening. The seeker carried on because they sought to confront the spirit of the dead of someone they knew, perhaps someone he loved.

The Sybil would say: "The left tunnel leads to Tartarus, the right to the House of Persephone." A priest hidden in the left tunnel would scream and burn harsh-smelling incense as a sign of torment. The seeker was led to the right tunnel down into yet another tunnel and then to the River Styx. The tunnel was filled with 100 lamps for illumination. We do not know exactly what the lamps were for, but my theory is that one, it was to give the tunnels an "Otherworldly" illumination and two, may have represented the spirits who dwelled in Hades. To the seeker, this must have been a fantastic and eerie sight!

At the River Styx, the seeker was led to another priest that was personifying Charon, the ferryman. His appearance was like an ancient filthy demon. Once on the other side of the river, a dog barked ferociously to represent Cerberus. This was a trained dog that recognized the Sybil.

They then went up steep stairs to another level and down a corridor. Then the seeker left the mistletoe in a niche in the wall as an offering to Persephone. In the inner sanctum, there was an altar with a tied up sacrificial animal. A priest cut its throat and let the blood poor to the ground for the shades. It is important to remember that the ancient view of sacrifice was different than our own. It was not looked down upon in ancient times to kill animals for their blood to give to the spirits of the dead. It was believed that the energy or life force of blood would give spirits of the dead, or shades, energy to manifest physically in the Middleworld.

After the blood was spilled, the shades would appear. Another priest

would act as a medium. It is believed that the priests may have used elaborate costumes to invoke or aspect the spirits of the dead. The spirit of the dead that the seeker wished to speak to would then "manifest." They would then answer the seeker's questions. Sometimes the seeker would receive answers in a clear direct manner, sometimes not. After a while, to end the session the vast shades of the dead would appear to come out and overcrowd the spirit. This was done by other priests who would dress in all black, making horrible noises to frighten the seeker which would make them want to end the session quickly. To the seeker this was perceived as the many shades of the dead that were gathering around to taste the lifeforce (blood) that was nearby. When this happened, the seeker was then escorted out through a secret tunnel. The priest would warn them not to look back or else they would have to stay eternally in Hades. The seeker would then arrive at the room near the entrance. The Sybil and the priest went over what was said in the session so that the seeker understood what was trying to be communicated to them.

The Kidnapping of Persephone

One day, Demeter, Goddess of the fields and agriculture, and her daughter, Persephone, were picking lilies and violets. While they were enjoying the beautiful day, Hades, the God of the Underworld, gazed upon her. He became enamored by her beauty and could think of nothing but having her as his Queen. He quickly grabbed her and carried her away on his chariot. Persephone screamed in terror and her mother came running after her. Before Demeter could see her daughter being carried away, Hades used his magical trident to create a hole in the side of the mountain, a gateway down into the Underworld. Persephone was lost.

Demeter mourned the loss of Persephone. For days she walked the Earth in great sadness not knowing what had happened to her daughter.

In her mourning, the land began to dry up, the fields withered, and the cold dark skies covered the land. Snows fell for the first time. Then, a water nymph came to Demeter and told her that she had seen Hades kidnap Persephone and take her down into the Underworld. Upon hearing this news, Demeter flew right away to Olympus to give her grievance to Zeus. Zeus understood her grief and the unfairness of the kidnapping. He promised to bring Persephone from the Underworld if she did not have anything to eat or drink there. Hermes, the messenger of the gods, was sent down into the Underworld and told Hades of Zeus' demand to release Persephone. Hades complied. But before Persephone left the gates of Hades, he gave her a pomegranate to subdue her hunger for the long trip back to the Middleworld. She then ate the pomegranate seeds, not knowing her fate. The Fates themselves could not undo what was set into motion by Hades. Zeus had to explain to Demeter what had happened. However, Zeus took pity on Demeter and Persephone and agreed to a compromise. For half the year Persephone had to remain in the Underworld as the Queen of Hades, but for the rest of the year could go back to her mother in the Middleworld. Demeter agreed to this compromise. But, whenever Persephone returned to the Underworld, Demeter would once again walk the Earth with sadness and winter would return to the world.

Rites of Eleusis

The Eleusinian Mysteries are perhaps the most famous rituals in the ancient world. People would travel vast distances to be able to partake in the most sacred mysteries of the ancient, civilized world. These rites were akin to a scholar going to graduate school to receive a degree that would put you in the ranks of other great scholars. Many philosophers and even the god of healing, Aesculapius, was said to have gone through

the mysteries. It was thought that to obtain an adequate idea of the gods and spirituality, one must go through the Eleusinian Mysteries. It was expected that both men and women were to be initiated. These rites were so sacred and so secret, that it was forbidden to speak of these rites with anyone who was uninitiated to the Eleusinian Mysteries. The punishment for doing so was death. And, indeed, punishment was carried out.

The Greeks most certainly kept written records of their philosophies, histories, and magick, however, there are no written records of the Rites of Eleusis. Remember, if the uninitiated found out about the rituals, they would face the punishment of death. The only records we have about the ritual are from art, such as pictures on vases, the occasional testimonial from a seeker of the mysteries, and those who spoke too much in front of non-initiates after too much drink. Archeologists and historians have spent many years trying to piece it all together.

It is believed that the mysteries were broken up into two sections, the Lesser and Greater Mysteries. The Lesser Mysteries began with the sacrifice of cattle to Persephone and Demeter. Before one could begin initiation, they had to fast for a certain number of days and keep their spirits and bodies as pure as possible. Essentially, there were three degrees. The first degree instructed the seeker in the myths of Demeter and Persephone and the rituals in which they should be honored.

For the second degree of initiation, the seeker was led into the temple. Their hands were purified with consecrated water. The priest led them into the first chamber. The candidates were locked into a dark room. The temple transformed into Hades itself. The sounds of the dead could be heard. Sorrowful sounds of morning, pain, and dread was heard from all sides. The shades of the dead were coming to get them! The door of Tartarus was opened, and all the demons and monsters of Hades could

be seen. There were reports that the actual demons and monsters of legend materialized before them! In each of the cold, dark rooms the candidates were pushed, pulled, and hit by the beings of the Hades looking for life. Somehow the seekers had to make it through. They could hear the painful laments of the shades who died from war, disease, murder, and accident. The dead were coming closer and closer to the seekers. They had to keep moving all the while suffering the brutal pushing and beatings of the demons of Hades. Finally, as they cleared the last chamber, the door of Tartarus was closed. The dark spirits and monsters were shut back into the dark corners of Hades. At last, a light was illuminated. The lights shone on a great statue of Demeter, the goddess of agriculture. Nature spirits danced around her with much joy! The initiate now understood the joys of living. Hades is a place of the sorrowful dead. Pain and suffering are all you would find there. It was discovered by the initiates that through living a life well lived, that Demeter granted blessing in this life, not the next. Life was meant to be joyful even in the midst of pain and suffering here on Earth. Demeter would sustain us all!

During the festival, the sacred marriage took place. A high priestess and high priest would invoke either Demeter and Zeus or Persephone and Hades to perform the sacred act of ritual sex to ensure the union of the divine to one another.

The third degree held the mystery of the ear of grain (wheat). The candidate, who was ready for the final degree, was taught about the magical properties of the ear of grain and its significant with the regeneration powers of Demeter. This final degree taught that during the quest for enlightenment, demons and monsters of the candidate's own making would try to sabotage them from obtaining the truth of the gods and the universe. What this means is that the candidate's personal fears, weaknesses, and imbalances would be revealed. The candidate must understand that

these are the things that keep them from discovering personal growth and enlightenment. They would learn that the universe had a creator and that the gods were mortal men and women who had ascended to godhood. The initiates were taught that through death and enlightenment one could ascend to become immortal and divine. That those trapped in Hades, under the protection of Persephone, would never ascend and become greater than their fates had prescribed for them.

Exercise:
Meditation of the Ear of Grain and Regeneration

Sit in a comfortable position. Take a deep breath and allow the stresses of the day to fade away as you exhale. Take another deep breath and as you exhale, allow the muscles in your body to relax. Take one more deep breath and allow the chatter in your mind to fade away. Close your eyes. Be at one with peace.

Visualize yourself in a barren field. The ground beneath you is hard and cold and you can smell the clay of the Earth. There is nothing around you for miles and miles. It is night, and the stars above are bright and magnificent. You walk through this barren land. This is the place where the ancients would plant their wheat, but that was thousands of years ago. As far as you can tell, there is no life now. No life. Only the harsh Earth below and the black sky of night filled with the stars. You feel a faint call to your heart. Something is leading you to the very center of the barren field. The soil cracks and crumbles as you trample upon it. It has not rained for so awfully long.

As you finally make it to the center of the dark field, you realize that you have discovered a great treasure. There is one single stalk of wheat growing in the lifeless place. Somehow it has survived. In all the death that is around you, you have found one single piece of life. You sit down

on the ground touching the lonely stalk of wheat. As you sit and place your hands on the wheat you feel the faint call of Demeter, the goddess of agriculture. It is more of a call to your heart than to your ears. You look up to the celestial heavens and the stars seem so much brighter now. They seem to be waiting for you to do something. But what?

As you sit upon the cold ground your eyes become better focused in the blackness of night. You then can faintly make out a few grave markers, old rusty guns, and fragments of some kind of machine; is that an army helmet you see? You realize that you sit upon a battlefield from ages ago. Was there a war that had taken place on the field that once supported life with wheat to feed the people? Death was once here and even death has gone away.

You connect your energies to the stalk of wheat. You feel its life-force pulsing through the roots and up the stalk to the leaves and grains. Take a moment to meditate with the wheat and your surroundings. What does the wheat tell you? What does the Earth itself have to say? What do the stars tell you? Take as much time as you need.

When you are finished, journal your experience.

The Ghost Dance

The Ghost Dance is a spiritual technique practiced by some Lakota and other Native American tribes from the plains region of the United States. The Ghost Dance is more than a Native style of dancing. It is considered a religion unto itself. The Ghost Dance was given to a Lakota Healer named Jack Wilson in a vision. During the dance, the dancers evoke the spirits of the Ancestors to come and dance with them. By doing so, the spirits of the dead are "resurrected" in spirit form. This is done to bring the spirits back from the land of the dead so that they may aid the people with their troubles in life such as food, shelter, tribal matters, and disputes

over land with the United States government. It was believed that the wisdom and power of the Ancestors would help guide the tribes to a better future.

There were many tensions between the Native American people of the plains and the United States government. All of the treaties were broken one by one, and the land allotted to the Lakota people by the U.S. became smaller and smaller. In one instance, men found gold in the Black Hills region, which at the time belonged to the Lakota. The government soon took that land away from the Lakota because of the profits that could be given to the U.S. The U.S. military wanted the Lakota people to stay on the reservations. The Lakota, being a nomadic tribe, followed the bison wherever the herds went. In response to this, the U.S. military attempted to wipe out the bison. Luckily, a few bison remained, and their population eventually increased. In the late 1800s, however, the bison were nearly all destroyed, and the Lakota were starving. They were forced to do what the U.S. wanted them to do. They were angry at the way the treaties were broken and their people were left to become sick and die of starvation and cold. The native peoples felt hopeless.

During the winter of 1889 there was a solar eclipse that caused great unease among the Native American Plains people. The natives living at that time did not know what a solar eclipse was and were very afraid of the giant spirit that blocked out the light of the sun. Some were so afraid that they shot their rifles at the shadow trying to kill it or at least move it away from the sun. As the sun became dark, a Lakota healer named Jack Wilson became deathly ill. As he lay in his bed, his spirit flew up to the Heavens and there the Creator gave him a vision. In his vision, the people danced the Ghost Dance. By living a virtuous Native life, making peace with the Whites, and not going to war, the Ancestors would return and assist the people in gaining back their spirituality, their tribal power, and

their lands. When Jack Wilson awoke, he taught the people this powerful dance. He taught the people that by walking the "good red road" and living a "good honest life" the Ancestors would return from the land of the dead and give the people power over themselves and their lives.

In Native American customs, the Ancestors were always remembered and honored. For the Natives, the land of the dead was simply hidden from view by a veil, and yet was all around us. The Ancestors were always with us, but the Ghost Dance gave the people the energy and power to summon the Ancestors in a more tangible way to help guide the tribe. The Ghost Dance became a religion. Jack Wilson would "preach" his teachings to anyone who would listen. Many Native people came to hear him speak and were profoundly moved by his vision and the idea of the return of the Ancestors. The people would then report back to their tribes of the wonder and power of the Ghost Dance. The Ghost Dance caught on throughout the U.S. Plains region.

The U.S. government heard rumors of this Ghost Dance and thought it nothing more than superstitions of the primitive peoples. However, they did notice that the once broken Native people were becoming empowered again. It may be helpful to remember that the white soldiers were Christian and thought of the Native spirituality as nonsense at best and devil worship at worst. They took great pains to break the spirits of the Natives and were profoundly upset when the Natives began to regain their personal power and will. The control of the Native People became more and more difficult. They even went so far as to tell their soldiers that the Ghost Dance was supposed to call up the dead so that they could push back the White people to take back their lands. If any Native People believed this, which is unlikely, it was not based upon the teachings of Jack Wilson.

The Ghost Dance religion became more and more popular and

practiced throughout the Western United States. The Lakota people on the Pine Ridge reservation freely danced the Ghost Dance and became more and more defiant of the ruling military stationed there. Tensions were high between the Lakota people and the military at Pine Ridge. Each side mistrusted the other and the soldiers were looking for any reason they could to kill and destroy the natives. Sitting Bull was a defiant Lakota Chief who was looking out for the best interest of his people. The soldiers came to arrest him, and one anxious Lakota man shot his riffle. The soldier shot Sitting Bull at point blank range in the head. Sitting Bull's horse was trained to trot when he heard gunshots. When the horse seemed to dance the Natives took that as a sign as the return of the Ancestors of the Ghost Dance. Shots were fired on both sides. 153 Lakota were killed that day. This would be known as the Massacre at Wounded Knee.

Whites feared the Ghost Dance not because they feared the return of the spirits, but because it represented the empowerment of a people whom they were trying to destroy. The massacre was brought on by hate, racism, and fear. The Ghost Dance religion taught tribal values and abstinence from war. Many Natives died during this time of being forced onto reservations and having little to no food and shelter. The Lakota, as well as many other tribes who took to the Ghost Dance, were rejoicing in the fact that they could dance with their lost loved ones, and they could once again become part of the tribal community. There are other shamanic cultures that teach a form of dancing with the Ancestors. What made the Ghost Dance stand out is the way that Jack Wilson preached about the values of a "good clean life" and how it would empower the people once more.

Exercise: Dancing With the Ancestors

Dancing with the Ancestors is a very empowering practice. Whenever I dance on a dance floor or around a drum circle, I always make sure I dance a little bit with the Ancestors who are willing to dance with me. I will say, almost always the Ancestors want to dance with you. The more you work with your Ancestors, the more you will notice when they appear more prominently in your energy field. The Ancestors, being energy themselves, can easily incorporate themselves in your aura. When our gods and Ancestors have a strong connection with us, they connect with our energies and give us strength, power, and guidance upon our spiritual paths. The Ancestors are always there, but we have to take the time to notice them. Dancing with the Ancestors is one of the best and most fun ways of working with them. When you first start dancing with your Ancestors, begin with music that has a simple beat. Any type of music that makes you feel spiritual will do as long as it has nice beat to it. There are a few things to keep in mind when dancing with your ancestors. Your ancestors will still have the same likes and dislikes when it comes to music. Remember, your grandmother who did not like heavy metal in life will not like it in death. However, I have noticed that even if tribal music was not something they listened to in life they will enjoy it in death. Most likely, this is because the drumbeat, which represents the heartbeat of the Earth, is a universal phenomenon and resonates through all of time and space. This is one of the reasons why we can travel astrally so freely with a shamanic drumbeat. The Ancestors appreciate new music too, but you may need to experiment with this a little bit before you find the right kind of music for them. Also, be aware that some ancestors may like one type of music while others will hate it, and vice versa. Try to find something that most of them can agree on unless you are working with one specific ancestor.

1. Light the candle on your Ancestor altar and say a prayer for your Ancestors in the usual manner. Fill the water bowls with water. Instructions on how to create an ancestor altar are in chapter 3.

2. Explain to your Ancestors that you would like to share energy with them by dancing with them.

3. Turn on the music of your choice. I light additional candles for ambiance, but this is a personal preference and you may do as feels appropriate to you. If you like, you can light incense such as sage or any other scent that makes you feel magical and connected with your Ancestors.

4. Begin slowly swaying back and forth with the music. Circle around the room with the rhythm of the music. Allow yourself to go into a light trance. Try not to go into a heavy trance until you are used to dancing with the Ancestors. We do not want you to fall down!

5. Visualize your Ancestors dancing with you. See them swaying back and forth with the music as you do. You may hold their hands if you wish, but this is not necessary. Do what feels right to you. The energy exchange will be stronger if you hold hands, but they will still receive energy from you and you from them if you do not hold hands.

6. Continue to dance as long as you wish. During the dance try to connect to the energies of your Ancestors as best you can. All the energies will flow around you and into your heart. At the end of your dance, thank your Ancestor for dancing with you and sharing this experience.

7. When you are ready, say your goodbyes to them and blow out the candles.

Exercise: Ancestor Dance Ritual

In my religious group, The Fellowship of the Phoenix, we have a yearly ritual around Samhain called Shadowdance. In this ritual, our focus is calling upon the Ancestors and connecting to them on a deeper level. The veil is thin at this time of year, so it is much easier for novices to do ancestor work if they have never had training. Our rituals are public, so we invite the greater public to participate. Each year we try to perform a different ceremony, but the core is the same, dancing with the Ancestors. We call to our ancestors in every ritual, but during Shadowdance our main focus is dancing with our beloved dead and the hidden company of the witches. This ritual is great fun and I encourage you to create a ceremony with simply yourself, a group of friends, or your religious group to share in power of magick with the Ancestors.

When organizing the Ancestor Dance Ritual, it is important that everyone involved understand what is to occur. You are going to summon the Ancestors through communal dance and connect with them on an energetic personal level. It is better to perform this dance with friends and colleagues who share your same spiritual philosophies. This is one of the easiest ways to work with the Ancestors. Many cultures have been doing this sort of dancing for all of human history. These cultures, however, have been taught from birth that working with the Ancestors is a fulfilling spiritual practice and there is nothing to be frightened of. In our modern society, as we have learned, people do not honor the dead and do not believe that their spirits stay close to us. When performing this dance with others it must be with the understanding that the Ancestors who show up are there because they love us. It does occur that sometimes novices or people inexperienced with Ancestor work have a strong tangible connection to the dead who come to dance with us. For some, this may be frightening or unnerving. It is best to have experienced magicians and

clergy on hand to help people who may have trouble or fears with this practice.

When it comes to public dances at a drum circle or Neo-pagan gathering, especially with the Ancestor Dance, remind people that drugs are never a good idea. Drugs alter the mind in a way that distorts the energies, and the mind can have a difficult time interpreting what is happening around them.

1. You may perform this ritual indoors or outdoors with a small bonfire or lantern. You can have one person or as many as you like. As a ritual facilitator, it might be wise to begin with a smaller group. You will have to keep an eye on the energies that are being summoned and hold space for the group.

2. I think it is important to give offerings to the Ancestors such as food, flowers, and other gifts. You can place them on a sacred space or altar, or place them directly on the ground outside of the dance space

3. You may use tribal or spiritual music or anything with a nice beat that makes you want to trance out and summon the ancestors. The music can be recorded our performed live with drummers or other musicians.

4. Begin by having the participants start swaying to the beat. They may begin moving into a circle in a clockwise (sunwise) manner.

5. Ask them to think about a specific Ancestor, or simply one of their Ancestors who wishes to join in the dance.

6. As they circle around, have them take a breath in and exhale energy next to them to allow the Ancestor to manifest for them. To do this successfully, they must have a deep longing desire to have the

spirit of their loved one to dance with them. It may help to open the heart chakra and send the Ancestors heart centered energy. Have everyone visualize the Ancestors dancing with them. The more desire one has, the more tangible the experience will be for each person.

7. If someone does not feel an Ancestor next to them, that is okay. Learning to feel the spirits around us often takes time and practice. Simply knowing the Ancestors are dancing with them will work just as well. Remind each dancer to visualize the Ancestors to the best of their ability.

8. Some of the dancers may receive visions or insights. Some may have wonderful conversations with their Ancestors, while others will simply have a wonderful energy exchange experience.

9. This is very healing and many sorts of emotions can come up. Joy, happiness, ecstasy, and perhaps even grief. Try to keep this as joyful as possible. If you notice someone grieving and unable to dance, gently guide them to the edge of the circle and either you or another helper can speak to them, or better yet listen to what they have to say. If they do not wish to speak, simply being there with them for support is perhaps all they need.

When you observe that the dancing is winding down or perhaps people are becoming very tired, you may end the dance. Give thanks to the Ancestors and each other for a wonderful experience.

For those of us practice an ancient religion or practice magick, Ancestor honoring is part of our heritage. As we have learned, ancient cultures from around the world honored the ancestors in some way. Death was an important part of the lives of ancient people. They did not run from it, they embraced it with both arms, heart, and soul. The dead and

their magick was important for the survival of the community. Without the dead, the village or tribe would surely fail. It was also the mysteries of death and the ancestors that taught us the value of life.

3
Honoring Our Ancestors

Those Who Come From The Mountain
(Japan/Shinto)

The snow hasn't fallen yet tonight. I suppose it will. It usually does all through the month of January. So cold. Mother convinced me to come out here to the rice fields, reluctantly, I might add. Grandmother is getting old; she says this may be her last time to see the Ancestors come down from the mountain. I have never seen such a thing, but my grandmother still believes. In such modern times, why she would want to hold on to old superstition is beyond me. But we love her, and she is very stubborn when we ask her not to do something she wants to do. I think she wants to catch a glimpse of Grandfather. I personally think doing this is silly. Mother never asked me to do this thing before. Neither did Grandmother. They mostly let me do what I want, but this year they are being very weird about it. Fine. I hope whatever we are doing doesn't take long.

The rice fields look cold, bare, and empty. Not much here to see but hard ground and the promise of snow. Everyone Grandmother knows is here, all the elders in the community. They seem happy, I guess. I don't know. This all seems strange to me. The sun has finally set behind the mountain so maybe we can get this going. The sooner it starts, the sooner I can go home. The wind seems to pick up from over the Mountains. I can hear it from where I am standing. That's weird. Usually, I can't hear the wind from that far away. Grandmother used to tell us stories about how the Ancestors lived inside the mountain. She would pray to the spirits of our family who she believed lived in the mountain. She said

that if we prayed to the Great Spirit of the Dead, he would help our Ancestors become great spirit guides and spirit helpers in the village. The wind seems to be getting louder now. It is pushing in the nighttime fog over the village.

The fog rolls down the mountain and sweeps through the countryside and begins getting closer to the rice fields. The old women are happy about this. "What's going on?" I ask Grandmother.

"They are coming," she says to me in a hushed voice. "They will be here soon."

"The Ancestors?" I ask.

"Shhh!" She startles me with her impatience.

The fog comes closer and closer to the fields. It seems to have a brightness about it, like it is glowing in the dark. That's weird. Perhaps a streetlight from the village is making it look like that. But the village seems too far away for that to happen. Weird. The fog is suddenly stopping over the rice fields. Did the wind stop? No, it can't really be the Ancestors. Can it?

"Look closely," Grandmother points to the fog. "There they are…"

I can kind of make out what looks like a silhouette of … people. The fog seems to be taking the form of people. Are these our Ancestors? Maybe this is a trick. Maybe Grandmother's stories have finally gotten to me. I cannot make out their faces, but I can see people made of fog walking over to the rice fields.

"They will mix their Kami, their spirits, with the rice fields for a better harvest," Grandmother says. "They will infuse their energy with the rice to ensure that our harvest is plentiful this year. Then they will return to the mountain after the crops are harvested."

I don't know what to say. Maybe Grandmother is right. Maybe our Ancestors are never gone but stay with us watching over the village as

spirit guides just like the old folk say in their stories. Maybe. Maybe I'm just seeing things. But …maybe she is right.

Modern Pagan Honoring of the Dead

Honoring the beloved dead is one of the most important parts of neo-pagan and magical spirituality. We often honor our gods and goddesses and even nature spirits, but sometimes forget the most important spirits to honor, our beloved dead. Our Ancestors are our family. They are our grandmothers and grandfathers and our great-grandmothers and great-grandfathers before that. They hold an energetic and magical link to us. We may not realize it, but there is a current of power that goes from us to our ancestors and from them back to us. It is strong. It is powerful. It is the bond of family. For Pagans, it is important to not only remember our Ancestors, but to incorporate them into our daily lives. Honoring the Ancestors is a part of our sacred duty as spiritual people. Archeologists believe that one of the very first spiritual things attributed to ancient peoples is honoring the dead. Working with the dead is a part of our spiritual makeup. It is who we are as human beings.

For modern people, to ignore the Ancestors is to ignore their own heritage both physically and energetically. If we do not nurture our bond to our Ancestors, then the spiritual energy in our bodies becomes weak and spiritual blocks may develop. A lot of people go their entire lives without developing a connection. In my experience, when the ancestral bond is weak in a family, then family problems become more common in that family. For instance, family karma cannot be resolved very quickly. The family is forced to deal with the energetic "backlash" of energy until someone in the family takes action. This could be one of the reasons that members of the same family often seem to have the same habits or bad luck. They have cut themselves off from a free flow of energy and

the current is blocked. It is far better to maintain a good solid connection with our Ancestors, both for our family and ourselves.

In the past, working with our Ancestors was very much a community-based effort. They were believed to continue to be a part of the community even after death. Our modern view of death and the afterlife has changed quite a bit. It is modern pagans and indigenous cultures that are continuing this age-old tradition of Ancestor-honoring. Now in modern times, working with the Ancestors has become more of an individual practice versus a communal one. However, there are still pagan groups and indigenous tribes that are re-establishing that magical current between the living and the dead. Our modern purposes for working and honoring our Ancestors may vary from our forefathers. We no longer have elaborate temples or groves dedicated to our Ancestors. In ancient times we had temples that lead into caves and the earth. These temples were used to contact the dead and the Underworld Gods. The Temple of the Dead in Baia is one such temple. The best we have in our modern society are cemeteries and mausoleums. These are wonderful places to work with the dead, but it is more powerful for our purposes if we build a family ancestral shrine.

The ancestral shrine is an altar or sacred space that is set up in your home. This acts as a focal point for you and your Ancestors to commune with each other. I like to think of it as a sort of "light house" that beckons the Ancestors to you. The Ancestors may not find it easy to navigate their way to us from the Underworld. The spiritual energy that you put into the ancestral altar calls to them. This is why when we build our shrines, we put photos and objects that belonged to our Ancestors. Not only does it help us tune into them, but it also helps them tune into us. It is very much a spiritual battery that has many benefits!

When building an ancestral shrine, it is important to remember that

it is for your benefit as well as the benefit of your Ancestors. It must be in a prominent place in your home such as the living room, dining room, or kitchen. We should treat the Ancestors as we would an honored guest in our home. Just because they have no physical body does not mean we do not treat them the same. Think of it like this, if you were to have your grandmother over to your home, you would not stick her in a closet and then go about your daily routine. This is how you must view your Ancestors when you begin to work with them. They become a permanent resident in your home. I have seen in some spiritual/magical traditions where the Ancestors are only honored around Halloween or the pagan holy day of Samhain. Though this is a holy day for the Ancestors, it is far more powerful to honor the Ancestors every day! Your Ancestors are with you always; it is up to you how strongly you would like their presence felt. Remember, the more we honor the Ancestors, the more they will have an influence in this world and the Underworld. To honor them only once or twice a year is like calling your grandparents once or twice a year then asking them to buy you a new car. The chances of that happening are slim.

We should take a moment from thinking about the Ancestors energetically and think of them emotionally. Just because they are dead does not mean they have necessarily evolved to such a state that they have understanding and patience with human mistakes, frailties, and simple lack of courtesies. If we ignore our Ancestors, especially those of us who know they are here still with us, then it will hurt their feelings and potentially cause them to become angry with us. This could cause more blocks and family karma for you and your family. If for nothing else, it is good karma and energy to give honor to those who gave you their very blood.

The ancestral shrine itself should be something pleasing to you. It

can be on the fireplace mantle or on a bookshelf. It can be on a little table somewhere in your living room. I have seen examples where people have placed their shrine on top of a family heirloom such as a china cabinet or end table that was in the family for generations. Some of us are not that fortunate, so any table that feels energetically acceptable will do. The shrine should feel like it is a natural part of the living area. It can be as intricate or simple as you like. I find that in the beginning, when you first build the shrine, you make it the way you want. Then the Ancestor will tell you what they like and do not like. This is perfectly fine!

I will caution on one thing when making an ancestral shrine. It should be comfortable for both you and your Ancestors. It should not be designed in such a way that looks scary or like something out of a horror movie. I am not trying to squash individual taste or other spiritual traditions but hanging plastic bats and putting frightening things on your shrine may make your Ancestors a little uneasy. With that, in Vodou and some witchcraft groups, they may use skulls and bones and items of that nature. This is fine if your spiritual tradition holds these things as sacred. The more sacred you feel your shrine is the more sacred it will become. Even so, ask the Ancestors if they are pleased with the shrine.

Building an Altar

The Ancestors have the ability to watch over us and offer us guidance and wisdom. As we have learned, just because we cannot see the influence that they have on us directly does not mean that they are not helping us in a significant spiritual way. As we work with the energy of our Ancestors, we will be able to see the influence that they have more profoundly. To do this, we must create a sacred space for them in our homes. This is commonly referred to as an Ancestral altar. At first, this idea of building an altar to the dead may seem strange. There are many religions in which

ancestral altars and devotions are performed. I think it may help to clear up some misconceptions about the Ancestral altar and the work ahead. First, we are not "worshiping" our dead as one would a god. However, this was certainly done in some pagan societies because it was sometimes believed that when a person died, they became divine and protected the tribe or clan in a very powerful way. The altar is a sacred space in your home that acts as a focal point for you and your Ancestors to commune with each other. Over time, this is the place where a lot of your power for magick will come from. To have an Ancestral altar in your home will only help you build your connection with your Ancestors and develop your magical practice.

As we build our Ancestor altar, we need to keep in mind the reality of the Ancestors themselves. The spirits of the dead in our contemporary society are most likely not magical or a part of the "spiritual community". Therefore, it is probable that they are not used to working with the living in such a direct way. Sometimes, the Underworld can be disorienting and a very tricky business for the recently deceased. The concept of space and time, according to the dead's point of view, has changed dramatically from what they knew when they were living. Also, no one is magically transformed into this "all-knowing" or "all powerful" being upon death. I was once told as a child that when you died you knew everything that ever was and everything that ever will be. In my experience with working with the spirits of the dead, and the experience of my colleagues, this is simply not the case. When a person dies, their hopes, fears, desires, and prejudices remain intact. And NO, they do not know everything. However, as we discussed before, they do have a front seat view to the upcoming events that are soon to happen in our physical world. But this too, is something that the dead must learn to do. In the Underworld, spirits are taught by divine Ancestors and spirit helpers who help them acclimate to

the Underworld. Part of this acclimation is learning to understand that in the world of spirit, time and space are not the same as the physical world. The dead can see the past and the future, as well as things in the present that we cannot. But, again, all these things take time and training.

Imagine for a moment that you have died, and you are trying to figure out the whole new Universe of the Underworld. Without proper training (such as a book of the dead), you may be confused and not understanding fully what is happening to you. Most of today's society come from a patriarchal religious view with either Heaven or Hell. We either are with God or the Devil. The fact is, that when we die, we do not necessarily go to the world of the divine. We go to the land of the Ancestors. A place of rejuvenation and healing. When most people die, this is confusing to them because they expect Heaven or Hell. The newly dead will need help navigating this new world of the afterlife. Also, the newly dead do not know everything. They are the same person they were when alive, the only difference being that now they are dead. When we are first beginning to work with the dead, have compassion for them and understand that sometimes they are just as confused as we are, if not more so. Often, they are surprised you are able to summon them back to the physical world. We need to help them out physically, magically, energetically, and emotionally. The best way to begin this process is to create an altar. This will help them focus on where you are. As you do your devotions and prayers to your Ancestors, the connection between you will become stronger and stronger. Over time, you will feel the power of the Ancestors and they will feel yours. Eventually, you will be able to have them perform divination for you, they will be able to help protect you and your home, and they will have other abilities you have yet to discover.

We will begin to build our family ancestral altar. As we journey

through this process, it is important to know that it is a holy and magical experience. We are not looking for ingredients for a spell or ritual. We are designing a vessel so that our family's spiritual lineage can come through in a profound and powerful way. Many spiritual and religious traditions may have specific ways to set up an ancestral altar. I will explain how to build your altar in the way I was taught. The instructions I give you are merely guidelines. Please feel free to design an altar according to your spiritual beliefs and preferences. You may also notice over time that your Ancestor altar evolves and grows as you evolve and grow spiritually. Or perhaps it will be designed according to the will and wishes of the dear Ancestors who love you. This is fine. Here are the steps to get you started:

1. First, go through your family's genealogy or family tree and decide which of the Ancestors are appropriate for your altar. Start with three or, perhaps, at most four. They can be from your mother's side, father's side, or both. If you are adopted, you can certainly use your ancestors from your adapted family. You may find that one Ancestor may come through very strongly while others may not. This is normal. Do not worry about who may be the strongest or more powerful spiritually. You want to choose the Ancestor that feels compatible with your energies. Do what feels right to you. Do a divination to see if that Ancestor is right for your altar. You may use runes, the tarot, or a pendulum to determine which Ancestors are best suited to be there. Any Ancestor who does not like you, or who do not approve of your lifestyle, sexual orientation, or religious choices may not be the best fit for your altar. However, the Ancestors love to be a part of your life and I've seen spirits of the dead put aside their prejudices so that they may commune with you.

2. Once you have decided which Ancestors to put on your altar, try to

obtain photos of your Ancestors and any personal items such as watches, jewelry, or something that may fit on an altar that would be appropriate to place in public view. It is better to make sure there is one person per photograph. The reason for this is that when you work with the spirits and gaze upon their picture you are giving them energy from your heart and mind. By having more than one person in a photo you may inadvertently give energy to Ancestors who you may not necessarily want on your altar. When you do this, they will be drawn to your altar, and this may or may not be appropriate for your other Ancestors.

3. In front of each picture, place one small offering bowl for water and another offering bowl for food. Each Ancestor should have his or her own offering bowls. Try not to mix them up between Ancestors. Over time, the Ancestors will have their own energy signatures on their items, and they will not want to have the wrong food and water dish. The bowls vibrate with the energy of that Ancestor, and they do not like it when they do not have their own bowl. The Ancestors are not used to this type of spiritual work and need to adjust to the energies that they are receiving for nourishment. It may take them a while to connect with the energies of the physical world again. It is better to make sure they have their own items so that they receive the energy you are offering in a more tangible way. If you like, you can take a marker or ink pen and write their name or initials at the bottom of their dishes to help you distinguish whose dish is whose.

4. At this point you will want to obtain one central candle for the altar. The candle serves a few purposes. First, it impresses on your consciousness that the presence of your Ancestors are here when you light the candle. It also gives them spiritual energy so that they

can manifest in your physical space more easily. I find a large, white candle works well. I also love beeswax, but larger beeswax candles can become expensive. I would refrain from getting scented candles unless your Ancestors specifically ask for them. Scented candles usually contain chemical perfumes that can hinder the energies of the spirits. I, personally, get unscented candles and place a few drops of peppermint essential oil in the wax and then anoint the candle itself. Peppermint is one of the essential oils that the Ancestors love, and it will give them power.

You may make the altar as elaborate or as simple as you like. The altar should be placed in the living room or a room where people gather to visit and be with each other. We want the Ancestors to be with us in spirit just as you would if they were in a physical body. You would never invite your great grandmother to your home, sit her in a hallway or bedroom, and then visit with everyone else in the living room or den. This is considered just as rude in the spiritual world as it is in the physical world. If you have roommates, explain to them that this is a religious practice. Most roommates do not have a problem with this. If you discover there is a problem, you may need to re-evaluate your living environment. I, personally, prefer to keep my ancestral altar simple, but if you would like to add decorations that make it feel "homey" and welcoming, feel free. Just be sure that it is not too cluttered so that when working with the altar and the Ancestors, you, and they, are not distracted by too many things getting in the way. Once you build your altar and have decided who to place upon it, let it sit for a couple of days so that it may find its grounding in the physical and spiritual worlds.

Honoring and Devotion

Before giving offerings to our beloved dead, set up your altar, light your ancestral candle and say a prayer to the gods and higher spirits on their behalf. You can say something to the effect of, "I ask the Gods to grant blessings, peace, and spiritual evolution to my Ancestors (name), (name), and (name)." Make sure you use their full names. This strengthens their connection to you, the altar, and your energies and spirits. Say this prayer every day for at least a week before engaging in conversation with your Ancestors. This will give your Ancestors time to acclimatize to the new altar and helps them understand that this is a focal point for energy and connection with you. Your Ancestors will hear your prayers in the Underworld. It is my belief that once you have decided to create the ancestral altar and work with them, the magical/spiritual connection begins to be made, however faintly. During your first initial prayers to and for the Ancestors, the energies and higher beings are preparing your Ancestors to come to the physical plane and work with you.

After a week or so, you may begin giving your Ancestors the offering of water in their water bowl. Different traditions will have different ways of doing this. In some, it is believed that it is better to give the Ancestors water after you speak with them. In others, you only put the water in after they speak with you. This is done to encourage them to speak and to overcome the astral/energy challenges which may block them from speaking with you. I understand this in principle, but to me the Ancestors should be honored whether they speak to you or not. I feel that only giving water to your Ancestors after they speak with you is more of a task-reward scenario. Again, we treat spirits, especially our own Ancestors, as we would if they had a physical body. WE NEVER TREAT THEM AS LESSER BEINGS. NEVER. I feel it is important to honor them regardless of how they choose to manifest. Some of the Ancestors will

manifest very strongly and some will not. I do not reward or punish my Ancestors because they lack strength in their ability to manifest. A word of advice, we treat all spirits the way we would want to be treated when we have passed on and we become one of the Ancestors! I have heard of and seen other spiritual traditions that treat the Ancestors as children who misbehave and should be punished or rewarded. I never worry if an Ancestor will become powerful or not. Over time they will come into their power and strength. The more they work with you and the more energy you give the Ancestors by offerings and devotions, the more powerful they will become. You must be patient and loving. For my practice, I simply light my ancestral candle first, say the prayer, then pour water in each of the water bowls as I begin to talk to the Ancestors. If you follow this practice, you need to do this once a day until the energetic connection between you is strong and solid. The spirits understand that we humans become busy with our human affairs. We may not always have the time and energy to have long conversations. However, you should say a simple prayer every day. This helps them stay connected with you and feeds them energy.

Speaking with the Ancestors helps build the energetic bond between you. Speaking, singing, or chanting has the power to manifest magick. In many religions when God or the creator deities speak, the Universe is created. Likewise in magick, when we speak or sing with intention, we are bringing spirit down to the physical plane to manifest our will. When we talk with emotion and intention, the energetic bond between you and your Ancestors is strengthened. The more you speak to them, the more energy you give to them and, in turn, the more energy they give back to you. This also establishes an emotional relationship bond. Just as we must nurture our relationships with our friends and family, so too, we have to nurture our relationships with the dead. Our Ancestors have an

investment in us because we are their family and their legacy. It is important to them to maintain family connections. They want to see us succeed. They want us to be happy and fulfilled in this plane of existence. The more powerful the family line is from this world to the spirit world, the more powerful the family influence is in all the worlds. Some of our Ancestors may not even know this, especially if they have not been in the Underworld for too long. However, our Ancestors who have been in the Underworld for generations have spiritually evolved to such a point that they are able to understand this concept and very much want to nurture this. These ancient Ancestors have their own mysteries that we may never come to understand in this life and plane of existence.

When you begin speaking with your Ancestors, at first you may not know what it is you should say or what the Ancestors would like to talk about. Typically, you can say anything you want. What do you think your Ancestors would be interested in? It is important to realize that they are your family. Your family is interested in what is going on in your life. To begin with, I would talk to them about what is happening to you day-to-day. You may speak with them about how work is going or about your romantic life if you feel that they are interested in that. Usually, grandmothers are interested in who we are dating and who are partners are. I think of speaking with the Ancestors as a magical phone call. I can light the ancestral altar candle, pour some water out to them, say my opening prayer, and then talk about my day, my hopes, fears, dreams, or anything that I think they want to hear about. There are no strict rules. However, if there are things you would not tell your Ancestors when they were alive, you may not want to talk about it when they are dead. I, personally, would not want to talk to my grandmother about my sex life while she was alive, so I would not do so during my conversations with her on the altar. As I said before, they will likely have the same worldviews

and prejudices as they did when they were alive. However, they may slowly come around to new and strange ideas like magick, spirits, gay, and alternative lifestyles. They have a different perspective now and can see different sides of the energetic "coin." I will say that this sometimes takes a while, and you may have to be very patient with your Ancestors.

If, while working with your Ancestors, one of them refuses to accept things such as magick, working with the living, or does not approve of your lifestyle, it is important that you explain to them that if they cannot be accepting of you and your work, then you will take them off the altar and no longer give them offerings. Your Ancestors will soon see the energetic benefit of working with you and may have to change their views. But there have been several cases where a particularly stubborn family member would just rather be taken off the altar. This is completely fine. You should not change their destiny and spiritual evolution. You cannot rush spiritual transformation. Perhaps they will come back in time. It is always better to have a harmonious relationship with your Ancestors. One of the most common questions that is asked of me about the Ancestor Altar in the living room is: "Will Grandma and Grandpa see me having sex in the living room or my bedroom?"

This always makes me giggle, but it would be mortifying if they did! The truth of the matter is that whenever you do not want to be seen, your psychic mind automatically puts up a shield around you and whatever you are doing. On some level you want privacy, even if you are not consciously thinking about it and Poof! The shield goes up, cloaking your actions. This is true about your bedroom as well. Your bedroom is your sanctuary. Most people know never to go into someone's bedroom without permission and these same courtesies go for the Ancestors as well. However, just to be safe, I would not leave the candle on my Ancestor

altar burning if I decide to become intimate with someone. Grandma may get a shock.

At times, some of your Ancestors may not work well together on the same altar. Sometimes, they take their stubbornness and disagreements into death with them. If your grandmother is very upset because Uncle Johnny stole a great deal of money from the family during life, she may take this anger into death with her. It is tedious, but you can play mediator between them. You may have to explain to them that what happened in life was a long time ago and they need to work on making amends, if not for their sake, then for the sake of the family and future generations. There have been family feuds and disagreements that have lasted so long no one really remembers how they got started. Even these can be resolved. If their minds are made up and they refuse to make amends after mediation, then you may want to consider taking one of them off the altar. When working with your Ancestors, you want the energy to be loving and focused. You do not want Uncle Joe's water dish being thrown off the altar. Yes, I have seen this happen!

After your conversation, say your goodbyes and extinguish the candle. You may use a candle extinguisher, or you may blow out the candle. Blowing out the candle is not disrespectful. It is the same as hanging up the telephone. When you are finished communing with your Ancestors, they may hang around a bit in your home or they may go back to whatever they were doing in the Afterlife before you called to them. I personally do not mind my Ancestors hanging around after the candle is blown out. Just as we said before, your Ancestors on your shrine are permanent residents in your home.

On special occasions, or whenever it feels correct, you may give them flowers and/or food. The kind of food is up to you. Generally, too much salt drains their energy so avoid salty foods and foods that have a

lot of preservatives. You should also de-shell or peel food as needed. Give meat sparingly. There are many spiritual traditions that give meat and animal sacrifice to the Ancestors. I do not interfere with those traditions, but for myself I prefer to keep the meat to a minimum. I give them meat on special occasions and holidays. If they did not like a meal during life, they won't like it in death either. Alcohol is fine on holidays and birthdays, but drunken spirits are not always the easiest to control or calm down. If they had a drinking problem in life DO NOT GIVE ALCOHOL. There may be times when we did not realize that one of our Ancestors had a drinking or drug problem. A lot of the time the dead have the same addictions and problems after death. If you have an Ancestor who continually asks or demands alcohol outside of a special holiday treat you need to be firm with them and explain that you are not going to provide it for them and if they continue to ask for it, they will be taken off the altar. I do not like to threaten Ancestors any more than I like to threaten a human being, but we must remember that those spirits with drug and alcohol problems need you to be firm and loving.

How the Dead Appear

As you are doing your work with your Ancestors, you are building a psychic connection at the same time as developing your astral and spiritual sight. When you begin, you may feel like you are imagining the voices of your Ancestors. This is a good thing. The idea is not to "make up" the conversation in your head, but to just let it happen naturally. It may feel like you are making it up, but you are not. This takes practice so do not rush it. For some people it happens very quickly and for others it takes longer. This has nothing to do with how much psychic ability you may or may not have, but rather how strong your connection is with the spirits of the dead. When you have your conversations, give each Ancestor water

in their bowl whether they spoke to you or not. It is not often that all your Ancestors will speak with you. Perhaps only one or two will speak, and often only one. When you feel it is appropriate, you can give food offerings to your Ancestors, and this will give them strength to manifest more easily on this plane of existence. When your psychic skills are improved and your Ancestors are stronger, it will be much easier to have conversations with them.

Once you begin having regular conversations with the dead, you may start to see them in your mind. This is a good indication that your connection to your Ancestors is becoming stronger. The vision in your mind may be hazy or fuzzy at first, but it will clear up in time. Often, after the Ancestors have been dead a while, they will appear as they did in the prime of their life. I often hear that they appear as the age of 33, but in my experience, they appear as the time in their lives when they were the healthiest and happiest. This happens because your consciousness has an immensely powerful effect on the astral and spiritual bodies. In energy healing, we teach that your thoughts have a direct effect on your energy bodies and your health. The same applies here. The spirit body will appear in the way that is the most pleasing to the spirit. In other words, if your grandmother died at 85 and had some debilitating disease at the time of death, she may very well appear later to you as a young and healthy woman. I have even seen adults appear as children. This is rare but it does happen.

After working with your Ancestors regularly for a time, you may no longer just see them in your mind. They may manifest in spirit right in front of you in your living room. If this happens, most likely they will all appear at the same time. I have never seen only one or two of my Ancestors appear while the others on my altar did not. At this stage of development, the only difference between your Ancestors and any other houseguest is that your Ancestors do not have a physical body. You may

even see them roaming around your house! Do not worry, only you and other clairvoyants will be able to see them. They usually only appear before you when you light the candle on the ancestral altar and say a prayer to them. Once the candle is extinguished, they disappear. This does not mean that you have banished them, but you have temporally "turned off" the connection that brings them to the forefront of your consciousness. They are still there on the astral and spiritual planes.

Evolution and Transformation of the Dead

In many cultures around the world, it is common for the living to pray to and for the dead. This is done for a variety of reasons. Prayers are heard throughout all three worlds and on all levels of existence. When we pray, we are using energies from our minds, emotions, spirit, and in some instances, our bodies. It is interesting to note that in indigenous cultures it is often common to pray to the spirits through dance and ordeals such as the sweat lodge and Sundance Ceremony. The sweat lodge, or *inipi* in Lakota, is a ceremony where the seekers go into a small lodge or hut. There, water is poured over hot rocks making hot steam. During the ceremony, powerful spirits and the Ancestors are called into the lodge, and they are prayed to for healing. The Sundance is a four-day event where the seekers dance all day and pray to the spirits for a vision that will aid the people in the times to come. When we pray with reverence and heartfelt feelings, our prayers are made stronger and more powerful. This is not to say that people who "care" more get better results necessarily, but it does mean that if we do not put much feeling and energy into our prayers then they may or may not get to the party intended. I personally believe that our personal gods and Ancestors are with us all the time and they always hear our prayers, but the difference is that they can tell how much we mean it when we pray.

In Shinto, the Japanese indigenous animistic religion, it is believed that the Ancestors need to be purified after death so that they may transcend to higher levels of existence. The higher levels of existence are more refined. This means that spirits who dwell in the "higher" planes of existence need to be in harmony and balance with these energies to be able to exist there. The benefit of transitioning to a higher realm is that, once there, the spirit can evolve and transform on a deeper level. The Shinto belief is that when the Ancestors have achieved this level of transformation, they are better equipped to become teachers and spirit guides for their families and community.

As living beings, we can help our Ancestors to evolve and transform through our prayers. When we pray for the purification, teaching, and transformation of our Ancestors, there are certain helping and healing spirits that will hear our prayers and help them to evolve and transform into more than they were at the time of death. There are Divine Ancestors, those Ancestors who have reached a high level of transformation, perhaps even becoming gods themselves, who have a personal investment in their bloodline and who will be able to help the dead learn to transform into higher beings. There are also healing spirits who can help the Ancestors heal from past hurts and tragedies and even unfinished business that cause the Ancestors to hold onto things that prevent them from moving to a higher level of being. In Native American cultures there are the Holy Medicine People. These are spiritual beings of great power that are wise in the ways of healing and transcendence. It is believed that their divine purpose is to help humanity find balance to evolve and transform. They will help both the living and the dead find the spiritual teachings they need to find their divine purpose in life and in death. We pray to higher beings because both the living and the dead have free will. Enlightened beings will only help us and those we love if we ask for it. When the

Universe created life, it did so with the idea of Free Will. The Universe allows us to make our own successes and mistakes and will not interfere unless it is necessary. It is true that one of their purposes is to help us, but they cannot interfere with our decisions for good or for ill. They will respect the path that we are currently on and help in the limited ways that they are able until we ask them through our prayers.

Once we put our intent in motion of helping our Ancestors evolve, then the higher beings take the Ancestors to a place where they can be taught how to become higher beings themselves. When this happens, our Ancestors can become more powerful and enlightened. They are then able to help us on the physical plane in more profound ways. They may become spirits guides and act as "guardian angels" for us. They will be able to help our family and us in more profound and tangible ways. They will also be able to help other people in a way that is beneficial to everyone.

On an energetic level, what is happening is that our prayers open our mind, energies, emotions, and our spirits to our Ancestors and higher beings to establish a strong and powerful connection. Through the connection we make with the spirits, they can use this energy and power to help our Ancestors evolve to a higher state of being. This is done over time, so it is important that we pray to our Ancestors and higher beings every day. It is also important that we give our Ancestors water and food offerings from time to time so that they can maintain their energetic connection with this world. You will begin to see how the Ancestors manifest in the physical plane quite easily. However, it is important to remember that it does indeed take time. In the Underworld, there is no concept of time how we are used to thinking about it. The Ancestors literally have all the time they need. You cannot rush spiritual evolution. Some of our Ancestors may learn and evolve very quickly and other may

take more time. There is no right or wrong way. It just is what it is. From our point of view, it may seem time consuming, but to our Ancestors point of view it may seem to be happening very quickly, or vice versa. The important thing to remember is to give your Ancestors the love and respect of being your family and your guides. After a while, this process will seem very natural to you and will become a part of your daily life.

Dreams with the Dead

Dreams are the gateway into the three worlds. Many pagan cultures, believe that the dream world is more "real" than the physical plane. One reason they believe this is because the dream world closely resonates with the spirit world. It has been in existence far longer than the physical plane and will be there long after the Earth, the physical universe, and all physical reality is long gone. The Dreamworld is a world or plane of its own, but it is also a portal or gateway into the Underworld. The gods, Ancestors, and nature spirits are able to easily communicate with us through our dreams. When the Ancestors come into our dreams we may ask the question, *are we dreaming of the Ancestors or are the Ancestors dreaming of us?* In dreams, things seem odd and magical. We can be in our homes and then instantly be across the world. In dreams, Ancestors can appear as they wish. Perhaps they appear as they did in life, but they can appear in any form they wish. The magick of dreams is closely related to the Underworld. In dreams we can certainly travel to the Underworld, but most often we are traveling in the Dreamworld itself.

A safe and effective way to speak with your Ancestors and the dead is through the ritual of incubation. In necromancy, incubation refers to speaking with the dead through dreams. This is a relatively easy process and sometimes happens without our even realizing it. A benefit of dream

incubation with the dead is that we are not inviting them into our space in the physical plane, but we are meeting them in an in-between place.

Before performing your Incubation Ritual, you will need to take a purifying bath or shower. You may add purifying essential oils to your bath such as peppermint, eucalyptus, lavender, or sage. You should also smudge your sleeping area with sage, sweet grass, frankincense, and/or lavender.

Ancestor Dream Ritual

1. Begin by creating sacred space. This can be a circle or simply a declaration to the spirits that your bed and bedroom is sacred and magical.

2. Say a prayer to your personal gods, asking them for guidance and protection. Then say a prayer to Persephone, Hella, Gwyn Ap Nudd, Osiris, or whichever Underworld god or goddess is most appropriate to your religious tradition, asking them to allow your Ancestors to speak with you. You can say something like this, "Hella, Goddess of the Underworld and of the Dead. I ask that you grant my Ancestors temporary leave of your kingdom so that I may learn from their insight."

3. Next say a prayer to Hermes, Hecate, Mercury, Cernunnos or whichever god or goddess of the crossroads, gates, or ghost roads is most appropriate to your religious tradition. It should be a deity who allows the dead to travel to the Earth plane from the Underworld. For example: "Great Hermes. You who travels the worlds. Grant my Ancestors safe passage to the world of dreams"

4. On your altar, or other sacred place in your home, lay out an offering in a bowl for the gods. The Greco-Roman deities I work

with like red wine, honey, beans, chickpeas, barley, and milk. You can also research other cultures to see what offering they left their gods. You can also use your intuition. Sometimes this is a particular deity speaking to you asking for something they especially like. If it feels right to leave out something other than what the sources tell you, then do so.

5.   In a separate bowl, leave an offering to the Ancestors. You can choose water, milk, rice, bread, fruit, or whatever you feel is appropriate.

6.   Then lie down. Just before you go to sleep make one last statement to the Otherworld. "I travel to the world of dreams so that I may speak with my Ancestors."

7.   Allow yourself to drift off to sleep. Know that you will see your Ancestors in your dreams. Try not to have any preconceived notions about what will happen and how they will appear. Allow the dream to unfold. The Ancestors may appear as they did when they died, or they may appear younger and healthier. They may even appear in another guise. Don't worry, in the dream worlds you will know them instinctively. Sometimes they will appear as animals or simply an energy or fog. You may not immediately succeed or be aware of your success at first if you are not used to doing this sort of magical work. Do not become discouraged. Keep at it. Eventually, you will achieve success. This may range from a dramatic encounter in the Dreamtime, a curious gut feeling about something that you experience upon waking, or something that drifts into your consciousness over the course of the next day.

8.   Upon awakening, thank your gods, the gods of the Underworld and the Gatekeepers, and your Ancestors. Even if you do not

remember your dreams, you must still thank all those spirits that you called upon.

9. Journal your experience. Write down impressions, thought, or insights. Sometimes when we perform the Ancestor Dream Ritual, we may not remember seeing our ancestors but they were there. In the beginning it may take a few attempts before we are able to see them clearly. Try to remember how you felt and what was happening. Maybe the Ancestors were observing you or maybe they were sharing energy with you without taking form. I try not to judge my dream experience. Journal what you can and try again the next night.

Exercise: Meditation on Being an Ancestor

I believe the relationship between a person and their Ancestors should be even stronger than their relationship with their gods. In an effort to better understand what it must be like for your Ancestors, I am providing a guided meditation that will allow you to have a better understanding on what it is like for your Ancestors. This is important because it helps us open or heart to them in a more compassionate way so that we can have a basic understanding on what it might be like for them. In this meditation, you will perform a guided visualization that will help you better understand the death experience. This is simply for you to better understand your Ancestors. You will not be harmed in any way.

Meditation:

Lie down and make yourself comfortable. Take a deep breath in and exhale the day's stress away. Take another deep breath in and allow the chatter in your mind to quiet. Take one more deep breath and release the tension in your muscles. Center yourself in your body.

You are in hospice hooked up to life support machines. You have lived a full life and now your body is weakening moment by moment. Your family and friends are at your side. There are tears in the room, but you are not sad. Your time has come to leave the physical plane and enter the spirit world. You will miss your family and friends, but you know that it is time for you to move on. The doctors have turned off the life support machines, and you can feel your body and life fading away. As this is happening you feel a strong spiritual presence all around you.

There are spirit helpers, spirit guides, and your Ancestors standing all around your bed. There is a sense of safety and mystery surrounding you. The machines have registered that your heart has stopped. Your life force is gone. You can feel your astral body separating from your physical body without effort. One of your Ancestors reaches out to you with their hand and helps your astral body off the bed.

A portal opens about the size of a door. There is a bright light coming from the magical doorway. Your Ancestors lead you through and your guides accompany you as well. You do not know what is on the other side of the door, but you know that it is the afterlife. After going through the door, you find yourself in a city. This is the land of the Ancestors. What does this place look like to you? Are the buildings large or small? Are they modern or old? Who is there when you get to the land of the Ancestors? Is there anyone here that you recognize? After a time, you start to become acclimated to this wonderful place. You meet Ancestors from your family lineage that go back thousands of years. You also meet friends and spiritual teachers who were once your companions in life. All family. All Ancestors.

Not too long after you have met your Ancestors in afterlife, you hear a spirit voice call your name. The voice is getting stronger and stronger, and it seems to pull you. It is almost as if your blood is dragging

you back across the great spirit veil that separates you from the world of the living. You cannot resist the magical call. You follow the call through the veil. You find yourself standing in an unfamiliar living room next to an altar of some kind. You walk closer to examine the altar and you discover your picture on top of the table with a bowl of water for you. You look around and see a young person saying prayers for you. In a moment, other Ancestors appear, ones you recognize.

"She has called you!" One of your Ancestors says.

You look at the young person and you do not recognize them. Their clothes seem strange and not what you remember at all from life. You look around the living room and notice that the furniture seems odd, like something from a science fiction movie. You see a calendar on the wall and see the date. It is 60 years after you died.

After the young person finishes their prayers for you and the other Ancestors, they pour water in the bowls on the altar. "Drink it," an Ancestor says.

You take a drink of the water placed in front of your picture. You feel refreshed and powerful. You feel a strong connection to the young person. Without asking them and without anyone telling you, you know their name. You've always known their name. You feel an incredible bond with them. You will do anything for them. You will open the gates of the spirit world for them. You will protect them. What they ask of you, you will do...out of love. They are your family. You are their Ancestor.

Trickster Spirits and Negative Entities

Occasionally you may attract spirits who are not your Ancestors. Most of the time these are spirits who have noticed your work with the dead and pass by because of curiosity or would like to ask your help in some way. You are not obligated to help them. For me, this is a part of my

spiritual work so if I am able, and my spirits advise me that it is right, and then I will help in whatever way I can.

Sometimes, entities or negative spirits may not have the best intentions in mind. Most of the time these spirits are looking to consume the energy that you are providing to your Ancestors. It is not a good idea to allow this to happen. It is very probable that the spirit will become stronger and more manipulative to obtain the energy and power it desires. It is better to deal with it before it becomes too powerful.

To deal with trickster spirits, the easiest thing to do is to touch your ancestral altar and call upon your spirits. Explain to them the situation (trust me when I say they already know!) and ask them to get rid of the spirit. Then visualize you and your ancestors making a circle holding hands while you are physically touching the altar. Visualize a brilliant white light that is purifying surround you, your Ancestors, and the altar. Know that this light is sending the trickster spirit far away and to another entity or god that may help this entity on its spiritual path. As you perform this little ritual, make sure you are doing it in a way that is compassionate and healing. We are not aiming to harm the trickster spirit, simply send it to another being who is able to give the spirit the healing it needs.

If you should encounter tricksters or negative entities, do not panic. Most of these beings are simply lost or confused and know that the energy you are providing for your Ancestors can give them "life" and nourishment. Just as stated above, they are easily persuaded to leave. Occasionally, you may have an entity that attaches itself to you and drains your life force. The best way to prevent this is to make sure you have healthy dietary habits, exercise regularly, solid spiritual beliefs, and practices that include devotional work. If you do manage to acquire a spiritual attachment, there are a few things you can do to remove the entity.

1. You or a friend can take a consecrated knife or dagger and cut the

spirit away. Visualize a cord between you and the spirit and see the knife cutting the cord. If the spirit is still there, refer to the "Banishing" techniques described later in the book to banish the spirit. This is the most aggressive of the techniques and should only be done when the others do not work.

2. You can take a bath in salt water. Salt drains the energy of spirits and they will quickly go away. I like to think of it as like putting salt on a slug to kill it.

3. Ask your gods and goddesses to remove the spirit. You can light a candle to them and send them a prayer asking them to take the spirit to a place of healing. Then visualize your god or goddess coming to remove the spirit and taking it away.

4. Ask your healing helpers, holy medicine people, and divine Ancestors to come and remove the spirit from you and take it to a place of healing.

You may use any of the above techniques that suit you or you may use a combination of them.

Finding an Ancestral Teacher

While working with the dead and your Ancestors, you will need to be able to maneuver through the Underworld. One of the best ways to accomplish this is to find your Ancestral Teacher. This is a distant Ancestor who has evolved spiritually to an advanced level and has chosen to remain in the Underworld to watch and guide your family line. This teacher no longer has the need of things associated with the physical plan, yet still retains the memories of life and understands what it is to be human. Your Ancestral Teacher has many abilities that they can teach you to work more effectively with the Ancestors and the dead. One of the most

important things is that they can teach you is how to better navigate the Underworld. There are places that the novice Underworld traveler should avoid until they are better prepared. It is not necessarily that we wish to avoid frightening and dangerous places, but also that there are certain strange realms that it is important to know and understand the customs that belong to that world. For example, if you find yourself in Svartalfheim, the land of dwarves and dark elves, you might find yourself in a jam because Dark Elves rarely make friends with outsiders, and they prefer to be left alone. Because of this, it is best to avoid them and leave them on their own or you may find yourself betrayed for your imposition. The Ancestral Teacher will help better prepare you for what is to come when you encounter such entities.

Your Ancestral Teacher has been watching your family for a long time and has spent years spiritually guiding your family throughout the generations. This teacher can assist you in your spiritual development when it comes to the dead and the Underworld. Whenever you have questions about your family lineage, your teacher is the best one to go to for advice. Your Ancestral Teacher can also assist you in learning Underworld divination and how to advance your magical experience using the ancestral and Underworld energies.

To Find Your Ancestral Teacher:

1. Sit in a comfortable chair or lie down. Relax your body and clear your mind. Begin to breathe slowly and connect yourself with the universal energies.

2. Visualize a Great Tree in front of you. It is the most magnificent and magical tree you have ever seen. You know this is the World Tree and will take you to anywhere in the three worlds you wish to go.

3. State your intention to find your Ancestral Teacher.

4. Your spirit animal greets you at the tree. You will both journey forth together. You see a door in the trunk of the tree. You open the door and see that there is a spiral staircase that seems to go down forever. Using your astral body, quickly move down the spiral staircase until you find the very bottom deep in the roots of the Tree.

5. As you step out of the tree's roots, you find yourself in the Under-world. What do you see? What can you hear? Smell?

6. Again, state your intention to find your Ancestral Teacher. The blood in your veins begins to vibrate. It seems as though your blood is guiding you now. Your spirit animal will guide you to your Ancestral Teacher.

7. As you journey forth, take notice of the landscape. What does it look like? Are you in a forest, desert, or prairie? Are you in a town or a city?

8. After a time, you find your Ancestral Teacher. Your teacher will make themselves known to you. You know this is your Ancestral Teacher because your blood vibrates stronger now in your astral body and you feel a family bond with this teacher. What does your teacher look like?

9. Spend some time asking your Ancestral Teacher questions and get to know them. When you are ready to leave say your goodbyes and journey back the way you came. Go back to the root of the tree, go up the spiral staircase and make your way back to the Midworld.

10. When you are ready open your eyes. Journal about your experience.
    Ancestral Patterns

Our family history is in our DNA. That which is spiritual manifests on the physical and that which is physical manifests on the spiritual. Our family passes physical attributes down to us. Likewise, they pass spiritual influences and karma. That is not to say that their religious beliefs are necessarily part of our genetic makeup, but rather that they pass down energetic patterns and unfinished business as well as blessings and curses.

We may notice patterns throughout our entire family. Sometimes these patterns go back to our grandparents, but other times these patterns go back for generations. We have the ability to change and alter these patterns and energies forever. We have the power to make a difference in our family lineage.

It is important to remember that this is not about blame or resentment. We have to understand that our Ancestors come from a completely different time and environment than we live in today. Most people simply were doing the best they could with what resources they had. They were human just like us. They made mistakes, had prejudices, hopes, fears, and disappointments just like we do now. To learn to clear ancestral patterns and karma, we need to have compassion. In fact, if you do not have the utmost compassion for your Ancestors then this work is not for you. Period.

Astral Traveling to Experience the Ancestors

This technique will help you learn more about the lives and history about your Ancestors. The purpose is to simply observe. Do not attempt to manifest yourself or make yourself known to your Ancestors or manipulate them in any way. Remember that in this exercise you are an observer. You are observing an energetic "echo" of lives that once were.

1. Lie down and find a comfortable position. Close your eyes and

relax as much as possible. Take a few deep breaths and release the tension in your body.

2. Visualize an energetic cord extending from your navel chakra. As it implies, this is the energetic center just below your navel. I see this cord as a blood red (blood/Ancestors), but you may see this cord as any color that feels appropriate. Know that this cord is of your blood and DNA and leads back to your Ancestors. You may also see the cord coming from the heart chakra if this works better for you. Bring your conscious awareness to the chord. From your point of view, the chord looks like a great tunnel that leads to your Ancestors.

3. Travel up this cord with your mind to your father. It does not matter if they are living or dead. You may use this technique in either case. See life through his eyes. When you are ready, come back to your body.

4. Travel up this cord with your mind to your mother. See her life through her eyes.

5. Now, pick either your mother or father and travel up the cord to your grandmother or grandfather. It doesn't matter which one. Just pick one at a time and experience his or her life through his or her eyes.

6. You may use your family tree to see what it was like to live in the world and time of that Ancestor. You do not need to know the names of your Ancestors in order to travel back and observe.

With this technique you will have a better understanding of what happened in the lives of your Ancestors and the feelings and energies surrounding them. When we have empathy for our Ancestors, we will

have a stronger emotional bond with them. This bond will make your magick and Ancestor work rewarding.

Traveling to the Ancestors to Release Ancestral Patterns

This technique is similar to the previous technique, but this time your intent is to find ancestral patterns that are affecting your life. These may be mental, emotional, spiritual, or physical patterns and ailments.

1. Lie down and find a comfortable position. Close your eyes and relax as much as possible. Take a few deep breaths and release the tension in your body.

2. Visualize an energetic cord coming from your navel chakra. I see this cord as blood red (blood/Ancestors), but you may see this cord as any color that feels appropriate. Know that this cord is of your blood and DNA and leads back to your Ancestors.

3. Call upon your Spirit Animal and Ancestral Teacher. Ask them to journey with you and guide you to the Ancestor and the point in their life that caused the negative ancestral patterns.

4. With your Spirit Animal and Ancestral Teacher, travel forth into the Ancestral cord. Set the intent of finding the negative ancestral patterns. Use your intuition to decide if it stems from your father's side or mother's side. Then use your intuition again to decide if it's on your grandmother's side or grandfather's side, and so forth.

5. Many times, you will only have to go back a few generations, but at times you may have to travel back several generations. Use the guidance and advice of your Ancestral Teacher. If you are stumped and do not know which Ancestor to try, then you must try everyone! This can be time-consuming, but you will learn about your

family history and have a better understanding of your lineage.

6. Once you discover which Ancestor and event caused the negative pattern, it is at this point that you call upon your patron god and/or goddess to aid you in healing the energetic cord and the Ancestor. In the case of hate and jealousy, for instance, ask the gods to help your Ancestor to ease their pain. You may help them further by using basic energy work. You can do this by visualizing the negative pattern, emotion, or event turning into light and evaporating away from your cord and into the cosmos to be transmuted into something more constructive.

Make sure you are sending healing energy to the Ancestral cord and the Ancestors it directly pertains to. See this healing energy flow down into the Ancestral cord healing their offspring and then the next generation and then next until it comes to you.

NOTE: The perspective of the person and the events taking place may vary. You may be watching it like a play or movie; you could see it from a bird's eye view, or you may experience it from one of your Ancestors' point of view.

Family Karma

There may be family karma that has been carried down from generation to generation to you. You may have heard the rumors of the curses of the Kennedy family and the House of Windsor. Sometimes the actions of our Ancestors have created an energy rift or echo that travels down to us. Not all family karma has to do with devastation, murder, and chaos. It can be something more along the lines of angering a spirit or god. It could also be a lesson that your Ancestors must understand before they can evolve to the next level of their development.

You may use the above technique to find the karma on your ancestral line. Once you find it, you must ask the gods, Ancestors, and teachers you are working with what needs to be done on this plane and this time to rectify the situation. It may be as easy as giving offerings and prayers to a god or spirit. But it may be more difficult, and you may not be able to resolve the situation completely in this lifetime. Then again, you may. The best thing to do is listen to your gods, Ancestors, and spirits. They would never ask you to do anything dangerous and foolish. They will never tell you to kill yourself, or give away all your Earthly possessions, or do something illegal. If a spirit mentions this, you must banish them immediately without hesitation. Ask your Ancestors on your altar to help you do this.

If you agree to the advice the gods and Ancestors give you, then you must carry it out. If it is a donation to an organization then do it. If it is prayers and offerings to a spirit or god, then do it! It may take weeks or even years to heal the karma, but it must be done. If not by you, then the next generation of your magical lineage.

Performing Tasks for Ancestors

While working with the Ancestors, there may be times when they ask you to do tasks for them. It is completely up to you if this is something you would like to do to strengthen your bond with them. It is not a good idea to promise them something without hearing what it is they would like you to do first. Most of the time they will ask you to tell them how your family is doing. Yes, they can find out for themselves, but remember that your Ancestors love to sit and talk about Aunt So-and-So or gossip about Great Great Uncle So-and-So. Don't forget the tea and cookies when you do this! They may also ask for a favorite food or drink. There is no harm in this, and it will be a lovely treat for them if you do so. There

may be times when they ask you to perform a task that is more difficult. For example, they may ask you to perform a task like obtain mementoes or pictures from their life. For some this is easy, for others it can be more of a challenge. Other times, they may ask you to obtain some object or do something that is virtually impossible, such as find the vase they once owned in 1754. Remember, time in the Underworld is different so they may have a hard time understanding that their vase has long since been destroyed. When something like this happens, explain the situation to the best of your ability.

Magick with Ancestors

Once you have a strong working relationship with your Ancestors you can ask for their aid in various types of magick. In the beginning of your relationship with your Ancestors you will need to build up their energy and trust. Unless the Ancestors you are working with on your altar are pagan or magical in some way, it will take a little bit of time before they are ready to work magick with you. Most likely, your Ancestors had little direct contact with the physical plane for some time. They may have observed you and your family, but that was probably the extent of it. Now, you are going to work with them in a very direct and powerful way. It will take time for you to build up their energy for them to influence the physical plane. The best way to do this is to continue to say your prayers to them, give them water every day, and offerings of food when you think it appropriate—such as holidays, sabbats, birthdays, and deathdays.

You will also want to increase their magical knowledge. You could teach them energy work and magick just as you would any student, but I prefer to let them learn at their own pace and in their own time. We do not honor the Ancestors because we want them to do things for us. We honor them because it shows them love and it strengthens our energetic

ties to our past, present, and future. When they are strong enough to influence the physical world, it is just an added bonus. When you are meditating, working with the gods, or doing magick of any kind, invite the Ancestors into your ritual space and ask them to observe. They have the ability to see the ebb and flows of the energies that you are using better than you can. They will be able to see the matrix of how it works and why, so do not be surprised if they learn very quickly. Every little or large work of magick I do or any healing I do, I invite the Ancestors into my ritual space. I also answer any questions they might have. If you have an Ancestor that is angry that you are doing "witchcraft" explain to them the mechanics of energy work and magick and why you do what you do. If they still protest take them off the Ancestral altar. I have had colleagues that did this, and the Ancestor suddenly became more tolerant and open-minded once they found out they were not getting any more offerings.

When you notice that your Ancestors are more visible during rituals you may see that they are helping with healings, giving your spells energy, and helping you open portals and gates to the three worlds. Do not force them to do this or get upset if they are not learning as quickly as you would like. Let them go at their own pace. Just as any student of energy work and magick has strengths and weaknesses, so will your Ancestors. Some may enjoy divination with tarot and runes, whereas the rest may not. Some Ancestors may enjoy spell casting and ceremonial magick, and there are some Ancestors who may simply lend energy to whatever task you are doing. All these things are powerful blessings. Having your Ancestors present in ritual space is a special gift.

Eventually, your Ancestors will get to a place where you can petition them for magical work or aid. Almost all pagan and tribal cultures in history have practiced Ancestor petitioning. The thought here is that because our Ancestors have an invested interest in our wellbeing and

happiness, they will do whatever is in their power and ability to help us, even more so than the gods. Ancestor petitioning is simply asking the Ancestors to help you obtain or accomplish something. Often, the Ancestors will be proficient in giving you advice whether you want it or not. But when they obtain skill and magical power, they are able to influence the physical world from the Underworld. To petition your Ancestors, light a candle on your ancestral altar and say a prayer for them. Then, place your hands on the altar and tell them of your day and what is going on. Next, explain the situation that you would like their help with and explain to them what you would like the outcome to be. When you are finished, give them offerings of water and food. Keep in mind that the Ancestors have the ability to see into the future better than you can. If your desired goal will cause you spiritual, emotional, or physical harm they most likely will not help you in that desire. This is not to say they will hinder any magick you may do for it, but they will not help their loved one cause themselves any harm.

Working with your Ancestors in magick is such a wonderful blessing. My rituals do not feel whole, balanced, and grounded until I call my Ancestors into the space. I truly feel your magick will feel more powerful and inspiring with their presence.

Calling Ancestors in Ritual

The Ancestors are a part of my everyday life. Not only do I light the candle on their altar and speak with them, but I also invite them to be with me in my everyday life. I may not always see them, but I know that they are there. They are my spirit guides in the truest sense of the word. We have talked about how the Ancestors have a vested interest in you because you are their blood and their future. They want you to succeed and become more evolved spiritually. The bond between you and your

Ancestors is strong and will remain as such for all eternity. I have found that asking your Ancestors to attend and aid you in ritual and magick is immensely powerful. Ancient pagans made it part of their spiritual practice to call upon the Ancestors. Native American, African tribal religions, Celtic, Hindu, and many other religions call upon the Ancestors in ritual.

As we have discussed, not all our Ancestors may have been magical when they were alive. However, they can learn magick easily since they no longer have a physical body and are able to see the energies at work in the Underworld. They can see the comings and goings of time and space and can see how magick and energy work are able to manifest in all the worlds. When first working with the Ancestors, you may find that they may have their own fears and prejudices of magick and may not understand why you are working with such energies. How I taught my Ancestors about magick was to invite them to observe my daily magical practices, prayers, and energy work. I did not force or even ask them to do any magick at first, but simply invited them into the ritual space to observe.

The Ancestors love it when you light your altar candle, pray for them, fill their bowls with water, and invite them to watch the different aspects of your life. They feel included in your life and a part of the family again. Remember, you may be the only living family member who speaks and works with them directly, so they will be naturally curious about your daily comings and goings. To begin with, I invited them to watch the daily practice of my energy work which included techniques from the Kabbalistic Lesser Banishing Ritual of the Pentagram. My grandfather, who grew up Jewish, recognized the names of God and found that ritual particularly interesting. My Ancestors seemed to be very fond of the energy healing work I did. After a couple of years of observation, learning magick through me, and their own spiritual evolution, they began to learn how to contribute to my magick in their own way. At

first it was only a little bit, but after a time, it became more and more profound and powerful. The Ancestors have a great amount of access to the magick and energies from the Underworld and it can be used for powerful ends.

I never ever force my Ancestors or the dead in general to aid me in magick. I feel that this is completely unethical and an abuse of power. You would not like spirits forcing you to help them if you did not want to, so you should give them the same courtesy. Most of the time, the Ancestors will want to help you in your magick, so forcing them to do so is not necessary. So, what if they decide they do not want to help you in ritual and magick for whatever reason? If this turns out to be the case, then you should still honor them on your altar as members of your Ancestral family. You should let them know that you will be seeking out another Ancestor who is willing to work magick with you. If they are upset, then perhaps you need to have a conversation with them about remaining on the ancestral altar. Magick, ritual, and energy work is a part of your life, and you should never change your ideals and beliefs because your family, living or dead, wants you to.

The most powerful and spiritual magick you can do is through the Ancestors. They can help you do many things such as divination and helping you influence your fate. Above all, they are your family in spirit. They care for you even more than the gods do. You are everything they worked for during their life. You are the fruit of their labors and hard work. Even though they can become powerful spiritual allies, they are still flawed. Even though they are in spirit, they are still human. It is true that over time they will evolve spiritually, but they will still make mistakes and defiantly have their own opinion. My grandparents on my father's side are on my Ancestral Altar. My grandmother will ask me many questions about my life and the lives of my brothers—and have an opinion

about it. She will often protest when I make a choice she does not like. She will tell me stories beginning with, "In my day..." At first, I would look at this like a cute things grandma says. Now, I see it as wisdom beyond the ages wrapped up in a tiny German lady who was able to take care of her family and teach her son how to take care of his and so forth. This is magick. This is why we light our candles.

4
Necromancy

Baldur's Dreams (Norse)

Baldur, the Norse god of beauty, wisdom, and light, began to have horrible dreams of shadows, skulls, and death. He dreamed of dark things in the night that were threatening him. He dreamed of monsters that told him stories of the darkness. The blackest darkness seemed to cover him. He dreamed that all would be lost and that he would die. Odin was told of these horrible dreams. He feared that perhaps his beautiful son, the blameless one, the most bright, dreamed of the future. Odin wasted no time. He mounted his eight-legged horse, Sleipnir, and traveled down to Hel. It is there he would find his answers.

In Hel, he rode over the dark bridge that led to the gates of the dead and past the dreaded hellhound that guarded the way. Odin's son was in danger. He must act quickly! As he rode, he noticed that the Realm of the Dead was decorated in gold. It seemed they were expecting someone of great importance. At the eastern gates of Hel, Odin found the burial mound of a great seeress. The All-Father used his magical charms and summoned her from her grave. The seeress was forced to obey the magick. She appeared before Odin.

Odin asked the seeress why Helheim was decorated in gold. The seeress was unhappy about being summoned from her grave. She explained to the Great God that Baldur would be taken down to the depths of Hel. She wanted desperately to return to her slumber. With magick, Odin forced her to stay. The desperate father of Baldur wanted only to save his son. The seeress told him that his own son, the blind Hod, would kill Baldur. Odin further questioned her about who would avenge his son's

death and how the tragedy would come to pass. The seeress spoke of oaths of brothers who avenged their siblings and women who howled during the time of the mourning of Baldur. She then returned to her grave with the strange warning that she would never return again until Loki escaped from his bonds.

Necromancy

Necromancy is an ancient magical art of summoning the dead and working with them for a variety of reasons. Originally, Necromancy was a means of divining the future. Necromancy means divination of the dead. *Necro* means "dead" and *mancy* means "divination". During the Middle Ages and the Christian uprising, to use magick was considered evil and to summon the dead was even worse. The clerics taught that the magician was not calling the dead, they were really calling demons from hell. *Necromancer* came to be a common name for an evil witch or dark magician. We know through researching ancient cultures that this is not the case. Necromancy is a way that magicians could work with the dead and the Ancestors in a profound spiritual way.

As we remember, communion with the dead goes back to when the Shamans sought their help for the tribal community. The dead were the respected Ancestors of the tribe who wanted to aid the living. The honored dead protected the tribe from evil spirits, gave advice to the leaders, and divined the future for the tribe. The Ancestors were consulted to foretell of the winters to come, enemies that were planning attacks, and where to find food. Summoning the dead was important to the survival of the tribe. As the tribes progressed into cities, the use of the Ancestors progressed as well. The Shaman summoning the dead for the tribe became the magician summoning the dead for political reasons and even for the common person seeking the aide of the spirits.

Reasons for Summoning the Dead

Working with the dead was a very sacred and spiritual act. The Necromancers who specialized in this art knew to treat the dead with great respect, and they only utilized this art so when it was thought necessary. There were many reasons to summon the dead. One of the most common reasons was to get advice from the spirit in question. It was thought that the spirits of the dead could see things that the living could not. They also retained the talents and wisdom that they once had in life. Therefore, it was common practice to go to the burial place of a king to get advice on matters of the kingdom and the land. You could also summon the spirit of a poet or bard to gain understanding of song and lyric. Another reason the dead were summoned was to gain power from the Underworld. As we have seen, there is much wisdom and magical treasure to be found in the Underworld. The dead had the ability to help you find these places of power. Also, the dead were summoned for works of divination. Just as stated before, the dead could see things come to be in the Underworld before they manifested in the physical world. They had firsthand knowledge concerning things that were soon to come.

Sacred Places

To summon the dead, the magician or necromancer needed to find those sacred places that were gateways or entrances into the Realm of the Dead. Entrances and gateways were places or objects that became a catalyst for the dead to manifest, or a part of this world that seemed to blend into the Underworld. The most common places to summon the dead were graves and gravestones. Some believed that a part of the soul remained near the body after death and could easily be summoned there. Others believed that the grave or bones of the dead acted as a "doorway" to the Underworld. I personally have found that the grave/bones of the

dead act as a signature or magical DNA. Meaning that the DNA of someone never changes and can act as the magical "phone number" to get into contact with that person. If we take a look at how our DNA works, it is the building blocks of our human bodies and ancestral lineage. Even though we share our DNA with our ancestors, part of our DNA is uniquely ours. No one on earth or the spirit worlds has DNA exactly like ours. Even DNA between twins is somewhat different. Because of this the bones and remnants of our bodies can be used to "tune" into us after death.

Lakes were thought to be entrances into the Underworld much like the sea. The lakes seemed to go deep under the Earth and to the ancients it made sense that the lake led to the Realm of the Dead. Burrows in the ground were thought to have a similar function. I often think of *Alice in Wonderland* and how the rabbit hole led to a magical land. Mounds were thought to be the Underworld rising up to greet this world. Sometimes these mounds are referred to as "Faerie Mounds." I have often been asked if Faerie Mounds and Burial mounds are one and the same. I think the answer can be yes and no. I believe that natural hills or mounds are an access port to the Underworld. They do not necessarily have to take you to the land of the dead, but they certainly can. Remember, the Underworld has its own laws and rules and as soon as we think we have figured it out we learn quickly that there is always more to learn. Then there are forests that are dark and very ancient. Of course, this would be a perfect place to summon the dead because of the feeling of darkness and death that might be nearby. The darkness of the forest was very foreboding to the ancient people who believed that monsters lurked deep within. Danger could be lurking all about in the form of wild animals, thieves, and murderers. It was also secluded; and necromancers knew that most people

would stay far from the dreaded dark forest because of the very thing they were about to do.

Sacred Times

Magical timing was also important to Necromancers. There were certain times of the month and year that were better suited for the practice of calling up the dead. The phases of the moon, sun, and stars could amplify the power needed for summoning. The dark and full moon were ideal for this purpose. Each had a special advantage over the other. The full moon has a powerful effect on magick. The energy emitted by the full moon helps the spirits to become more visible to the magician. During this time of the month, it was common to summon the dead for wisdom, advice, and power. The dark moon has its secrets as well. During this time, works of a darker nature were undertaken, such as binding spirits, divination, and summoning spirits to attack enemies.

There were certain times of the year that were especially powerful for calling forth the dead. The Celtic Fire Festival of Samhain, which happens around November 1, is thought to be the most powerful time of year for spirit work. Samhain is the Celtic holy day that begins the dark half of the year on or around October 31 in the modern calendar. At this time of year, the weather turns cold and the last of the crops is harvested. The Celts could see the power of decay and death all around them. The winds howled and the land around them seemed to die. Naturally, they thought that if the land was dying then it was turning into a sort of "land of the dead" and it would be easier to call upon the dead for works of magick.

Another powerful time was Yule. This holiday comes from the Nordic peoples and is another name for the time around the Winter Solstice, December 21. Traditionally, the Celts did not celebrate the solstices and

equinoxes, only the events that fell in-between these days. It was not until much later that the solstices and equinoxes were observed. Nevertheless, to the Northern European people this was a powerful time for calling the dead. Yule is the longest night of the year. The world around these ancient people was barren and most likely frozen over. The Land of the Dead was truly upon them, and the dead could surely be found in the woods or in some forbidding corner of the landscape. The energy was perfect for calling forth the dead.

Cemeteries

To me, cemeteries have always had a holy and sacred feel to them, as well as a sense of Otherworldliness. When we visit cemeteries during the day, the grounds feel like they are holy and protected by higher spirits. However, after dark, cemeteries may have a strange and sometimes foreboding energy to them. This is not because the spirits are most active at night. The spirits are active all the time, we are just aware of them mostly at night. During the day, the sun emits a very large amount of ion into the atmosphere. This solar energy can drown out the spirits astral and spiritual bodies. At night, we are able to see and feel the spirits more clearly because the moon only emits a small amount of ion and the spirits can be easily seen. This is not to say that you cannot see spirits during the day. You certainly can. It just takes more psychic ability to do so. The grounds, themselves, are usually blessed by a local priest or rabbi so that no lower energetic beings will bother the spirits that are laid to rest there. Cemeteries were first built for several reasons. One reason was to keep the dead bodies away from the living. When a corpse is decomposing, it releases toxins into the ground. Those toxins can sometimes make their way into the drinking water of nearby people. Another reason was to keep the

dead bodies close to the church or temple so that they would be spiritually safeguarded from negative spirits and from grave robbers.

Some belief systems say that the spirits of the dead stayed close by their graves and that a necromancer could easily summon a spirit by going to their grave. One reason for this is because to effectively summon the dead, you need to know their name. In modern times, the name of the deceased is often placed upon the grave marker. Another reason is that when the necromancer is close to the remains of the deceased it is easier to summon the spirit because there is an energetic imprint on the remains that link them to the spirit. In my belief, a spirit does not actually remain in the graveyard unless it chooses to. But when summoned, the grave acts as a portal that can easily summon the spirit back to its remains.

There are several stories and legends about the ghosts of the dead that haunt graveyards for a myriad of reasons. One can pick up any horror novel or movie and find such a story. The spirits of the dead have other business to attend to and do not "haunt" graveyards unless there is a particularly good reason.

Cemeteries do a have a spirit Gatekeeper. The Gatekeeper is a spirit that can be found close by the actual gate of the cemetery or sometimes in the very center of it. The duty of the Gatekeeper is to keep away unwanted energies, people, and spirits who wish to harm or desecrate the graves in some way. When a magician wishes to work with the spirits in the cemetery it is wise to ask the permission of the Gatekeeper. To do this, you simply use your intuition to find the Gatekeeper. They can be found in a statue, a tree, or some other object. Then you can ask for their permission to allow you to do your work. The Gatekeeper may or may not speak to you directly. Gatekeepers vibrate on a higher level and do not always speak in the ways we are used to. I allow my intuition to guide me. When asking the Gatekeeper's permission, you will feel if it is correct

to go further with your work. If it feels correct, continue. If not, pay your respects to the Gatekeeper and try again another day. There may be several reasons why the Gatekeeper barred your way into the Cemetery. Perhaps there are several people visiting relatives that day and they would disturb your work. Or perhaps the spirits are unwilling to be bothered. Know that the Gatekeeper has the best interest of the spirits in the cemetery and will always be looking out for them. You do not always know what is happening energetically in the cemetery and you must trust that the Gatekeeper knows what is best.

When I am in the cemetery, the ground feels sacred and magical. It literally feels like I am in a sanctuary. However, you may find that if you dig up a little dirt and take it beyond the borders of the cemetery, the energy of the dirt changes. It may seem to become infused with the energy of death and decay. There are several Hoodoo spells that require graveyard dirt for magick and cursing. Some of those spells are intended to harm and even kill its target. I have to laugh when I see graveyard dirt "substitute." There is no such thing. Graveyard dirt is graveyard dirt and there is no substitute. It just does not exist. If you choose to dig up graveyard dirt in the cemetery, you must remember a couple of rules: First, ask the spirits before you go digging up their sanctuary. To do so without permission is very disrespectful and you may get an energetic slap in the face. I would not chance that. Second, leave money or coins where you dig up the dirt. Believe it or not, the dead do like money. Remember, the ferryman Charon requires payment before he will carry the spirits of the dead across the river Styx. There are other rules, each according to the custom of the religious beliefs of the dead and that of the magician. Just because you do not know the customs does not mean that the spirits will not hold you accountable.

When working rituals and magick in the cemetery there is also a

chance that spirits will follow you home. I have heard of magicians that say that you must walk backwards out of a cemetery and all the way home so that a spirit will not follow you back. If you live several miles from a graveyard then this will be tricky indeed. I do not personally feel that this is necessary. If you pay respects to the Gatekeeper going in and out of the cemetery and are respectful to the sanctuary and the spirits within, you should be fine. However, sometimes a spirit may still follow you out. When this happens, there are a couple of choices. You may ask the spirit what it wants from you and decide if you are able and willing to help it. You could banish the spirit. You could also put the spirit back into the graveyard and allow the Gatekeeper to take care of it. Sometimes the spirit will attach itself to you with an energetic cord or simply latch on to you. If that is the case, I see no harm in coming to an agreement with the spirit. It may ask for offerings of food and water to aid you. It may need your assistance with a task. Ask the spirit what the task is and decide if you are able and willing to perform the task. If you are able to perform the task and you agree to it make sure you do what the spirit asks in a reasonable amount of time, otherwise the spirit may become upset and cause havoc in your home. It is best to negotiate the timeframe with the spirit at the moment you make this contract. If you cannot help the spirit for whatever reason, then explain this to the spirit and ask your gods and Ancestors to help the spirit find a magician who can.

If the spirit is hostile to you and your home and will not leave, then you must banish it. There are several ways to banish a sprit, and these will be discussed later in this book.

Mausoleums

When you tour a cemetery, you may find two types of mausoleums. One type of mausoleums are the small structures that house caskets. It can

house a single casket, or it can house a whole family of caskets. They come in a variety of shapes and sizes. I am sure they were inspired by the Egyptian pyramids and the Northern European grave mounds. The purpose of mausoleums, in a mundane sense, is for the family of the deceased to be able to visit the caskets above ground. In large cemeteries, you may find many mausoleums in a variety of styles. The more lavish mausoleums usually belong to well-to-do families.

The magician can use the mausoleums as portals into different times and dimensions. It is a useful magical technique that the advanced magician can utilize during his work with the Ancestors and the dead. I have been transported back in time to whence the mausoleums were created or to when that family was alive and well. Very rarely will you come across a mausoleum that was specifically designed and created for magick. It happens seldom, but it does happen. Living in Chicago, I have been fortunate enough to come across such mausoleums several times. The best way to find these special portals is, of course, energetically. They seem to hum with an energy that is waiting to be used for magick. Another way to tell if the mausoleum was intended for magick is to look at the design of the structure. You may find magical symbols engraved on the structure and statues of gods, goddesses, spirits, and other magical beings. If you find such a mausoleum count yourself lucky. A magician may use any mausoleum for magick; however, some are energetically stronger than others.

To use the mausoleum for magick you must first speak with the spirits on the inside of the mausoleum. There may be a family guardian spirit around the entrance. If so, remember to state who you are and what your intentions are with the mausoleum and the spirits who dwell inside. The guardian of the mausoleum will be able to tell from your energy if you mean well or not. If the guardian spirit accepts your

intentions, there are a couple of options you may have to work with the structure. You may touch the door of the mausoleum and astrally project yourself going through the door. The door may be a portal in itself or you may simply go inside. If you do not wish to physically place your hands on the door you do not have to. I find that it provides a stronger connection. However, some magicians feel that by touching the mausoleum they are invading the space of the family of spirits inside. I personally feel that if you clearly explain your intentions to the guardian spirit and you have permission to use the structure as a portal, then you also have permission to touch the building. Once you are astrally inside the mausoleum, you may see other portals and doors to other places. Feel free to explore them all. They may take you to different times and dimensions or ever alternate universes. All these can provide you with opportunities to learn and grow spiritually.

If a family guardian does not give you permission to be inside, respect the wishes of the family and find another mausoleum. Never magically force your way in. Doing so will not only upset the family, but the cemetery's Gatekeeper may bar your way inside the next time you come to the graveyard.

There are also large mausoleums that can be the size of a small public works building, like a school. They can have many floors and wings and may house hundreds of caskets. This is essentially a necropolis, or a city of the dead. If you take the time to search through these structures, you may find many old sections that have been long forgotten. I will often see spirits roaming the hallways visiting other people. It is quite a strange locale, but a wonderful place to do spirit work. These large mausoleums have a different energy than the private family ones. The larger ones feel like a city or great temple. It is easy to imagine that the

great halls of the Underworld gods and goddesses must feel quite similar to this.

Tombs and Mounds

Ancient peoples honored the land in such a way that it was very much alive to them. The land is what gave them their food, homes, and everything necessary for survival. The Earth was sacred to them, and it was held in the highest holiness. To people who honored the land as sacred, such as the Celts, the land and the king were one. What happened to one would happen to the other. The king, other royalty, and heroes would be placed in a sacred tomb or burial mound. These became very sacred places over time. They were not places to be frightened of, but places of holiness and spirit.

If we remember, to those people who honored the land in this way, the spirits of the dead were near to and became part of the land. It was common practice to go to the mounds or tombs to seek guidance and wisdom from the spirit of the person buried there. Necromancers would go to these places to seek out the wisdom of the dead spirit's particular profession. If the current king wanted advice about the land or a better way to rule the kingdom, he might go to the mound and petition spirits of former kings for guidance. This was done by sleeping on the mound or in the tomb or by bringing a priest or magician to summon the spirit. By sleeping on a mound, you allowed the spirit who rested within to enter your dreams. Dreams are a gateway into the world of the dead and one of the easiest ways to commune with spirits.

The spirits of kings and warriors had the ability to join with the land after death and become a spirit guardian. The function of a spirit guardian was to protect the land from invaders, aid as oracles, and keep the energies of the land healthy for vegetation. When builders try to tear down some

forests and sacred lands, they have sometimes found that their machines have broken down without any explanation. At other times, if a building is built it will have many weaknesses in the structure and may collapse. This is the guardian of that land trying to keep intruders out of the sacred place. There is the tale of the British war chief Vortigern who tried to build a castle, but the castle would not stand and kept tumbling down. Time and time again, Vortigern tried to build the castle and time and time again the castle collapsed. Merlin was called in to do magick to keep the castle standing. When Merlin took a closer look at the land, he found that two dragons, one red and one white, were fighting beneath the Earth and would not allow any structure to stand in that location. When working magically with the land, or simply wanting to build something, it is always best to get the permission of the guardian spirit. Otherwise, you may face many challenges with your endeavor.

It was common to leave offerings in graveyards or the sacred lands of the dead. The bones and remains of the dead were thought to be a powerful link to the Ancestors. The belief was that if one had human bones, one had power over that person. Offerings to the dead included food, wine, honey, blood (both human and animal), material gifts (especially jewelry and other valuables), and flowers.

Graveyard Meditation

One of the best and easiest ways to learn to work with the dead is to contact them at their graves. There are many stories and legends about people going to the cemeteries and grave mounds of kings, heroes, witches, and poets to learn a certain skill or simply to gain advice from that person. Necromancers would also go to graves to summon a spirit to the physical plane, sometimes forcibly. Our purpose here is not to learn how to force

a spirit to do something against its will, but rather to learn how to communicate with the spirits of the dead in a very direct way.

If you can find the grave of a teacher within your own profession or the grave of a trusted magician, that would be ideal. Most of the time, however, I ask my Ancestors to guide me to the grave of a spirit that would benefit both of us for this type of work. Sometimes I may see one of my Ancestors walking towards a grave. Other times, I may be "pulled" or "guided" to a grave. Make sure to bring an offering. The most common offerings I use are:

1. Juice
2. Food (bread, cookies, fruit, honey, milk)
3. Coins (silver dollars work well. I usually leave at least two or three)
4. Flowers
5. Water

It is not a good idea to give spirits you are not familiar with alcohol. Alcohol may be too intoxicating for the spirit, and you basically are being introduced to a new spirit who's drunk. Also, we need to keep in mind the spirit's ethics have not changed much since they were alive. If they had a religious taboo against alcohol, then you may be violating their religious beliefs and the spirit may find it disrespectful.

In Greco-Roman necromancy, it is common for magicians to use blood and meat to give the spirit enough energy to manifest and speak with the living. For our purposes here we are giving a token of goodwill and will be visiting the spirit in the astral world and do not need for them to manifest physically. For this meditation, you may go to the graveyard during the day, but if you have access to a graveyard at night, then all the better.

1. Ask your Ancestors to guide you to a grave of someone from

whom both of you can benefit. If you have not found your Ancestors yet, then use your intuition and ask your healing helpers and
guides to guide you.

2. Once you have found a grave, take a moment to sense the area.
    How does it feel? Is it comforting and welcoming? Does it feel as
    if there is an important task at hand? Does it feel dangerous?

    NOTE: If it feels dangerous and yet your Ancestors and guides
    want you to work with this spirit, there could be an important
    reason. If you are beginner, find another grave and come back to it
    after you have spoken to your Ancestors and guides at some length
    about what is happening. If you are experienced in necromancy
    and spirit work, then do the meditation and see what you can do –
    it may be that the Ancestors wish you to help the spirit for some
    reason. Do, however, make sure that said reason is congruent with
    your own ethics.

3. Look at the gravestone and find the name, birth, and death dates
    of the person. Begin to focus on them. The name of the person
    acts as an astral beacon and you will be able to call upon the person
    with just their name.

4. Leave your offering on or near the grave. Try to be as respectful to
    the grounds as possible. Cemetery keepers do not like it if they
    perceive that you are leaving "junk" on someone's grave. One of
    the advantages of liquid, such as milk, honey, or water, is that it is
    absorbed by the Earth and does not leave anything behind.

5. Sit comfortably on the grave in a meditation posture. Close your
    eyes and focus on your breathing. Clear your mind of your daily
    routine and focus on the work at hand.

6. Call out to the spirit of the grave. Ask the spirit if they are willing to meet with you.

7. Begin to imagine yourself seeing the spirit of the grave come to you. How do they look? What clothes are they wearing? Do they look like what you thought they would, or are they different from what you expected?

8. At this point, introduce yourself and ask them questions. You may ask them about their life and what it is like in the afterlife. You may ask them about their profession in life. You may also ask them why your Ancestors chose them. Is there a message the spirit has for you?

9. The spirit may tell you some fascinating things or they may tell you things that are quite ordinary. If they ask you for your help in any way, decide if you are able and willing to aid them in their request. If you can, then great. If not, be polite and explain to them why you cannot help them at this time. If you like, and feel it is appropriate, ask the spirit if it would like to speak with you again. At the end of the conversation, thank the spirit for their time and open your eyes.

10. When you get back home again, make sure you eat, drink, and do things that bring you out of trance and will help you ground.

The Hidden Company

The Hidden Company is a term we use in Traditional Witchcraft. Traditional Witchcraft is Witchcraft that predates modern Wicca and Neo-Paganism. It is said to come from a magical tradition that stretches back to at least the 17th Century and perhaps longer. This kind of magick was more community-based. The witches included in this grouping were the

Wise Women and Cunning Men, Toad Men, Hedge Crafters, and some Shapeshifters. These people practiced in secret to not alert the local authorities of the local town or village. Contrary to the documentation of that era, the townspeople did not always fear these men and women. Western medicine was a far cry from what is today. With little knowledge of surgery and medicine, people often died while in a doctor's care. The townspeople were sometimes poor and could not afford a doctor. The local Hedge Witch or Cunning Man was wise in herb craft, potions, ointments, and magick. At the time they did not call themselves witches. In fact, most of these wise ones were Christian and felt that they were doing the Lord's work by performing healings and magick for the village. To call them a witch was considered an insult, which could bring up charges of heresy against them.

Along with healing, the Traditional Witch also worked with the dead. They had no fear of the dead and often sought out their counsel on a wide variety of subjects. A lot of the old Pagan beliefs were still held by the villagers. There were many rituals for good crops and blessings that would keep good spirits close and malicious spirits far away. To Traditional Witches, the Ancestors were still a part of the greater community. They believed that upon death, the Ancestors stayed with the land.

The Hidden Company were those Ancestors who were witches, healers, and magical people. If you belonged to a group or coven then you had a spiritual lineage to these magical Ancestors. Also, if your family Ancestors were magical then you had lineage through bloodlines. If a witch needed assistance, then they could summon the Hidden Company in ritual. The spirits of witches long gone would come to the ritual space and commune with the living. The Hidden Company were powerful and wise and could help the summoners with spiritual knowledge, wisdom, and magick. They could also aid them in prophecy. One only conjured

the Hidden Company when one truly needed their counsel. Today, the Hidden Company are still conjured by Traditional Witches. The Hidden Company are powerful allies to have.

If you belong to an older magical order or coven, then you may conjure the Hidden Company of your group. When treated with the utmost respect, they can help you with your spiritual journey and magick. If you do not belong to a magical order or coven or your group is young, then you may ask to speak to the Hidden Company in general. These would be the spirits of witches and magicians who are willing to aide you in magick even though you do not belong to their magical lineage. These spirits have the ability to add potency to your magick. However, they will only give what is needed and only if they deem you worthy of their influence. I personally never conjure the Ancestors with the intention that they must aid in magick. When they do so it is a benefit and never a requirement. When they lend their powers to you it is a blessing indeed.

The Rose Castle

The Rose Castle is a magical sanctuary for the dead that lies somewhere between the physical plane and the Underworld. It is a place to await the Goddess of Death to take you to the realm of the Ancestors. There is great power and magick in the rose. In magical herb books, the rose is commonly associated with love and sex, but it is much more than that. The rose is an ancient symbol of life, desire, sex, blood, and death. If we allow ourselves to look into the mystery of the rose, we will discover its deeper meanings. Red is the color of birth, life, death, and rebirth. We are born from our mothers covered in blood. This is not something to be disgusted by it is natural and part of the birthing process. The blood that courses through our veins gives us life. Red is also the color of desire and of lust. It is sex that allows the rebirthing process of the future souls

to be reborn. Red is also the color of the blood that leaves us at death. Without the magick of blood we die and begin our journey to the Rose Castle.

The Rose Castle was created from desire itself. The realms of the Underworld are created from our dreams and beliefs. The resting place of the Ancestors appears as it does because those who exist there wish it to be so. That is why for the Greco-Romans it appears as Elysium, to the Norse it is Valhalla for warriors and Hel for those not slain in battle, and to the Welsh it is Annwn. For those who follow the path of Traditional Witchcraft there is the Rose Castle. The Rose Castle is a four-walled castle that can be seen when the sun sets over the western seas. During the in-between time of twilight, when the fire of the sun meets the waters of the sea the Rose Castle can be seen.

When the Traditional Witch dies, their spirit is taken to the Rose Castle by a boat or ferryman similar to Charon. Once there, the deceased sees a deserted island with no life. It is barren. There is nothing but the castle itself. This is to keep those away who do not belong here, or perhaps to a spirit whose final resting place is beyond the Island of the Rose Castle. Before the deceased enters the castle, they must have the desire to be with the Goddess. It is desire that created the magick of the castle and it is desire to be with the Goddess of Death that awakens its magick. It is then that the island comes to life, blooming with roses of the afterlife that surround the castle.

The castle is the resting place of the deceased Traditional Witch. It is a place of magick and mystery. The Hidden Company of the witches may be found there. Above all it is the residence of the beautiful and mysterious Goddess of Death. In Traditional Craft she is known as Hulda, Diana, Hecate, Innana, and many other names. She is beautiful and terrible.

She is the magick at the end of desire and the Mother of the Dead who takes us to our place beyond the waves.

Ritual of the Rose Castle

This ritual can be used to meditate upon the Rose Castle and learn about the mysteries, the Goddess of Death, and the Hidden Company. It can also be used to summon the spirits or the goddess to your physical temple.

Items needed

1. A skull. This can be crafted from clay, wood, or ceramic if you do not possess a human skull.

2. 3, 6, or 9 roses

3. Red String, yarn, or chord

4. Four white candles

Place the skull in the center of your working space. This can be used to symbolize the Goddess of Death. Place the roses around the skull. Next, place the four white candles around the skull and roses. Place one in the north first, then south, then east, then west.

Place the red string around the skull and candles making a spiral that is three circuits around counterclockwise. Make sure the space in between is large enough to walk around. The red string is the chord of Fate and it is also the connection of the of your blood to the spirit of the ancestors. It is your direct connection to the dead.

1   Proclaim your intention to the spirits to cross the veils into the Rose Castle to learn about the Hidden Company and the Goddess of Death.

2. Take a moment to center yourself and still your mind. Know that

this is a holy solemn ritual with the intent of a deep understanding or gnosis.

3. Begin at the outer most edge of the spiral of blood/Fate. Begin to walk counterclockwise. At the first circuit, take a moment and contemplate your own death. Your astral body has left the physical plane and you are now on a journey to meet the ancestors. At the second turn, your astral body releases all those things that kept you tethered to the physical plane (relationships, hopes and fears, desires for the future). At the last turn, your spirit is pure, and you feel the power of the connection of the ancestors. The power of the blood and spirit.

4. As you reach the skull, light the white candles in the following order: north then south, east then west. Gaze upon the skull. Visualize the Rose Castle around you coming to life with the bloom of roses. You are in the inner sanctum of the Castle. The skull is the vessel of the Goddess of Death. Call upon her energies and ask her to inhabit the skull for the duration of the ritual. You may visualize the goddess' energies entering the skull.

5. Allow yourself to go into meditation. It is in your mind and heart that the Ancestors will come to visit you. What do you see? Close your eyes and see if the Ancestors come to you in vision. Visualize the Goddess of Death manifesting in the skull. You may spend some time speaking with her. What wisdom does she give you? If you like, you can also summon the Ancestors and the Goddess of Death to the physical plane. This takes more magical power and can be done alone or in a group.

6. When you are finished, thank the Ancestors and the Goddess of Death. Visualize the ancestors and the Goddess returning to the

Underworld. Extinguish the candles.

7. Begin your journey back to the world of the living. Begin your journey by walking clockwise. At the first turn, you re-affirm that the ancestors are always around you acting as guides. At the second turn, you remember who you are (your desires, your hopes and fears, your dreams for the future). At the third turn, you enter your physical body and return to the physical plane.

This is a powerful and profound ritual and is one of my favorites. To me, there is nothing like being with the Goddess of Death and the Hidden Company in this manner. It seems like a simple ritual, but it holds much power and gnosis. Please remember to center and ground after this working and journal your experience.

Summoning Spirits of the Dead

To call upon the spirits of the dead in magick and ritual is a practice as old as magick itself. Every pagan culture from the Greeks to the Egyptians had rituals to call upon the dead. It was not seen as evil or diabolic until the patriarchal religions came into power. This is because Christian cultures taught that the dead were either in heaven or hell never to return and you were not summoning the dead, you were summoning demons. Pagans did not share this philosophy. To summon the spirits of the dead was as common as it was to summon deities in ritual. When we summon the dead in magick it can be for many reasons such has healing, wisdom, finding lost objects, and oracle work, to name a few purposes. I have given you a basic ritual outline below. This is a simple outline that is taught to magicians. It is only a suggested outline. If you would like to come up with something different that works better for you, by all means please do. This is just to get you started using a traditional formula.

Ritual Outline

I.   Purpose for summoning the dead

Before doing any magick, no matter what it is, you must have a purpose. You must decide what it is you want from the spirit and whether or not it is worth their time. Put yourself in their shoes. You would not want someone pulling you out of a perfectly happy afterlife just because they wanted to see if they could do it. You may do a divination such as with runes or tarot to see if it is a favorable time for this type of magick.

II. Establishing sacred space

It is important that we have a safe and comfortable space for the spirits when we call to them. You do not want any distractions or energies that may take away from the experience.

Cleansing/banishing

The first thing you will need to do is cleanse and banish the space. If you are working indoors you will need to physically clean your ritual space. You will also need to cleanse the space magically to get rid of any negative energies that may inhibit your work. Also, as a rule of thumb, negative energies attract negative spirits. We want to be as spiritually clean as possible. For banishing, you may simply use a witch's broom to sweep away the negative energies or if you prefer a more ceremonial technique you can perform the Kabbalistic Lesser Banishing Ritual of the Pentagram. You may find this ritual in Donald Michael Kraig's book *Modern Magick: Twelve Lessons in the High Magickal Arts.*

You may use the Lesser Banishing Ritual of the Pentagram or you may use a modified version of the ritual below to banish unwanted energies.

The Pentagram Rite of Protection

1. Stand in the middle of your temple area facing East. Say a prayer to the gods that you fallow. If you have not chosen a god or goddess, you can pray to the creator or the Universe. Ask the gods to protect you and your temple space.

2. Walk to the eastern part of your temple room. With your dominate hand trace a flaming blue pentagram in the air, beginning at the bottom left point, draw clockwise. Know that it will protect your temple space from negative energies and banish unwanted energies as well.

3. Place both hands over the center of the pentagram and call to your god or goddess and say, "I call upon the highest power of (name of god/Universe). May this pentagram protect all those who stand within."

4. Go to the southern part of your temple room. With your dominate hand trace a flaming blue pentagram in the air, beginning at the bottom left point. Place both hand over the center and say, "I call upon the highest spirit of (name of god/Universe). May this pentagram protect all those who stand within."

5. Go to the western part of your temple room. With your dominate hand trace a flaming blue pentagram in the air, beginning at the bottom left point. Place both hand over the center and say, "I call upon the highest being of (name of god/Universe). May this pentagram protect all those who stand within."

6. Go to the northern part of your temple room. With your dominate hand trace a flaming blue pentagram in the air, beginning at the bottom left point. Place both hand over the center and say, "I

call upon the highest form of (name of god/Universe). May this pentagram protect all those who stand within."

7. Return to the center of the temple space. Visualize all four penta-grams surrounding your temple with bright light. Know that all those you conjure may enter your temple. All others cannot.

Circle

When working with the dead, I personally do not draw a circle because I treat the dead exactly how I would treat a visitor in my home. I would never say, "Excuse me Sir, please stand beyond this boundary because I do not know you." I also understand that as a beginner you may feel the need for a magical circle to keep out unfamiliar spirits. At this time draw your circle, if you are going to do so, using your tool of choice such as an athame, dagger, broom, or your index finger. Just remember to visualize your circle as a sphere or dome of flaming blue light.

Stand in the east with your athame, broom, or dagger. Visualize your tool absorbing powerful spiritual energy from the Universe. See your tool glowing with power. Project the energy out from your tool and create a powerful blue arc from above your head down into the floor. Half of the arc is in your temple the other half is under the floor. You will create a solid sphere. Place your tool to the side of the arc and visualize your tool sending out energy as you open the arc to form a perfect sphere. Take your time as you open the arc and walk to the south, then west, then north. Finally, join the arc in the east forming your sphere of light. Stand in the center of your protective sphere and feel the power of the sphere.

Calling Gods, Ancestors, Nature Spirits

You will want to call upon the gods that you work with to oversee the ritual. However you prefer to call them is fine. If you do not have a specific god and goddess that you work with, simply ask that the Great God and Goddess who created all things be present and watch over your ritual. I also call the Ancestors that I work with to be present. Make sure that you invite your Ancestors into your circle. They are honored guests and should be treated as such. The circle will allow them in. A magick circle only keeps out the things you want out. Otherwise, the gods and other spirits are welcome in. If you work with nature spirits, elves, faeries, and the like, feel free to welcome them into your space if you know them well and trust them.

III. Vessel or catalyst

In the beginning of your necromantic work, you may find it helpful to use something that the spirits of the dead can use to reside and manifest in while they are in your magical space. It takes a lot of energy for the dead to manifest in the physical and/or astral plane, so having a place for them to reside will help them tremendously. When you become an advanced practitioner, you will not need a catalyst because you can simply use magical energy for them to manifest. However, do not do this until you are adept at summoning spirits.

Incense smoke

One suggestion for a catalyst is a fumigation. There are many herbs that resonate with the energies of the dead. A few of them are mugwort, wormwood, dittany of Crete, myrrh, dragon's blood, bay leaf, and flax seed. Simply purchase or make a blend you prefer and burn on non-toxic charcoal briquettes. A couple of recommendation for books on this are *The Complete Book of Incense, Oils, and Brews* by Scott Cunningham and *The*

Element Encyclopedia of 5000 Spells by Judika Illes. Remember, toxins drain the spirit's energy. Burning non-toxic charcoal will help the spirit manifest easier. When the spirit manifests, it is common to see the shape of the person's face in the smoke. It sounds funny but remember to crack a window or you may have the smoke alarm going off in the middle of your ritual, which is very disruptive.

Poppet

Again, it takes a large amount of energy for the dead to manifest in the physical plane. You may use a poppet to can act as a "house" for the spirit to temporarily reside in. The figure can be cloth or wax. It is traditional to use beeswax, but paraffin works well too. When you do your conjurations, tell the spirit of the dead that it may use the poppet as a vessel for the duration of the ritual. Some magicians believe that you use one doll per spirit and never use one doll for many different spirits. This is because the spirit leaves an energetic signature, and it confuses the new spirit. If you choose not to work with a spirit ever again, make sure you gently release the spirit from the poppet, send it back to where it came from, burn the doll, and then bury it as if it were a corpse. This will sever the tie between you and the spirit.

Skull and Bones

The skull and bones is one of the most ancient and primal forms of necromancy. The bones have an energy signature close to that of the energy of when the spirit was alive. There is also a connection with re-animation, but you will not re-animate the spirit with the bones, only communicate with it. This is one of the strongest vessels you can use. You may use just a skull or other parts of the skeleton. Traditionalists say to always use real human bones and never replicas. I say that the mind of the magician is the power behind all magick and if a skull replica works

for you then by all means use it. Using a skull replica for housing the spirit will also give your ritual a "necromantic" feeling and often adds more energy to the ceremony simply because it touches a deep part of our mind that honors death.

Candles

Most of the time the ancients did not use candles in their necromantic rites. If there was fire, it was a small bonfire or the flames from an oil lamp. Personally, being in the modern age, I will sometimes use black or white candles to give the spirit more energy to manifest. Black candles traditionally symbolize the night, dark magick, the Underworld, the dead, and the Great Mystery. White candles symbolize purity, the divine, pure spirit, day, cleansing. I leave it up to your intuition to use what is right for you.

If you want to be inspired by the Greco-Romans, you may use a cauldron fire to give the spirits energy in your rite. Pour a little rubbing alcohol in an iron or metal bowl or cauldron and light it with a match. Remember a little goes a long way.

IV. Offerings

It is proper to give the spirits you are working with offerings; be it gods, nature spirits or the Ancestors. Offerings give the spirits more energy to manifest. It is also a good gesture of energy exchange. If they do something for you, you do something for them. It is important to remember to only give offerings to spirits that are helpful. Never give offerings to demons or destructive or trickster spirits. They may take your good gesture and do negative or harmful deeds with it.

Milk, water, incense, wine, honey, blood, beans, flax

These are traditional offerings to the dead. Offerings that have large amounts of life force give the spirits a large amount of energy. I do not

recommend that beginners use blood as an offering, because this will give a spirit so much energy that it may be hard to get rid of them. Think of it as if you are giving someone heroin. It will give them a powerful high, but the spirits (like people) may sometimes do anything to get it again, even turning vampiric. This is very troublesome. Wine is a good substitute for blood.

Flowers and gifts

Sometimes flowers and gifts such as toys, trinkets, and knick-knacks are given to show appreciation. Each region and religion have different things that they give. My personal favorite is when some Asian cultures give the dead fireworks and spirit money. They burn the money so the dead have plenty of money in the Afterlife.

V.   The Conjuration of Manifestation

When you call upon the spirits of the dead, there are a variety of ways you may do this. If you prefer the ancient ways of the Egyptians, Greeks, Romans, or Babylonians, there is a very definite structure. The Greeks would ask the Gatekeeper Hecate to open the doors to the Underworld. Then they petitioned Persephone the Queen of the Underworld, with the name of the spirit they wished to summon.

It would look something like this:

"Great goddess Hecate! Lady of the crossroads and the keeper of the Keys, I ask that you open the gates to Hades. Blessed be your powers to protect us from harmful spirits and to prepare us for the journey ahead.

"Beautiful Goddess Persephone, Queen of Hades, Mother of the Dead! I ask that you find it in your gracious heart to allow the shade of (person's full name) to journey the death road back to the

realm of the living for a short time so that I may (purpose of ritual).

"I ask that (person's full name) journey forth into the world of the living for the purpose of (purpose of ritual). I ask that they remain here for the duration of this ritual until you are dismissed by me and the power of the gods summoned here tonight."

It is important to know that the Romans seldom conjured the name of Hades. Hades was the Lord of the Dead and to conjure him or to speak his name was to bring death and chaos into your temple or grove. He was respected, but greatly feared. Persephone on the other hand, was a goddess who dwelt half of the year in the Middleworld with her mother Demeter and could understand the desires and shortcomings of man. She had great love and sympathy for their suffering, and she would help them in any way she could. When this conjuration was used, it was common to give Hecate and Persephone offerings of love and gratitude.

If you follow other pantheons, you may substitute other names. Remember to call upon the god or goddess that opens the gates to the Underworld and then the god or goddess of the Underworld itself. If you do not know the Gatekeeper, you may simply say the conjuration of the God/dess and the shade desired. Remember that the above conjuration is something I modified from ancient Greco-Roman necromancy. If you would like to come up with your own summoning, you are certainly welcome. You can even be a little simpler and say something like this:

"I call to the gatekeeper who opens the gates between this world and the world of the dead. Open for me the gates to the Under-world. God and Goddess of the dead, we ask that you allow

(Name of Spirit) to travel from the world beyond to the physical world of here and now."

VI. Communications

This is the "meat" of the ritual, or the point where the purpose of the ritual comes to fruition. Everything up to this point prepared you, your space, and the spirits for this moment. This is a very sacred act. In medieval grimoires of necromancy, a spirit of the dead was sometimes threatened and commanded like a servant. One reason for this was because it was thought that necromancy was unholy and diabolical, and the spirits were really devils anyway and should be treated as such. Another reason was because of the fear of death and the spirits of the dead. Magicians feared that the spirits could jump into the magick circle and take the magician kicking and screaming down into the depths of hell. This all comes from Christian superstition and fear. In ancient pagan indigenous cultures, the dead were a part of the community and were to be welcomed and blessed. The rituals were simply to help the dead manifest in a way that the living could see and understand in a more profound way. The spirits of the dead are welcomed guests. Treat them as such.

I like to tell my students, "You would never invite someone into your home and start yelling at them: "Hey you!!! Stand in the corner and answer my questions or I'm gonna smack the crap out of you!" Being rude to the dead is the same thing.

I have listed only a few reasons one may wish to summon the dead. There are many others, but remember what we have talked about before. To summon any spirit, you must have a specific purpose. You would not be too happy if someone called your phone and asked you to come to their house and after you got there they said, "I only asked you to come over just to see if you would. Goodbye now!"

Divination

The spirits of the dead can see how events flow through the Underworld before they manifest in the Middleworld. They are not bound by time and space, and they can also travel back and forth in time and witness events firsthand. This is why the ancients used the dead in divination. We are reminded of how Odin conjured the seeress in the Underworld to know the fate of his son, Baldur. We must remember that the dead have hopes, fears, and prejudices just as we do, and they are not always removed from the situation you may be asking about. They also may interpret information their own way. We all know that three people can witness a car accident and then all offer different interpretations when questioned. Personally, I only use my Ancestors and specific spirits for divination, however I encourage you to experiment and come up with your own conclusions.

Teachings about Death, Vocation, Underworld, and Wisdom

The dead can be valuable when they are questioned about death and the Underworld. They have firsthand experience when it comes to what it was like to transition into the Afterlife and what their experiences are in the Underworld. This may help prepare us for the death process. It also can give people peace of mind from their own anxieties about death and whether there actually is an Afterlife. It is helpful to know that your beloved family member is happy where they are after death. Also, it was common for ancient cultures to ask the dead about their vocation. There are many stories of artists and poets sleeping on the burial mound of a great artist hoping to meet them in dreams to ask their advice. You may also conjure the spirit of a magician or witch to ask them information about magick. I will warn you though, not every spirit wishes to be conjured to the physical plane. I would ask my Ancestors to find them

and ask them personally if they would not mind coming to you during your ritual.

Closure

It may be important for you to conjure the dead for yourself or on behalf of someone who may need closure. If things were left unsaid or perhaps there was a great quarrel that left deep energetic wounds in the family, the spirit may be conjured to give closure for both parties. This is wonderful healing if it is done with love. When a ritual to call the dead is done for this purpose the spirit may still be angry and they may need to hear an apology or vice versa. Sometimes when there is an accident or death comes very suddenly, we do not have the time we would like to say our goodbyes. This is the time to do it. This can be very therapeutic. It allows both parties to move on and sever energetic chords that may be keeping them stuck in grief and frustration.

Unquiet Spirit

Hauntings do not happen very often, but they do indeed happen. If someone is experiencing unexplained phenomena such as items going missing, cabinets and drawers slamming, a chill in the room when the window is closed, or a "presence," you may have a haunting. There can be several reasons that a place is haunted, and you may need to conjure the dead to find out what to do to pacify the spirit. They may have unfinished business, or they may not know they are dead. They may be seeking justice for something. There are many other possible reasons. Conjuring the dead and finding out what to do is the best way to rid yourself of a haunting.

VII.   Dismissing the spirit of the dead

After you are finished speaking with the spirit you will need to dismiss them. You may simply thank them and give them a blessing on their way back to the Underworld or you may use a more formal speech such as:

> "(Name of spirit) I thank you for your attendance here tonight. I ask that you return to the Afterlife (or Hades, Hel, etc.) harming none on your way.

> "Goddess Persephone, take your child back into your arms where they are forever safe.

> "Mighty Hecate, I ask that you light the way for (name of spirit) and close the gates of Hades. I thank you mighty Queen!"

VIII.   Thanking the Dead and Gods, Ancestors, and spirits

After your conjuration is concluded you must thank the spirits, Ancestors, nature spirits, and gods for coming to your ritual space. I personally do not banish them in the traditional sense, but I will thank them for their energies and help, and welcome them to stay in my space if they like (but only if they are known and trusted spirits). If you cast a circle, dismantle it at this point. Leave appropriate offerings to the gods and spirits as you see fit.

IX. Banishing space

If, after your conjurations, you feel negative energy in your ritual space or feel like you may attract unwanted entities with your workings, then banish them from your space. Use the same procedure you used in the beginning to cleans and banish.

The Dead and Cursing

There are many old grimoires that speak of conjuring the dead to curse an enemy. This makes sense because in medieval grimoires, it was thought that the spirit of our Ancestors went to Heaven or Hell and they would not be able to help us in magick. It was only the tormented Earthbound spirits who were able to cause sickness, pain, and misfortune for one's intended target. These spirits were only too happy to cause harm to another because they knew nothing but torment and misery. In my personal work with the Ancestors and other spirits of the dead, my magick is used for healing, education, and wisdom. It is never meant to command the dead to do my bidding, especially to harm someone. It is important to know that it is possible to hurt another person, and there are some unethical magicians who have no problem at all with causing pain and suffering to others no matter what the cost. Binding spirits of the dead to harm another is extremely dangerous. If the spirit is ever freed, they may seek revenge on the dark magician (and rightly so). Never think that you are above the power of the Underworld Gods. These gods treat the dead as their children and will harm you if you harm them. I have known a few magicians who have used spirits, the dead, and other entities to harm others. This caused them psychological pain and suffering in the long run. Also, spirits talk to one another. The dead will not want to work with you if you have a reputation for causing harm to people or other spirits.

Healing and Removing Curses

The spirits of the dead can be used to help heal and to remove curses from someone or something. As we have talked about, the Ancestors have a stronger influence in the astral plane and the spirit world. They can see energies more clearly than we can and can aid us in strengthening

or weakening those energies. When it comes to healing, they may ask other entities of healing to help us. They may also be able to direct the energies in a more direct way than we are able to see or know. They can also weaken the energies of dark magick that are sent against us. If a spirit is causing the harm, then they can speak with that spirit and try to convince it to not harm us. They can also energetically weaken the magical stream that is being sent to us. For us to do this, we just simply have to ask them for help. I will visualize what I would like the Ancestors to do. They can see what you see and sometimes it is easier to show them than it is to explain it to them.

Forcing the Dead Against Their Will

I would like to take this opportunity to talk about using magick to force or bind the dead to do things that are against their will. In this book, we have discussed how important it is to treat all spirits with respect, be it gods, nature spirits, planetary entities, Ancestors, or spirits of the dead that you do not know. There are some magical practitioners who use magick to bind the dead and force them to do things even if they spirit wants to or not. You can find many books on necromancy, especially in medieval magick, that have pages and pages of cursing spirits of the dead and binding them to work the will of the magician.

Let us take a moment to discuss why magicians from long ago would do such a thing. Were magicians of the past unethical? The answer is not necessarily. In medieval times, magick and witchcraft were outlawed in Europe. Pagans and healers who worked with the Ancestors would not have written their magick down, and if they did, it would have not been available for anyone to see. Some ceremonial magicians did write down their magical techniques. Ceremonial magicians primarily came from a Judeo-Christian background. In this belief system, any spirit that was

not an angel from God was considered a demon from Hell or at best a mischievous spirit that needed to be controlled. Most grimoires talked about how to bind spirits and force them to do the will of the magician. They also most likely believed that if you were a spirit that could be conjured and bound then obviously you were not allowed into Heaven and you were supposed to be in Hell. To their way of thinking, there was nothing wrong with commanding a spirit of the dead that was supposed to be in Hell anyway. You may be horrified at this philosophy, but in that time, this was a common belief of Europeans, and this is all they knew of earthbound spirits.

There are some modern practices that have mixed traditions with ceremonial magick. Sometimes, when this happens, the magician may still believe that spirits of the dead who are earthbound, lost, or conjured from the Underworld (Hell in their point of view) deserve to be bound and controlled. The spiritual philosophy that I have presented here is far from those ideas.

Again, all spirits should be respected. Not all Ancestors or the dead have our best intent in mind. As we have learned, just because you have passed on from the physical plane into the Otherworld does not mean that instantaneously you become wise and evolve. It just means you are dead. The only time the dead should be bound is if they are causing sickness or harm to the living and then they should only be bound long enough for a healing spirit of the Underworld to come and take them to the proper place to be, a place of learning and healing, not a place of torment and damnation. When using the magical techniques of necromancy and Ancestor work, you must treat all spirits with the utmost respect, compassion, and honor. If you are careless, indignant, or cruel to the dead, then eventually the dead may turn on you. Remember, as you get older and weaker your magick may waver. The dead that you have

upset have literally all the time in the world. The dead can be very patient when they want to be.

When you treat spirits as family, friends, and colleagues, they will treat you with love and respect. I would much rather a spirit help me out of love and friendship than to have to force them to do anything. When you have a relationship with the dead out of mutual respect, the work can be rewarding.

Re-Animation
The Sorrow of Isis (Egyptian)

The great Mother Goddess of Egypt, Isis, had left her son, Horus, in the company of the gods while she was away curing a child who had been stung by a scorpion. The gods took great care of Horus, who would one day become the ruler of the cosmos. As Horus played by himself, scorpions scuttled across the floor. The gods took great care to keep the child-god protected from anyone who wished him harm, but they did not see the little creatures creeping down below. Before anyone knew what had happened, Horus was stung. His body lay motionless on the ground and foam spilled from his mouth. The gods did not know what to do. None of them had the power to return the dead back to life.

As Isis returned home, she was told the terrible news of her son. The Great Mother leaped to her son's side and held him close to her. She saw the wound where the poison had entered his little body. "Horus is stung!" She cried. "Horus is stung!"

Nephthys, with tears in her eyes, went to Isis and said, "Isis, pray to the skies so that the spirits who row the great barge of Ra will stop their rowing. The sun barge will forever sit over the place where Horus lies until Ra restores the little one to life."

In her anguish, Isis let out a cry for her dead child that only a mother

could. The cry was directed to those who rowed the barge of Ra. The bright disk above stopped. Not one of them had the heart to continue. The sorrow of Isis was too much for them. They were frozen by her cries. Then, Thoth appeared before Isis and her little son. He saw Isis' tears and felt great pity for her. "Isis do not cry for your son. Ra himself gave me the power of Ma'at! All things I say come to pass. For Ma'at is the law, and thus my word is law."

Isis held Horus tightly as Thoth approached. He held the little one's hands and spoke the magical words over his head that brought Horus back to life. He spoke of the protection the cosmos would provide for the little god in the Middleworld, Underworld, and Upperworld. He spoke of the adventures and triumphs he would have in days to come. He spoke of a boy who would grow up to be a fierce and honorable warrior. He spoke of a divine life. As Thoth spoke, so it came to pass. Horus returned to life and grew up to be an honorable and strong warrior.

Fears of Re-Animation

When it comes to working with the dead and necromancy, re-animation is the most controversial topic there is. In almost every religious philosophy, to re-animate the dead is the biggest taboo. In many stories, to do so has dire, even deadly consequences. I would like to discuss the topic and try to help the reader understand the reasons for re-animation. There are two common reasons to bring the dead back to life. The first would be when a loved one has been killed and the grieving family members and friends wish their loved one to be returned to them. The second is more diabolical. It is when dark necromancers wish to have control over the dead for a variety of reasons. When we examine the reasons for bringing a loved one back to life, it is hard not to be sympathetic to those people who are grieving. Almost everyone has wished that a

friend or family member who has been taken away could stand before them in the flesh again. This is especially true when one's child or spouse is murdered or killed by accident. We tell ourselves that they died too young and that if only the situation was different they would still be alive. When magicians and witches are overcome with grief and they understand that they have real power, there may be a thought in the back of their mind that says: "What if?" When someone is grieving, their thoughts and actions may not always be rational. Grief is powerful. Our desire to have our loved one back may be equally as powerful. There are many myths and legends of how the grieving have used magick, or hired someone to use magick, to bring back a loved one. Nowadays, most ethical magicians and witches would not consider such a thing. They would, however, have sympathy for the grieving person and help them through the pain of loss. But in the past, some magicians have not been so ethical. There are many stories of re-animation gone wrong. There are stories of the spirit of the dead being forced back into a rotting corpse and feeling the bewilderment and pain of being in a broken body.

There are myths of mortals, and even gods, seeking the aid of Underworld Gods to bring their loved one back to life. The gods of the dead almost always decline the request. However, once in a great while, they may grant the wish. But bringing the dead back to life always has special requirements. There is always some sort of magical "catch" and usually the mortal, and even the gods, fail at the requirements needed to bring back the dead. My personal belief is that when a strong mortal or god makes such a request to the Dark Gods, the gods understand that sometimes there is no reasoning with one who is grieving so the requirements they place upon resurrection are intentionally very tricky. I believe they know that the supplicant will fail and the dead will safely remain with the Ancestors. But what of the gods who have succeeded,

such as Osiris, and Jesus, and the like? If we take the myth of the resurrected god as a story, then it was written in a period of agricultural reliance and the people needed myths to explain the seasons of the sun and the cycles of the crops. Even though the crops died in the winter, they would be resurrected in the spring. If we take the resurrected gods as more than myth, then upon further inspection, we discover that the gods that died and returned to life have a shamanic initiation. What happens during a shamanic initiation is that the god or hero seeks to understand the mysteries of death and dies, at least temporarily. We see this in such myths as the Death of Osiris and the Descent of Inanna; also, with the sacrifice of Odin on the World Tree. When a god dies, it throws off the cosmic balance. The Universe intervenes in some way to restore the balance, otherwise the worlds will be thrown into chaos and death and destruction will rule in the place of life and order. The Universe may intervene in several different ways. One such way is that another god or gods seek to bring back the deceased gods through resurrection. When Set killed his brother Osiris, Isis searched the world for his body parts in order to bring him back to life to restore cosmic balance. While Inanna's sister imprisoned her in the Underworld, the Earth's vegetation and crops died. To stop this from happening, other spirits and gods conspired to help Inanna escape and return to the celestial realms. However, after the resurrection of the gods from the Underworld, they return with the understanding of the mystery of life and death.

There are stories about dark magicians, necromancers, and witches who used magick to bring the dead back to life for their own diabolical purposes. You can find many "old" grimoires that describe in detail how to bring back the spirit of the dead in order to re-animate a corpse. There were several different reasons that one might want to bring the dead back to life as a necromancer. One reason is to temporally re-animate

the corpse for divination and prophecy. Once the spirit was summoned into his or her corpse, they compelled them with magick to answer their questions. This took great skill and powerful magick. The magician or witch had to find a certain spirit in the Underworld with incantations and spells, and then force them to return to their corpse, and then bind them to the corpse for a certain amount of time. On top of that, they must compel them to tell the truth of future events. The whole process was considered painful for the spirit and was considered unethical even in ancient times.

The necromancer did not have to summon a spirit into the corpse that they once inhabited in life. The spirit could be summoned into any corpse the magician chose. This was even worse for the spirit. The corpse could be in any shape of deterioration and because it did not belong to the spirit of the dead in life it was harder to inhabit. Yet with great magick, the necromancer could bind the spirit to the corpse to speak prophecies.

A witch or magician could also use a severed head or simply a skull that was consecrated to the work of necromancy. The magical process was similar to that of binding the spirit to a corpse, but in this instance, it was bound temporarily to the skull. The magician only needed to hear the utterings of prophecies, so it did not need the whole body. It only needed the skull to speak. The skull would have magical sigils and incantations written on the crown, the jaw, and inside the cranium. There are also spells that require magicians to put magical writings on bay leaves and insert them in the skull's mouth. The necromancer then summoned the spirit of the dead into the skull for the spirit to mutter prophecies. The prophecies that the magician often sought out were mostly political in nature. It was most desirable to know the inner workings of the courts and minds of emperors and kings of the ancient world. Very often, someone would seek out a necromancer to hear the dark prophecies of

a skull or talking head. This was usually an enemy of the state or someone from the opposing country looking to find the weakness of the rulers to defeat them in battle.

Asclepius and Diana Bring Back the Dead (Greco-Roman)

Hippolytus was the son of Theseus. He was a vibrant youth who had strength and a great deal of wisdom at an early age. His stepmother, Phaedra, was close to him in age and fell in love with him. She tried to seduce him, but Hippolytus would not betray his father in such a dishonorable way. Phaedra was furious! No one dared to reject the beauty of the princess, for she was daughter of King Minos of Crete. She would have revenge on him! She was a devotee of the god Poseidon and prayed to him to seek revenge upon the boy.

One day, Hippolytus was driving his chariot close to the seashore, when a giant sea monster rose from the depths. The hideous creature splashed with a mighty roar and the horses driving the chariot were frightened. They ran away from the creature dragging the chariot with them. The monster chased after the chariot and with one mighty swing, the chariot was smashed to bits. Asclepius, the god of healing, found Hippolytus. The poor boy was dead. There was no longer breath in his beautiful young body. Asclepius wept for this tragedy.

The Goddess Diana of the Moon heard her nephew weeping. She descended from the heavens and appeared before Asclepius.

"Lady," Asclepius wept, "the poor boy is dead and my magick alone cannot bring him back to life."

Diana felt Asclepius' heartache and decided to help him. "Each of our powers alone cannot bring the poor boy back. But you have the

power to heal, and I have the power of mystery. Together, we may bring the boy to life."

Asclepius reached deep within himself and called upon the powers of healing that he received from his father, Apollo, and was instructed in by the centaur, Charon. His magick swelled up inside him until he could no longer restrain it. He touched the wounds of Hippolytus and sent forth the power of healing. Diana added her magick of mystery and the two gods' powers intertwined like a spiral of two serpents writhing around each other. For a moment, the Earth did not move, the bees did not harvest nectar, and the sun did not journey across the sky. Suddenly, Hippolytus opened his eyes. His death wounds were healed. Diana then took the boy away from his cruel stepmother and sent him to be protected by a nymph named Egeria.

My Thoughts on Modern Re-animation

Bringing back someone from the dead is something that almost every culture forbids or at least gives dire warnings against. Several cultures speak of it as being only a temporary fix that goes against the ebb and flow of nature. In some ancient cultures, it was a crime against the state and in others it was a crime against the gods. Most magical people either could not, or would not, bring the dead back to life. However, that does not mean that it was not done. There are spells and rituals that necromancers would use to temporarily summon the spirit of the dead into a rotting corpse. This ghoulish magick was intended to bring the necromancer information from the Underworld bringing knowledge that most magicians would never have.

I personally believe that there are far more productive ways to work with spirits of the dead than re-animating a corpse. The more you work with the dead the easier it will become to see them, feel their presence,

and to speak with them. I believe that the ancient spells used to re-animate a corpse were used because those magicians did not have the psychic skill to see nor hear the dead without the aid of a body. They also did not possess the skill to channel the spirit within their own body. Part of that was because they feared possession by spirits of the dead. The truth is, it is harder than you think for a spirit of the dead to possess and take control of your body. However, the ancient necromancers did not want to take that chance.

Say, for instance, that you had the power and skill to bring back a person who had just died or recently died. The person originally died because the body was damaged in some way that the body could not support life. The circumstances behind the death could be anything including old age, trauma, or disease. The body could not sustain life on its own. To have a minimal chance for success, you needed a master necromancer and a master healer as in the case of Asclepius and Diana. Even then, it took the two gods to bring one person back to life. When the person revived, Asclepius was punished by the King of the Gods himself.

I believe that when we obtain the gifts and blessings of the spirits and gods, we need to respect them and the natural flow of the Universe. To go against these principles would have bad karmic consequences for everyone involved. I continue to believe that there is a reason for everything. Sometimes the reason for a loved one's untimely death is beyond the understanding of mortals and the Ancestors. If we go against that flow of energy, then we can throw things out of balance. The spirits can and will intervene. You also risk losing the gifts that the spirits gave you.

As we advance in our magick evolution we will gain insight and power. Some of that power we will learn through working with the dead.

The dead can be powerful allies and guardians. They can help us turn back curses aimed at us and even aid us in healing. The dead can teach us their skills from beyond the grave. However, the dead should be treated with the utmost respect. The dead are not devils or spirits who will give us disease or bring death upon us, they are spirits who should be honored. When we work with the dead with honor, they will become powerful teachers who show us the mysteries of death, the Underworld, and when we are trusted they may show us deeper into the Great Mystery.

5
Skulls, Bones, and Blood

Odin Enchants Mimir's Head (Norse)

All-Father held the head of his dear friend. Poor Mimir was killed because the Gods of the Vanir felt cheated. After the great war between the Aesir and Vanir, two hostages of the Aesir were given to the Vanir: the wise Mimir and the less-wise Hoenir. In exchange, the Vanir gave Njord, Freyr, and Freya as hostages. The Vanir soon realized that without Mimir, Hoenir did not speak wise counsel. The Vanir were outraged. In retaliation, Mimir was returned to Odin without his body. All-Father could not bear to have his friend sent to the Halls of Hel.

Odin had powerful magick. He had the runes, and he had the enchantments of the Nine Worlds. Using the powers of the runes and his spells, Odin returned Mimir's head back to life. He used special resins to keep the head preserved. He put magical herbs inside the head to summon back the spirit of Mimir. Finally, with the runes he brought the head of Mimir to life once more. Mimir opened his eyes to see All-Father staring back at him. Odin took Mimir and placed him deep in the Underworld in a magical well. The well had magical powers of wisdom and life. Mimir would drink from the magick well and utter prophecies and wisdom to those who journeyed into its mysteries.

The Skull

One symbol of witchcraft, magick, and necromancy is the skull. The skull is the symbol of death in all cultures and in all time periods throughout history. By simply gazing upon the human skull our minds can be filled with thoughts of death and the afterlife. In modern times, the human skull serves as a warning to be careful, such as in a warning for danger or poison, or else we, too, may become nothing more than a skull. The skull reminds us that death is imminent. We are born and we must die. No one is safe from death. For a lot of people in our modern world, the skull can be a sorrowful symbol of the grief of having lost a loved one or the grotesque images of a body rotting down deep in the grave.

The skull has been used in magick ever since the first shaman began to understand the physical and spiritual components of death. Let us take a moment to have a further understanding of what the skull is. Physically, the skull is the bone structure that forms our head. It has a protective cranium for our brains, eye sockets, a mandible with our teeth, and nose holes for breathing. Without this structure we could not live.

When ancient tribespeople died, their bodies decomposed and all that remained was their bones. Their bones seemed to be eternal and did not decompose as fast as the rest of the body. Ancient people must have been fascinated by this. They looked at the bones as magical because they had the power to survive even after death. To ancient people this was great magick from the gods themselves! As the only part of the body of their loved ones that remained, surely they must still hold the essence of that person. Perhaps a little part of the deceased was still energetically present.

In an energetic and spiritual sense, the skull and bones were connected to the energies of death—not necessarily to bring death to

this world or to a person, but to understand that death was a part of the natural cycle of life. The spiritually minded person understands that the only thing that remains after death is the spirit. So, because the skull and bones were the only things that remained and the spirit was the only energetic thing that remained after death, the only logical conclusion to draw was that the skull was a representation of the human spirit.

When magical people use the skull and bones in their work, they do so for a variety of reasons and there are many ways to do it. One of the most common ways to use the skull in magick was to create a "Talking Head." Talking Heads were primarily found in Celtic lands and parts of Europe. As previously stated, the ancient Celts were headhunters and would keep the head of their enemy as a trophy because they believed that the soul resided there. The human skull would be enchanted to summon a divination spirit and the skull would then utter prophecies of the future. It is speculated that only a skilled necromancer could hear the words of the talking head, but there have been stories told that any passer-by would be able to hear the magical skull speak. After Alexander the Great was killed, his head was placed in a jar of honey. Honey is a natural preservative. It was said that Greek emperors would ask the talking head of Alexander for advice before going to war or before any great act of leadership.

The skull can also be used as a permanent or temporary vessel for spirits in magick. When the magician summons a spirit of the dead, it takes a large amount of energy for the spirit to be able to occupy the physical plane. For spirits to become effective in divination or carrying out tasks, they need energy from us. They need offerings and a temporary vessel. The most gruesome vessel would be the rotting corpse itself. Historically in most cultures, using necromancy to re-animate a corpse or using a decomposing body for spirit work was illegal because it

desecrated the honor and memory of the body, and it was a grotesque and time-consuming act. One had to dig up a grave or break into a crypt and then summon the spirit into the rotting body. If I were a spirit, I most certainly would not want to find myself in the body of a corpse with rotting limbs and a foul stench. A more civilized way to create a vessel for a spirit to use in necromancy would be to use a human skull. Once the session was over, the spirit would be released from the skull and the skull would then be physically and spiritually cleansed.

The skull can also be used as a gateway or portal when journeying into the Underworld. Each eye socket, nostril, ear hole, and the mouth are a gateway into a different part of the Underworld and the Realm of the Dead. The important thing to remember about such portals is that they may or may not always lead you to the same place twice. In the Underworld, time and space are subjective and many people who have mapped the Underworld and tried to go back to the exact same time and place have been disappointed to find themselves in an unexpected location. I find this to be one of the beautiful and mysterious qualities of the Underworld. It is an interesting concept to explore.

The skull can be used to summon dark and malicious spirits that you can use to curse and bring death to your enemies. This is something I would never teach to students or anyone who asked. I do think it is important to know that it is possible; not all magick is friendly. It is also important to remember that just because you have ethics and honor does not mean that your enemies do. It is important to understand that dark spirits can be summoned with the skull.

One question I am often asked is if one must obtain a real human skull. The answer is no, you do not. Remember, power and magick come from the magician and not from the tools. Tools are there to help us when we are learning and the more adept and powerful you become, the

less you will need to rely on your magical tools. You may use a skull replica or an artistic skull sculpture. I suggest using a skull that closely resembles a real human skull in the beginning. This will create the necessary spiritual link in your mind and energy field to do this kind of spiritual work.

The Celts practiced ancestor worship. This took a variety of forms. First and foremost, they believed that the dead existed among us and could easily be contacted. Some Celts believed that their Ancestors were directly descended from the gods. The Celts were headhunters. They believed that the souls resided in, and could be summoned back into, the skulls of the dead. They believed that the more heads a warrior collected, the more access to the spirits of the dead they had. This was done mostly to their enemies in war. The spirits of the slain warriors could be summoned back with magick and used as oracles and divination. To most modern people, this sounds very strange and very much like a form of "black magick." But, in ancient times, people had a different way of life and different ethics. One such ancient Celtic belief was that it was completely justified to use magick against someone if they threatened the survival of the tribe. Times were tough and sometimes cruel, and the way they viewed survival was different from how we view survival. The skulls of the dead helped the Celts with prophecies such as if an enemy was planning attack, harsh weather coming, or if spirits where working against them. These are only a few things talking heads could be used for. As we can see, having them gave the Celts an advantage for survival.

The Skull Meditation

1. Obtain a skull or skull replica.
2. Place it on your lap or on a small table in front of you.

3. Turn off all the lights. You may have a small candle nearby, but the room should be very dim.

4. Gaze upon the skull and allow any thoughts about the image or of death to come to mind.

5. Take a deep breath and allow those thoughts to fade away with each exhale.

6. Now, think about your spirit. It is the part of you that will never die. Your spirit can never be destroyed.

7. Know that the skull is a representation of your spirit. The spirit is your pure essence. It is that which is beyond time and space.

8. Continue to gaze upon the skull. How do you feel? What fears or hopes come to mind?

9. Now place your fingers on your head and feel your own skull. Feel the eye sockets, the nose bones, the cheekbones, the cranium, and the jawbone. Your skull is not your literal spirit, but it is a symbol of your spirit. Keep this in mind as you feel your own skull. What sensations do you feel? What insights pop up in your mind?

10. Journal about your experience.

Initiation of the Bones (Skeleton Meditation)

When working with the Underworld and the Ancestors, it is important for us to understand our inner nature and our core being. The spirit can often feel unfathomable for magical practitioners. We hear about the spirit from members of clergy in different religions and from books about spiritual enlightenment. But we cannot learn about the spirit through books and simply being a "good person." Our spirit is much more vast, complex, and timeless than we can understand. There also may be some

confusion about the difference between the soul and the spirit. In patriarchal religions there is often a lot of talk about saving the soul and what happens to the soul after death. The spirit is our core being: that which survives after death and even after the soul is gone. The spirit is our pure light of self. I use the term "light" because we tend to think of white light as pure and universal, that which is unchanging and unwavering. People with psychic vision often report spirits and benevolent beings looking like white light. I believe that the spirit can be that, but it is much more. Something to contemplate: Perhaps these ascended beings appear to us as white light because the true nature of spirit is too complex for our eyes and minds to understand.

The soul is the part of our selves that houses the spirit. While the spirit is the pure essence of our spiritual being, the soul is everything that makes you *you* in this life. Your soul contains your ego, hopes and fears, dreams and desires, and your memories. The spirit is unbreakable and resilient, but the soul is at times fragile and can easily break away from us. This is why shamanic soul retrieval exists. When we experience a tragedy or accident, sometimes the great psychological and/or emotional impact can be too much for our soul to handle, so a part of our soul "breaks" off and flees to another part of the three worlds. Depending upon the personality of the event, psycho-emotional factors, and other external circumstances, the soul can journey anywhere in the three worlds to hide, heal, and regroup. One of the duties of the shaman is to find the soul fragment and bring it back to us to help us reintegrate it into our being. The soul's purpose is to help us learn, evolve, and become higher beings in our own right. I like to think of the soul as an intermediary between our spirit and our astral selves.

When working with the dead, it is imperative to begin the process for understanding our divine nature. Often, the ego of the shaman, witch,

and magician gets in the way of their spiritual work and they begin to do it for the wrong reasons. This is not to say that when this happens the shaman is evil or bad, it is just to say that they have strayed from their divine purpose for that moment and need guidance. I have seen magicians who summon and work with the dead simply for ego-based reasons including power, greed, and arrogance. These things have no place when working with the Ancestors or any concept of the divine. To understand our spirit and our divine will we need to contemplate and meditate with our seemingly ineffable spirit.

As we have learned, to the ancient peoples the bones of our skeleton represented the unchanging and undying spirit. Bones are magical and resilient. They represent our divine selves. One way to meditate with our own spirit is to meditate on our own bones.

1. Sit or lie down and make yourself comfortable.

2. Take a deep breath and with the exhale allow your mind to relax.

3. Take another deep breath and with the exhale allow your emotions to find balance.

4. With one more deep breath, as you exhale allow all the muscles in your body to relax.

5. Close your eyes and visualize your body. See yourself exactly as you appear now.

6. After a moment, visualize the inside of your body. See your muscles, organs, nerves, veins, etc. Now, let that visualization fade away until you can see nothing but your bones. Know that your bones are powerful, unchanging, undying. This is your spirit. These are the bones of your Ancestors. These are the bones of your family for the generations to come.

7. See your bones becoming bright light. Watch them become brighter. Spend some time contemplating the bright spirit light of the bones. How does this make you feel? What insight do you get? What wisdom do you learn from the bones?

8. When you are ready, open your eyes, take a deep breath, stretch, and then journal about your experience.

Gravestones

The gravestone is an important tool when working with the dead. At the most basic level it acts as a grave marker. It lets us know where a corpse lies, the name of the deceased, and the dates of birth and death. On a magical level, it keeps the spirit of the deceased right where they are. People in the past used to fear that the spirit of the dead might journey out of the grave to haunt the nearby village. At worst, they may have feared that the body would be reanimated, get out of the grave, and walk around like a modern-day version of a zombie or a vampire. The magical powers of the stone and prayers said around it acted as a spiritual weight that prevented the spirit and the corpse from leaving the grave and running amok.

In necromancy and spirit work, the gravestone can be used for a couple of different purposes. First, it can be used as a temporary vessel for a spirit when you conjure them out of the grave. It is sometimes easier for the spirit of the dead to manifest if it has a vessel of some kind that it can use temporarily to commune with us. A magician would use the vessel during a necromantic ritual. After the rite was over the magician would dismiss the spirit and magically cleanse the gravestone. Another use for gravestones is as portals to different places in the Underworld while in the astral.

Oracles and Guides

The dead can be used as oracles. They have the ability to see the workings of time and space and they may be able to help you in seeing the past, present, and future. In the beginning during your practice, use your own Ancestors for oracle work. This may take some time at first, but with training and help from you and other Ancestors, they will be able to become quite proficient. When you become comfortable using the dead for oracle work, then you may use other willing spirits of the dead. It is better to use spirits that you know or who were magical in life. Sometimes spirits that we do not know will want offerings and libations and will tell you what they think you want to hear. Over time, you will be able to tell who is telling you the truth and who is not. For now, stick with your Ancestors and ask your ancestral teacher the best way to help your own Ancestors learn oracle work.

Blood Magick

Blood magick is important in the magick and use of the Underworld. It is through the power of blood that we are able to communicate more efficiently with the dead and learn about our Ancestors. Blood carries our life essence and our DNA. In Traditional Chinese Medicine it carries our Chi and in Ayurvedic Medicine it carries our Prana. Our blood literally is our life force. It is the liquid substance that carries information about every part of our physical and spiritual makeup. Blood is one of the transportation systems of our body, delivering vital information and nutrients to our organs and bones. It also can carry infection and disease to our bodies. The same blood that flows through our veins is the same blood that flowed through the veins of our Ancestors.

In magick, blood holds both power and taboo in its use. The ancients knew of the magical powers and abilities of blood. They knew that blood

had a life-giving power. There are several theories about how this came to be. One theory states that the ancients saw how people died if they had no blood and so they knew that blood was the substance that gave life. Another theory says that as blood was spilled on the Earth, the ancients saw how it helped plants grow stronger. Modern scientists say that it was simply the nutrients in the blood fertilizing the Earth, but shamans, witches, and magicians know it is more than this. We know that not only does blood contain nutrients, but it also carries our energetic life force. The ancient pagans used blood in sacrifice. It is for this reason that Judeo-Christian magicians would place great taboos and warnings on the use of blood in magick. They would teach that blood was used to conjure demons and steer the magician down the dark path of black magick. While I will say you can use blood in black magick you can also use blood in healing and ancestral magick.

Sometimes the ancients used their own in a blood-letting ritual and other times it was animal and/or human sacrifice. "Sacrifice" is a word that sometimes inspires caution in the Neopagan and New Age practitioner. They much prefer the idea of "offering" to the cold sound of "sacrifice." But we need to be clear. To give sacrifice is to give something up of yourself or something that you own. Take a moment to think about it. When someone gives you an offering, they are giving you something that they can easily obtain. But when someone gives a sacrifice to you, they are giving you something that has great meaning to them. In turn, they give it more spiritual power because of the importance of the object. So, receiving the sacrifice carries more energy to you. It is also important to remember that when you give sacrifice to a spirit or entity, you must do it because you want to do it and never give sacrifice begrudgingly. Think about times in your life you knew someone gave you

something, not because they wanted to, but because they felt they had to. It takes the specialness out of the item and you do not want it as much.

Sacrifice in the ancient past was common. The Maya gave human sacrifice to their gods. More specifically, they gave the blood and the heart of the victim to the gods so that they could manifest their powers more efficiently on the Earth. When the Maya gave sacrifice, it was not because they were bloodthirsty, but because they believed it would help the cycles of the crops, the community, and the Earth continue to thrive. The Celts also sacrificed humans for the same reasons. Some scholars say that the ancient tribes of Palestine sacrificed humans to their gods, but as time progressed, animal sacrifice was substituted. This may be the meaning behind the story in Genesis of Abraham preparing to sacrifice his son Isaac before seeing the ram caught in the bush. The Greco-Romans commonly gave animal sacrifice to the gods. Before and after a successful hunt, the hunters would give a portion of the kill to the Goddess of the Hunt, Artemis/Diana. It was also common to keep goats in the temple of Artemis/Diana so that the priests could give blood sacrifice to the goddess to win her favors. However, there were also times when the pagan gods would demand human sacrifice to keep the spirit of that person close to them. It is important to remember that the ancient pagan gods meant everything to the community and the individual person. It was common for mortals to be literally *in love* with their chosen patron or matron. To give your life to your god and eternally be by their side was, at one time, considered an honor.

Sometimes we may get upset when we hear or read that the gods demanded human or animal sacrifice. We may think that this is a cosmically "unfair" act because we are lesser beings than the gods. Yet it is important to realize that the gods experience this phenomenon too. In myth, we see that the gods were also sacrificed for the greater good of the cosmos.

Osiris was killed by his brother Set and sent to the Underworld. Because of this, Osiris is able to aid the newly dead through the labyrinth of the Dwat and help them join with the gods. Asclepius, the Greco-Roman god of healing, is killed by Jupiter/Zeus and then later exalted to godhood by his father Apollo. This enables him to have greater powers to help heal mankind. In Christian myth, Jesus is sacrificed on the cross to save mankind from sin and allow the souls of the dead to dwell in heaven. Ancient peoples believed that the universe did not have an inexhaustible amount of energy. When the universe needed to evolve to something greater it needed a large amount of energy to do so. By sacrificing the gods themselves this provided the energy needed.

The Blood of Creation (Maya)

There was only the darkness of the void. Before time, there was no time. Before space, there was no space. Before creation, there was nothingness. The first beings gathered together in a circle. They knew of themselves and they soon came to know each other. But the void remained. There was still nothingness. Their power was vast and unimaginable, but it was contained. The power of all things was contained inside their bodies. The gods had come together to begin creation and creation would be released from within them.

The gods fashioned a sharp dagger made of their own bones. The bones of the first gods formed the very core of the beginning of what was soon to come. Creation. But there needed to be more. The power within must be released. The gods took the sharp daggers and raised them high above their heads. They looked each other in the eye. Their minds were joined now. Their thoughts the same. Creation. In unison, the gods plunged the sharp daggers through their penises! Agonizing blood spilled out into the void. The power was released. The blood spilled

into the nothingness and began creation. The cosmos was forming out of the drops of painful blood that spilled from the penises of the gods. The cosmos formed other gods; the other gods formed the Earth, sea, and sky. The raw power of the blood from those great penises contained the essence of fire and creation. The new gods took the blood and continued to create the universe. The very DNA of all things was made from the DNA of the great gods. Creation continues from the blood of the old ones.

If we look closely at this myth, we can take the story and learn to use blood magick ourselves. Blood can create life and add great power to our magick. When we use blood in magick it puts our astral and energetic signature on magical work that we are doing. When using blood magick it is vital that no one other than you handle or have care of the items that contain your blood. Your blood is one of the most powerful energetic ways to link back to you. A magician could potentially use the item with your blood against you. Never allow this to happen.

Witchblood

Anyone who has studied Traditional Witch lore has heard of the term *witchblood*. This means a person who comes from a hereditary witch family. This does not have to be direct lineage from the immediate family such as father to son or mother to daughter. If there was a magical person in your family several generations back, it may be that the magical energy skipped a few generations before manifesting in you. If so, you may still have the witchblood. I have heard some modern witches, shamans, and magicians say that if you go back through your ancestral lineage far enough you will find someone with witchblood because everyone in ancient times was a witch, shaman, or magician. Let me tell you that this is not true. First, let me explain what a witch really is. Neopagans use a modern

interpretation of the word witch. Today, the word witch can mean anyone who follows a magical or spiritual path and works with the energy of the Universe. In ancient times witch meant anyone, be they Christian, pagan, or any religion who worked with the primal, darker forces of the Universe to obtain a desired goal. This could mean cursing, working with the dead, conjuring demons, or healing. They also summoned chthonic powers and spirits to benefit the community such as for weather working and to provide food for the tribe. Most modern witches would be aghast that I said such a thing, but it is true. There is nothing wrong with redefining a word, but it is important to know where the word came from and what it originally meant. Not every human in the far distant past was a magician, witch, or shaman. These were and are very specialized skills that use specific energies for the purpose of the conjurer. Many people who are witches believe that they have a distant relative who was a witch and the magick has passed down to them. I believe that this is perfectly fine to believe whether it is true or not. I look at it this way, if it makes your magick and spirituality more meaningful, then why not?

So how does witchblood work? The witchblood is like a spiritual calling card between you, your Ancestors, and the gods. The blood sometimes "boils" with magick and power. When one has "the blood", as it is sometimes called, a person cannot ignore the spiritual call of the ancient ones and the shining ones. To do so usually ends in psychosis and madness. I think of it as a genetic energy power surge that, if used, has the potential to help humanity reconnect with the three worlds. Not everyone has the witchblood. This does not mean that if you do not feel the fire in the blood that you are not a witch, magician, or shaman. This means that the magical blood begins with you. If you are the first in your family line to be a witch, then great! You may have just as much power as someone who is from a family of witches. Think of it this way: just

because you do not come from a family of doctors does not mean you will not be a skilled doctor once you receive medical training.

Hyndla and Freya (Norse)

The goddess Freya went to the dark cave of the giantess Hyndla. She knew that Hyndla was a seeress and knew how to use her magick to see the Ancestors of everyone in the Nine Worlds. Freya promised the giantess that if she would grant her a favor, she could convince the great gods Odin and Thor to grant blessings on her. Reluctantly, Hyndla came out of her dark cave. Hyndla wanted nothing more but to slumber in the darkness of the Earth. Freya appealed to the giantess to come with her. Hyndla agreed. She rode off on her wolf and Freya on her magical boar. However, Hyndla could not be fooled. She knew that Freya, the goddess of love, rode no ordinary boar. The boar she rode was her lover, Ottar, who was transformed into the animal. Yet Freya protested; she tried to convince the giantess that her boar was not her lover in disguise.

Freya asked the giantess about the lineage of Ottar. Hyndla knew Freya was up to something. The gods do not often make friends with the giants so easily. She decided to give Freya what she had asked for. She used her magick to tap into the blood of Ottar. Through magick of the blood, she could see deep into his family history. She could see deeper than all other beings in the Nine Worlds. She began naming off Ottar's lineage. She named the names of men that were long forgotten by time. She named those who deeds were legendary. She named those who may have wanted to keep themselves secret, even from the gods!

Freya was happy to hear the family names of Ottar. She told Hyndla to give Ottar the magick potion that would make him remember all that he had heard. Hyndla knew Freya was up to something. There would be no reward or treasures for this. She then told the goddess that if Ottar

drinks the potion it would do nothing but curse him. Freya feared not. With her own magick she would make sure the potion Ottar drank held no curse. With this, Hyndla returned to her cave to slumber ever deep.

Tapping into the Blood

As we can see from the story above, there is magick in our blood. Our blood contains every bit of information about our past, present, and even future. It has the DNA of our Ancestors. The blood that ran through your forefathers runs through you. Our blood can tell you the state of your current health as well as possible future troubles not yet detected. On a spiritual and energetic level, our blood contains many magical abilities. There are several legends about the bloodline of shamans, witches, magicians, and healers. When we say that magick "runs in the family", we are specifically referring to the power that is transferred to each generation through the bloodline. It is thought that the Ancestors and gods of the ancient past run in the blood as well. To access this deep, powerful magick, all we have to do is connect on an energetic and spiritual level to the blood. This can be done quite easily.

Exercise: Tapping into the Blood

1. Relax your body and take full slow breaths.

2. Bring your awareness to a meditative trance state.

3. Bring your attention to your heart. Feel the heart pumping blood to your entire body.

4. Become aware of the arteries and veins that make up the circulatory system of your body. This is the lifeblood that pumps within you.

5. Understand that the same blood that pumps through your body

also pumped through the bodies of your parents, your grandparents, your great-grand parents, and back to the beginning of the human race.

6. As you focus on your blood, take a breath and breathe in life force form the air. I like to visualize it a vibrant gold or orange color. See the life force enliven and awaken your blood. Visualize your blood glowing red like embers or lava from deep within the Earth. Your blood becomes enlivened from this energy.

7. Think about your Ancestors. Think about your family lineage throughout all of human history.

8. Call to your Ancestors. Ask them to be present within and around you. Feel the power of the blood give your ancestors energy to manifest in the physical plane.

9. Bring to mind the Ancestors you wish to speak to and have a deeper connection with. Think about what they look like and sound like if you know.

10. Connect with your ancestral altar. Touch it. Visualize all the Ancestors you work with holding hands with each other. Visualize them holding your hands. You and your Ancestors are forming a circle.

11. Take a deep breath and breathe the lifeforce to your Ancestors once again. See an energetic cord or line going to each one of them. Know that you are giving each other power and magick. The Ancestors are your past, and you are their future.

Journeying To The Blood

With this technique you will be taking a shamanic journey into the blood itself to speak with your ancestors. So, instead of journeying up or down the shamanic world tree, you will be using your blood as a catalyst to speak with your Ancestors that you already know, or you may use this technique to discover Ancestors from the distant past long forgotten. I enjoy using this technique to learn more about my ancestral heritage and the long-forgotten stories of my Ancestors.

1. Lie down or sit comfortably in a chair. Relax your body and take full slow breaths. State your purpose of seeing Ancestors known or unknown.

2. Bring your awareness to a meditative trance state. You may simply take nice deep hypnotic breaths if you like. With each breath allow yourself to go deeper and deeper into trance.

3. Bring your attention to your heart. Feel the heart pumping blood to your entire body.

4. Become aware of the arteries and veins that make up the circulatory system of your body. This is the lifeblood that pumps within you.

5. Have a deep understanding that the same blood that pumps through your body also pumped through the bodies of your parents, your grandparents, your great-grand parents, and back to the beginning of the human race.

6. Bring your awareness into your body; into your heart. Visualize yourself inside your own body inside the blood that pumps through the heart. What do you see?

7. With the powers of your visualization, journey deeper within the

DNA and Matrix of the blood. The DNA is a portal to your ancestors and those who share your bloodline in the future. Visualize yourself journeying into a magical energetic realm inside the blood. You may see people, places of the past, or some other magical place.

8. Visualize a place to meet your Ancestors or guides. You may see them somewhere in the Underworld, the astral plane, or perhaps somewhere in the history of your Ancestors.

9. When you see your Ancestors, greet them as you would any guest and speak with them for a while. When you are ready, say your goodbyes and bring your awareness back to your physical body and the physical plane.

10. Journal about your experience.

Blood in Magick and Necromancy

It is believed that one of the most powerful ways to empower something with magick is to use blood. Blood keeps us alive and has our life force and the DNA of our Ancestors. Blood carries the powers of the magician and witch. Everything we are and everything we hope to achieve is in our blood. We often hear people say: "It's in his blood!" Blood carries the components to heal our wounds and bring us back from sickness to health. To give something blood is to give it life and manifestation.

In necromancy, blood is a powerful way to summon spirits of the dead. Offerings of food, wine, and water help the dead manifest on the physical plane, but blood will give them the life force that they need to truly manifest on the physical plane and cause change. The spirits of the dead sometimes crave it. Its power can be seductive to them. In many cultures, the blood of the gods created life on Earth, and it is that same

blood that can resurrect spirits of the dead, even temporarily. In Greco-Roman necromancy, blood was poured into a hole dug into the ground which became a doorway into Hades. The blood would give the dead power and life force and the necromancer was able to ask the spirit of the dead advice and wisdom of the Underworld. The Nordics would empower the runes with blood to magically charge them. When this was done, the runes were alive with power, ready to do magick. Oaths were sometimes signed with blood. This would magically bind the person to their oath forever. In medieval magick, blood is sometimes considered black magick because of the idea that blood was used to feed demons and a witch's pact with the devil was signed in blood. In Vodou and some African indigenous religions, blood from animals such as goats, chickens, and small animals is sometimes used to give devotion and energy to certain gods. Shamans and Neopagans may give a drop or two of their own blood to the spirit of a tree or plant as payment for harvesting the plant.

I personally feel that if a magical person understands themselves and the magick at hand and takes full responsibility of the magick being performed, then "do what ye will." Blood magick is an ancient magical practice and very powerful. In my personal practice, I believe that anytime blood is used in magick it binds you to the spell or ritual in a strong and powerful way. This can be a blessing or a curse. Some pagans use their blood to bind themselves to ancestral lands. The sweat and blood of their Ancestors worked the land and harvested food and shelter, so magically they want to bind their magick to the land to strengthen their ties to it and help the spirits of the place prosper. It can become a curse if you decide to bind a love spell with your blood. This connection is powerful and is seductive to the obsessed lover, but if the love affair becomes sour or should end for a variety of reasons, then ending the spell is very difficult.

Mayan Ancestral Blood Summoning Ritual

I mentioned the bloodthirst rites of the ancient Maya earlier and their interesting way of summoning the Ancestors. To the Mayans, the Ancestors had the power to influence magick, tell the future, heal, and cause harm to others to protect the family or the tribe. To summon the Ancestors, they would put paper or wood shavings into a sacred bowl. They then would take a large bone needle and pierce their penis if they were men or their tongue if they were women. They would then let the blood drip over the paper in the sacred bowl and allow it to dry. Once the blood had dried, they would ignite the paper on fire and summon the Ancestors for magick.

To modernize this ritual, you may obtain a sacred bowl or small cauldron and place wood shavings inside. Then make a mixture of incense using dittany of Crete, dragon's blood, and a couple of drops of your own blood. Place the mixture on the wood chips and allow them to burn. You may also skip the wood chips and place the incense on non-toxic charcoal instead [charcoal can generate more carbon monoxide than woodchips – so be careful in enclosed space]. The kind used for hookahs works well. Once the smoke begins to rise, you may use a conjuration such as:

"I call upon my Ancestors (Ancestors' names)! Use this sacred smoke to draw energy and manifest yourself through the smoke and appear before me!"

You may adapt the words to your liking. The important thing is to let the Ancestors know that they can use the incense to manifest through the smoke to take shape. This may be challenging for your Ancestors if you have not been working with them for long. Remember, the Maya pierced themselves in the places of creation (penis) and manifestation (tongue the spoken word). I strongly recommend against performing

this ritual in the traditional Mayan way. However, it is up to you to take responsibility for your own safety and well-being.

Spellcasting Using Blood

Using blood in magick is a very ancient practice. I remember when I was first learning, a friend told me that if you signed your spell with your name in blood, the spell or person you placed the spell on was forever bound to you. Honestly, that may or may not be true. I feel that if you believe that it is true, then perhaps your belief makes it so. Blood in magick also has the reputation from the old witch-hunt fears that if you use blood in magick then you are attracting evil forces. That is not necessarily true. If you choose to use blood in magick, the devil will not appear and make you sell your soul. That is purely a superstitious Christian belief. But as we have learned, blood contains a powerful life force and the DNA of the person or animal it originates from. Life force has an enormous amount of energy, and spirits use energy as food. I leave it up to you to choose to use a few drops of your own blood for magick. I have friends and colleagues who practice the religion of Vodou and use animal blood in their devotions and rituals. It may seem cruel and barbaric, but I am fond of reminding meat eaters that it is more sacred to use a chicken for magick and devotion than it is to keep it in a farm where its beak is cut short, it is given horrible hormones, and forced to live in its own feces.

Blood is sometimes given to one's gods and goddesses as a form of devotion and to strengthen the bond. To give of one's own blood to a god is a very sacred act. You are giving your very essence and life force. This should only be done to one's patron or matron. These are the gods and goddesses that you will work with for the rest of your life and the lifetimes to come. I personally work with other gods that are not my

patron and matron and feel it is important to give to any gods that aid me in my spiritual growth devotion and offerings. However, I would never give those gods my own blood. The sharing of blood is a sacred act between my lifetime gods and myself. Another reason I don't share my blood with gods other than my matron or patron, is that I do not want just any god laying claim to me simply because they want my energy. This, to me, is vampirism.

When it comes to spirits and entities, especially demons and beings you do not know, you should not give them your, or anyone else's, blood under any circumstances. There are some grimoires that say to conjure certain spirits you should give them animal blood and/or human blood sacrifice. This is an unbelievably bad idea. First and foremost, to give them your own blood attaches them directly to you making them extremely difficult to banish. They also get a lot of energy from the blood, and they will no longer want other offerings. If you have a spirit that promises you power, love, or money in exchange for blood offerings, you should refuse! These are usually trickster and malicious spirits that have no real power of their own. The only way they can manifest your desire is to give them a power surge of blood. It is much easier to manifest your desires with devotions to a god or goddess.

Using bones and blood are the most powerful tools to use in magick. It is life. It is power. It is also makes an imprint on our consciousness and in the spirit world. These tools give spirits more power to manifest our will. They are most likely the first tools of magick and witchcraft. When we use these tools with reverence for their power, we tap into an ancient lineage of magick that goes all the way back to the first practitioner of necromancy and spirit work.

6
Magical Protection

When traveling in the Underworld or summoning its energies and entities, there is always a chance that something unwanted may follow you back to this world. It happens to the best of magicians. It is always a good idea to know some basic magical defense and protection. It is wise to remember that as human beings, we have more influence in the physical plane than most spirits do. You may come across powerful entities that become interested in you. Most are harmless and are simply curious about you and the magical talent that you possess. Some entities may see the life force within you and may be attracted to that energy. The Underworld is a place of the dead, demons, chthonic entities, and many things that we do not want to remain in the physical plane. If we are to work with the energies of the Underworld, then it is our responsibility to make sure that we put back anything that manifests on this plane because of us!

To protect ourselves and our temple space from Underworld entities, the first thing we must do is to makes sure that we treat all spirits with respect. If the being is grotesque and scary, we must still treat it with kindness. Sometimes spirits appear in your temple space unexpectedly because you may have opened a portal to their world. Being respectful brings you allies and equal respect from other spirits. If a spirit seems hostile to you there are a few things that you can do to send them back to where they belong.

Talking to the Spirit

The first thing you should always do with a spirit is to talk with it and find out what it wants. If you cannot hear what it says or it communicates in

a different language, use your intuition. Pay attention to your feelings. What images pop up in your mind? Do you "know" what the spirit wants? Sometimes, the spirit may recognize something special in you and want a working relationship. But if it feels sinister, dark, or even evil, the best course of action is to ask it to leave. If that does not work, a more aggressive course of action is required. In the case of a hostile spirit, never allow the entity to remain in your home or temple space. The longer it is there, the harder it is to get rid of.

The Broom or Besom

The witch's broom conveys to us the idea of magical power. We have all seen the depictions of witches flying to the Sabbat on a broom. The broom has many mysteries, but for our purposes here we will talk about the broom's ability to cleanse and banish unwanted spirits and energies. As with all magical tools, our broom needs to be set aside from our everyday household sweeping. It should be cared for as a sacred magical tool and placed in a position of honor by your altar or sacred space. When you hold your broom, know that you are holding a powerful tool that has an ancestral lineage into the European past. Witches used this tool to heal and to protect. The bristles sweep away negative energies and spirits. Use the broom to sweep these out of your ritual space. Walk counterclockwise as you sweep. This is counter sunwise or widdershins, so it is ideal for banishing energies. Walk counterclockwise three times while sweeping the energies and negative spirits away. Visualize the negative energy being swept away into the Underworld to be recycled into something more productive and useful for the Earth. You may also sweep away negative spirits who threaten you. If you place your broom in front of a door, window, or portal, it acts as a barrier. No spirit can get through.

Blast of Power

Emotions are a great storehouse of energy. A blast of emotional power can banish an entity in a pinch. The trick is to summon a feeling of great control over your environment and a dire need for the spirit to be thrown out of your home. Think of it like a security guard throwing a thief out the door! It will not work if your fear outweighs your feeling of control. Negative spirits feed on the energy of fear. All you must do is build up this great emotion of control and aggression. Then wave your hand in the direction you want the spirit to go and say, "Go!" Remember, this is a temporary fix. After the blast of power, you must set up wards to keep the spirit from returning.

Wards

One of the best ways to keep unwanted spirits away from your home is to set up wards. A ward is focused energy that holds the intent of protection and keeping unwanted energies away from a person, place, or thing. The more common wards are written symbols (be they astrally or physically written) or physical objects that are magically charged. Some common symbols include: the pentacle, the equal-armed cross, reiki signs, god symbols, family or clan shields, or runes. You can make a simple ward by binding two rowan sticks together with red string to form an equal-armed cross. If hung over the window or rafters, it offers wonderful protection. You may also want to trace the *Elhaz* rune over doors, windows, and the four corners of your home. This is extremely effective, and I use this particular ward myself every day. Feel free to come up with your own symbols or glyphs that feel powerful and protective to you.

Banishing Without Prejudice

A powerful way to banish spirits energetically is to use the pentacle. You may take a magical athame, sword, dagger, or simply your index finger and trace a large flaming blue pentacle in the air. Begin toward your left knee, as you trace the pentacle, visualize it as a flaming blue line, and trace up above your head. Then trace the line to your right knee. Continue tracing over to your left shoulder, then straight across to your right shoulder, then trace the line back down to your left knee so that it connects with your starting point. You should see a large star of blue flame in front of you. Take your dagger or index finger and summon pure white divine light from the heavens into your dagger or finger. Then take a deep breath and on the exhale, forcefully send a beam of that divine light through the center of the pentacle while at the same time shouting "Go!" or "Begone!" Visualize every aspect and molecule of the spirit instantly disappearing. There should be no debris whatsoever.

Laughing

One of the most effective ways to get rid of a negative spirit is by laughing. As silly as it sounds, it works! Remember that negative spirits feed on the great power of fear. If we are laughing, then we ground our fears and transmute them into joy! The spirit is quickly deflated and has little to no influence in this world. It's one of the easiest ways to banish unwanted guests.

The Magical Ring

A magical ring is any ring that is consecrated with the intent of magick and protection. The ring can be silver, gold, copper, or iron. Silver summons the powers of the moon and can aid you with your psychic powers. Gold summons the powers of the sun. In Underworld magick,

the sun can disperse negative energies and spirits and control demons. Copper has power over the dead. In Greco-Roman myths, copper was used to summon, control, and banish the dead. Iron is a metal that disperses spiritual energies. Only use iron to rid yourself and your space of negative energies. Other spirits do not like iron as much, so be careful and judicious with your use of iron implements. If you use a ring with a gemstone, make sure it is a stone of the sun such as heliotrope, tiger's eye, or sunstone. Sun energies help banish negative spirits.

Herbs/Crystals/Stones

Herbs have been used to protect people from negative magick and spirits for thousands of years! Different herbs have different energy signatures and spirits. Here are a few herbs that are easily obtainable from magical shops or online:

Sage - used to purify and protect

Osha Root - banishes negative/evil spirits

Frankincense - purification, exorcism, banishing

Rue - protection, banishes negative energy placed upon you

Rosemary - purification and cleansing

Onion - absorbs negative energy, can be placed in windows as a ward against evil

Lemon -very powerful plant. Lemon juice can be put in blessed water for purification of the body, home, magical tools, etc.

Lemon grass & Lemon Verbena - purification herbs. Can be used similar to lemon.

Quartz crystal - can be empowered with protective energy and spells. Quartz can be placed in a circle and charged forming a powerful protective circle or barrier.

Salt - grounds energies. Salt has a powerful "draining" effect on spirits. It can quickly diminish their power in the Middleworld.

Tiger's Eye - ruled by the sun. It has a powerful banishing and deflecting effect against negative energies.

Sunstone - powerful solar energies. Used to "frighten" negative spirits. The solar powers of the stone banish spirits and diminishes their influence in our world.

Coscaria - ground eggshells make a powerful protective barrier around you and your home. Placed on the back of the neck it defends against possessions.

Camphor - more of a chemical than an herb, but spirits do not like the toxicity. It has draining effect on spirits.

Bloodstone (heliotrope) -controls and banishes negative spirits.

Red Brick - made simply by powdering a red brick. Can be used to Dust "seal" or "wall" something out. Keeps negative forces away.

Vinegar - Keeps negative energy and spirits away. More natural than chemicals. Be cautious because it also keeps good and healing spirits away as well.

Chemicals

These are not healthy for the environment, but if needed, household cleansers such as Ajax, Lysol, and Pine Sol can quickly banish spirits.

Ammonia (in small doses) works well too. Spirits become quickly drained when a generous amount of cleansers are around. Their astral essence quickly dissipates. Do not use chemicals against spirits except as a last resort. Using chemicals to banish all the time can result in other spirits not wanting to work with you. Also, be aware that if there are any spirit allies in your temple it will have the same effect on them.

Incense and Fumigations

A wonderful way to keep unwanted spirits from your home or temple is to purify with incense and fumigations. A fumigation is simply an archaic term meaning the act of using incense to cleanse the space. One common way is to smudge your ritual space and your entire home, with sage or mugwort. You may also use a combination of any herb that is used to protect, purify, and banish. Just place your mixture on a charcoal briquette and let the fumes do their magick. Two good books I referenced before for this are Scott Cunningham's *Oil's, Incense, and Brews* and Judika Illes' *The Element Encyclopedia of 5000 Spells*.

Ancestor Magick

The Ancestors can provide a powerful defense against unwanted entities. They have a great amount of influence in both this world and the Underworld. However, you must work with them for a while to build up their power in this world. One way Ancestors can help is to use their energy and influence to escort the spirit away. They may also call upon a higher Underworld spirit to help with this. If a trickster spirit is in my home, I place my hands upon the ancestral altar. I visualize my Ancestors and myself holding hands in a circle. I then visualize brilliant white light forming a powerful sphere all around us. This magick sphere banishes the trickster spirit back to where it came from.

God Magick

The gods we work with are the most powerful force against negative spirits. This, in addition to the wonderful sense of connectedness and love you feel, is one of the chief reasons why it is so important to work with a specific god and/or goddess and give them offerings and devotions. Whenever you feel threatened, do not be afraid to call your personal gods. They are invested in you as you are in them and will quickly come to your aid.

I personally try to handle negative spirits myself before I call upon my gods. They can provide a wonderful defense against negative spirits, but this privilege should not be abused. Do not think that because the gods have great power over spirits that you can be irresponsible when you conjure spirits of any sort. If you abuse the power of the gods, they may not come to your aid. I only call upon my gods to deal with negative spirits when I have exhausted all other avenues. You can, however, invoke their energies when you are performing a banishing. This allows you to tap into their powers without them having to do the work themselves.

Talismans/Charms/Medicine Bags

You can make protective charms and bags very easily. You simply take an herb or a stone and put magical energy in them with the intent of protecting you and your space, or banishing a spirit completely. Remember, there are some powerful spirits that will require more than a charm to banish them. Medicine bags can combine several different items. You may use stones, bones, herbs, coins, powders, or anything you can think that will protect you and your space!

You can make a talisman with things such as coins, jewelry, wood, necklaces, or any object that feels powerful to you. Here is an easy ritual

to create and consecrate a protective talisman. It is best to perform during a waning or full moon.

> Items needed:
> Talisman
> Incense stick
> Candle
> Small bowel of water
> Salt

1. Find an object that feels magical to you. You may buy a protective talisman online or at a magick shop or you can simply look for stone or some other item that feels magical.

2. Place the talisman on your altar, the incense in the east, candle in the south, water in the west, and salt in the north.

3. State your intention to the spirits and gods of empowering and consecrating your protective talisman.

4. Purify with sage, the besom, or any purification herb you like.

5. If you like, you may draw your magical circle. Then, call to the four directions beginning with east (air), south (fire), west (water), and north (earth)

6. Place both hands over the talisman and send protective energies inside. Visualize yourself and your home being protected by pure magical energy.

7. Pass the talisman through the incense smoke and say: "I ask the spirits of air to protect my mind. Let no entity use my thoughts against me nor give me thoughts of doubt. May only mental clarity prevail!"

8. Pass the talisman through the candle flame (or above it if object is flammable) and say: "I ask the spirits of fire to protect my will. Let no entity make me question my purpose. May only my Divine Will prevail!"

9. Place the talisman into the water (or sprinkle a few drops on the talisman) and say: "I ask the spirits of water to protect my emotions. Let no entity use me emotions against me. May only emotional stability prevail!"

10. Place the talisman into the salt and say: "I ask the spirits of earth to protect my body. Let no entity cause me physical harm in any way. May only bodily strength and health prevail!"

11. Take your empowered talisman to the east. Face the east and visualize the air and the sylphs and say: "Sylphs, spirits of air. Bless and consecrate my talisman!" Visualize the yellow sylphs spinning around the east. See them go around and into your talisman giving it power and blessing.

12. Take your empowered talisman to the south. Face the south; visualize fire and the salamanders and say: "Salamanders, spirits of fire. Bless and consecrate my talisman!" Visualize the red salamanders spinning around the south. See them go around and into your talisman giving it power and blessing.

13. Take your talisman to the west. Face the west; visualize water and the undines and say: "Undines, spirits of water. Bless and consecrate my talisman!" Visualize blue undines spinning around the west. See them go around and into your talisman giving it power and blessing.

14. Take your talisman to the north. Face the north; visualize earth and

forest and the gnomes and say: "Gnomes, spirits of earth. Bless and consecrate my talisman!" Visualize the green gnomes spinning around the north. See them go around and into your talisman giving it power and blessing.

15. If you like, you may ask your god and/or goddess to bless your talisman. You may visualize the god/dess standing in front of you giving your talisman power, or you may visualize divine white light coming from above blessing your talisman.

16. Thank the spirits and each direction. In my spiritual tradition we don't banish or dismiss the elemental spirits because without them we could not exist. We simply say, "Thank you (name of spirit) for your work tonight. You are always welcome in the circle of my life."

17. Allow the power to absorb into the talisman. Keep it covered for a couple of days before use.

Mirrors

Mirrors can be used to scare or drive away negative spirits. If you hang a mirror in your window or outside your door it will reflect negative energy away. This also helps when someone is purposely sending negative magick at you as well. You can also hang multifaced glass crystals as well. These direct the energies to go away from your home.

Ritual to Banish Unwanted Spirits or Demons

You may use a formal ceremonial banishing ritual if you would like. This ritual will summon Kabbalistic energies to banish a spirit:

I.   Banish

Perform the Lesser Banishing Ritual of the Pentagram. This will

banish most negative energies and spirits and will clear the way for you to banish the more powerful spirits. Think of it like sweeping the floor before you mop it. Essentially, this is what you are doing astrally.

II. Circle

You will draw a circle or sphere that will protect you from any negative energies while you perform the ritual. Before you draw the circle, you will need to place a Triangle of Art or another device that will hold the spirit in place. You can use a clear quartz crystal if you like. Draw your circle using your tool of choice such as an athame, dagger, broom, or your index finger. Just remember to visualize your circle as a sphere or dome of flaming blue light through which no enemy or hostile entity can enter.

III. Archangels

At each of the four directions call the powers of the four Archangels. In the East is Raphael. In the South is Michael. The West is Gabriel. And the North is Ariel. You have already summoned the archangels in the Lesser Banishing Ritual of the Pentagram, but this will provide an anchor in your mind that your magical circle is protected by these mighty powers.

IV. Circumambulations/Raising Power

To raise power in your circle, walk clockwise fully around the circle (circumambulate) beating a drum or rattle. This will help you gather magical energy for your banishing.

V. Invoking Divine Power

To give your ritual added power, you may add the divine power of your god or goddess with which you work. If you do not work with a particular god or goddess, you may say a prayer to God or Goddess or The Creator. Ask the divine to give you blessings, protection, and to empower your

banishing. Ask the divine to aide you in banishing the negative energy or spirit.

VI. Banishing

Now you are ready to banish the aggressive spirit.

A. The Command

You must command the spirit into the Triangle of Art or your quartz crystal. You must feel the power of the god or goddess coursing through your body. You must know that you have the powers of the Universe at your disposal.

You may use your own commands or use the one below.

"(Name of spirit) (if you do not know the name of the spirit just say "spirit"), by the power of (god/goddess) I command you into the Triangle of Art (or crystal)! You shall be bound within until I give you command to depart! In the name of (god/goddess), so be it!

Visualize the spirit manifesting into the Triangle of Art or the crystal. They cannot escape! You could skip this part if you feel that you do not need to contain the spirit, but the benefit of containing the spirit is that it allows the buildup of magick and spiritual power to hit the spirit all at once. You also have a focal point for the banishing.

"I command you (name of spirit) to depart this physical plane never to return. You shall return to the realm from whence you came, harming no one or thing upon your return. Depart! Depart! Depart, I say!"

You must say this command with extreme authority and force! You have the power of the gods behind you! You are a god in your temple space. As you say, so it is!

B.   Banishing with prejudice

If the spirit has enough power to stay on the physical plane, even with your magical commands, then you may banish with extreme prejudice. Banishing with prejudice means that when you send energy to banish something you are doing it with full confidence and force that the energy or entity must be 100% destroyed. Do not do this with a spirit who has simply gotten lost and ended up in your temple space because of an accident for which you are responsible. Be respectful to the spirit but be firm. If a negative energy is trying to cause you harm and will not depart, then banish it without prejudice.

To do this, take your magical athame or dagger and point it towards the sky. Summon divine powerful white light into the blade. Aim it at the crystal or Triangle of Art. Take a deep breath and muster every ounce of magical force you have. Know that you wield the power of the gods! Then with a mighty yell, say, "GO!" or "Be gone!" and visualize the divine light striking the spirit like a laser beam. This beam evaporates the spirit. It is gone. It is banished back to the realm from which it came.

VII.   Thanks and Ending the Rite

When you are ready, thank the spirits and gods that you have conjured. Begin by releasing the energies of the deity whom you have invoked. Be sure to thank them and offer them your love and blessings. Then, beginning in the North with Ariel, thank the archangels one by one and bid them farewell. Afterwards, dismantle your circle.

VIII. Banish

End the ritual with the Lesser Banishing Ritual of the Pentagram, smudge, or banish with your besom. This will get rid of any spirit debris or left over energies after your banishing ritual. If you have a favorite way you enjoy cleansing the ritual space you may use the technique of your choice.

Valediction

We have come to the end of the first part of our journey. We have journeyed deeper into the depth of the Underworld and death. It is natural to fear death. We want to live happy healthy lives and death is not what most of us want. We fear what we do not understand. It is my hope that you understand the process of death is part of the spiritual process. We must face our fears to release our truest potential. Even still, a healthy respect for death is programmed in our psyche to help us survive. There are those who romanticize the dark and shadowy aspects of the Universe. Some witches, shamans, and magicians may seek out the Angel of Death himself, but as we have learned, he is not the hellish figure from popular culture or even medieval depictions. The Angel of Death is a healer in his own way, taking the spirit away from the broken body to the world of the ancestors.

In this book, we covered how ancient pagans honored death in numerous ways. Among those ways, necromancy in some form was commonly used to communicate with the dead. In the Temples of the Dead in Greece and Rome, many travelers would enter the temples seeking yearning to speak with their beloved dead one last time. They believed that they were traveling into Hades and speaking with the shades of their loved one. I believe that this is a form of therapy for the living. When they communicated with the dead, they were able to make their peace and move on. The Egyptians, of course, took great pains in preserving the body after death because they believed that for the spirit to remain intact, the body must be intact. As we learned, one of the most sacred ceremonies in ancient Greece was the Eleusinian Mysteries teaching the seeker the mysteries of death and rebirth. The Lakota Ghost Dance summoned the ancestors during a sacred dance to ask for aid for the benefit of the tribe. We saw that many cultures believed the ancestors

have the power to help their descendants with the things they need in life such as food, land disputes, and the governing of the people.

In modern paganism, it is important that we continue the practice of honoring our ancestors. We often honor our gods, but do not have a place in our spiritual practice for our sacred Ancestors. Having a shrine in our homes helps the Ancestors manifest in our magical practice and our daily lives. In Native American cosmology, the ancestors do not leave us for heaven or the Underworld, they remain here to help us on our spiritual path. When we honor them daily and give them offerings, they will gain the strength to aid us in our magick. But be patient. Unless your ancestors were magical, it may take them a little while to understand how magick works. If we stick with this practice, the Ancestors will learn as we learn and we can establish a fulfilling and powerful magical practice. They can even help us with healing ancestral or negative family patterns and sickness that manifest in our lives. This, to me, is one of the greatest aspects of healing.

Summoning the dead in ritual sometimes brings to mind nefarious magicians hellbent on doing dark magick, but the dead can be very helpful in magick. There are many places that will aide in spirit manifestations, such as cemeteries, mausoleums, and natural places like lakes and ponds. The dead can tell us prophecies, divination, wisdom, and help us to grieve when we summon a loved one. There are many myths that describe bringing the dead back to life. It takes an immense amount of power and usually it is usually the gods who can do this. Bringing back someone from the dead into a broken body is something we never want to do. When working with the dead in magick it is important to be respectful just as you would with any other spirit.

Working with the dead can help us understand our spiritual lineage in a deep way. Our ancestors can help us tap into the sacred magick of

our blood lines. They can also help us learn about own spirit and the magick that we possess deep inside the core of our being. There are many tools such as the skull and bones that can help us tune into our deepest nature of spirit. At first glance these things may seem macabre, but our bones are as natural as the earth itself. When we truly understand the depths of our spirit, it is then we can connect to the spirit world to enhance our magick, deepen our understanding of the Universe, and continue our journey into the depths of the unknown.

These two volumes of *Underworld* have been a very enjoyable process for me, and I have gotten great joy in teaching the myths and magical techniques to shamans, witches, and pagans. This work is a culmination of my experience and research for the past 25 years. One of my spiritual goals is to help people to reconnect to the three shamanic worlds. The two volumes of *Underworld* are only part of the work that needs to be done for fuller understanding of the spiritual Universe.

Other Works

Now that you have explored the Underworld and learned to build extensive relationships with the Ancestors, be sure to continue your journey through the worlds with my other offerings. In *Upperworld: Shamanism and Magick of the Celestial Realms,* we journey to the Upperworld to discover the many ancient beings in the above worlds that can help us learn about the energies of the Universe and transform our lives for healing, power, and spiritual evolution.

Bibliography

Angels, Demons, and Gods of the New Millennium. Lon Milo Duquett. Weiser. 1997.

Alice In Wonderland. Lewis Carroll. Bantam classics. 1984.

American Indian Myths and Legends. Richard Erdoes and Alfanso Ortiz. Pantheon Books. 1984.

Aspects of Anglo-Saxon Magic. Bill Griffiths. Anglo-Saxon Books. 1996.

Bardo Teachings : *The Way of Death and Reburth*. Lama Lodu. Snow Lion Pub. 1982, 2010.

Becoming Osiris: The Ancient Egyptian Death Experience. Ruth Schumann Antelme and Stephane Rossini. Inner Traditions International. 1995.

The Book of Fallen Angels. Michael Howard. Capall Bann. 2004.

The Book of Solomon's Magick. Carroll "Poke" Runyon, M.A. The Church of Hermetic Sciences Inc. 1996.

British Witchcraft and Magic. Emma Wilby. Sussex Academy Press. 2005.

Call of the Horned Piper. Nigel Aldcroft Jackson. Capall Bann Publishing. 1994.

The Cup of Destiny. Trevor Ravenscroft. Weiser Books. 1982.

The Celtic Book of the Dead. Caitlin Matthews. Grange Books. 2001.

Communing With The Spirits. Martin Coleman. Samuel Wieser, Inc. 1998.

The Complete Book of Incense, Oils, and Brews. Scott Cunningham. Llewellyn Publications. 1989.

Courageous Dreaming. Alberto Villoldo, PH.D. Hay House Inc. 2008.

Cunning-Folk and Familiar Spirits: Shamanistic Visionary Traditions In Early Modern British Witchcraft and Magic. Emma Wilby. Sussex Academic Press. 2006

Cunningham's Encyclopedia of Magical Herbs. Scott Cunningham. Llewellyn Publications. 1985.

Death: A History of Man's Obsessions and Fears. Robert Wilkens. Barnes and Noble. 1990.

The Deities Are Many: A Polytheistic Theology. Jordan Paper. State University of New York Press. 2005.

The Dreamer's Book of the Dead. Robert Moss. Destiny Books. 2005.

The Egyptian Book of the Dead: The Book of Going Forth By Day. Translated by Dr. Raymond Faulkner. Chronical Books. 1994.

Egyptian Mythology: A Guide To The Gods, Goddesses, and Traditions of Ancient Egypt. Geraldine Pinch. Oxford University Press. 2002.

The Element Encyclopedia of 5000 Spells. Judika Illes. Element. 2004.

Eleusinian Mysteries and Rites. Doudley Wright. The Theosophical Publishing House.

The Essence of Shinto: Japan's Spiritual Heart. Motohisa Yamaksage. Kodansha International. 2006.

The Exorcist Handbook. Josephine McCarthy. Golem Media. 2010.

The Faery Teachings. Orion Foxwood. R.J. Steward Books. 2007.

Forbidden Rites: A Necromancer's Manual of the Fifteenth Century. Richard Kieckhefer. The Pennsylvania State University Press. 1998.

From Artemis to Diana: The Goddess of Man and Beast. 12 ACTA Hyperborea. Edited by Tobias Fischer-Hansen and Birte Poulsen. Museum Tusculanum Press. 2009.

From Distant Days: Myths, Tales, and Poetry of Ancient Mesopotamia. Benjamin R. Foster. CDL Press. 1995.

Gods, Demons, and Symbols of Ancient Mesopotamia. Jack Black and Anthony Green. University of Texas Press. 1992.

God Is Red. Vine Deloria Jr. Fulcrum Publishing. 1973.

The Gods of the Egyptians: Studies in Egyptian Mythology. E.A. Wallis Budge. Dover Publications. 1969.

The Goetia: The Lesser Key of Solomon the King. Translated by Samuel Liddell MacGregor Mathers. Samuel Weiser, Inc. 1995.

The Grail Legend. Emma Jung and Marie-Louise von Franz. Sigo Press. 1986.

Greek and Roman Necromancy. Daniel Ogden. Princeton University Press. 2001.

Greek and Roman Mythology. Thomas Bulfinch. Penguin Books. 1979.

Hecate's Fountain. Kenneth Grant. Skoob Books Publishing. 1992.

Heimskringla or The Lives of the Norse Kings. Snorri Sturluson. Dover Publications. 1990.

Hoodoo Herb and Root Magic: A Materia Magica of African-American Conjure. Catherine Yronwode. Lucky Mojo Curio Company. 2002.

Indian Mythology: Tales, Rituals, and Symbols from the Heart of the Subcontinent. Devdutt Pattanaik. Inner Traditions International. 2003.

Jotunbok: Working With The Giants of the Northern Tradition. Raven Kaldera. Asphodel Press. 2006.

Julian of Norwich: Revelations of Divine Love. Translated into modern English by Clifton Wolters. Penguin Books. 1966.

The Lost Secret of Death. Peter Novak. Hampton Roads Publishing. 2003.

Low Magick. Lon Milo Duquette. Llewellyn. 2010.

Magic and Superstition In Europe: A Concise History From Antiquity To The Present. Michael D. Bailey. Rowman and Littlefield Publishers, INC. 2007

Magical Use of Thought Forms: A Proven System of Mental and Spiritual Empowerment. Dolores Ashcraft-Nowicki and J.H. Brennan. Llewellyn Publications. 2002.

Masks of Misrule. Nigel Jackson. Capall Bann Publishing. 1996.

The Master Book of Herbalism. Paul Beyerl. Phoenix Publishing Co. 1984.

Modern Magick: Twelve Lessons in the High Magickal Arts. Donald Michael Kraig. Llewellyn Publications. 1988.

The Mythic Path. David Feinstein, Ph.D. and Stanley Krippner, Ph.D. Tarcher/Putnam Books. 1997.

The Myth of Isis and Osiris. Jules Cashford. Barefoot Books. 1993.

Netherworld. Robert Temple. Century Publications. 2002.

The Nightbattles: Witchcraft and Agrarian Cults in the Sixteenth and Seventeenth Centuries. Carlo Ginzburg. Translated by John and Ann Tedeschi. Penguin Books. 1983.

Norse Mythology: The Guide To The Gods, Heroes, Rituals, and Beliefs. John Lindow. Oxford University Press. 2001.

The Norse Myths. Kevin Crossley-Holland. Pantheon Books. 1980.

Osiris and the Egyptian Resurrection. E.A. Wallis Budge. Dover Publications. 1973.

Our Name Is Melancholy: The Complete Books of Azrael. Leilah Wendell. West Gate Press. 1992.

The Pathwalker's Guide To The Nine Worlds. Raven Kaldera. Asphodel Press. 2006.

Popol Vuh. Translated by Dennis Tedlock. Touchstone. Simon and Schuster Publishing. 1985, 1996.

The Practice of Dream Healing: Bringing Ancient Greek Mysteries Into Modern Practice. Edward Tick, Ph.D. Quest Books. 2001.

The Prose Edda. Snorri Sturluson. Translated by Jesse L. Byock. Penguin Press. 2005.

The Poetic Edda. Translated by Lee M. Hollander. University of Texas Press, Austin. 1962.

The Robert Cochrane Letters: An Insight into Modern Traditional Witchcraft. Robert Cochrane with Evan John Jones. Capall Bann. 2002.

The Roebuck In The Thicket: An Anthology of the Robert Cochrane Witchcraft Tradition. Evan John Jones and Robert Cochrane. 2001.

The Sacred Pipe: Black Elk's Account of the Seven Rites of the Oglala Sioux. Oklahoma Press. 1953.

The Secret Commonwealth of Elves, Fauns and Fairies. Robert Kirk. Dover Publications, Inc. 2008.

The Shaman's Secret: The Lost Resurrection Teachings of the Ancient Maya. Douglas Gillette, M.A., M. Div. Bantam Books. 1997.

The Spiritual Universe: The Existence of the Soul. Fred Alan Wolf, Ph.D. Simon and Schuster. 1996.

Summoning Spirits: The Art of Magical Evocation. Konstantinos. Llewellyn Publications. 1996.

Temple of the Cosmos: The Ancient Egyptian Experience of the Sacred. Jeremy Naydler. Inner Traditions International. 1996.

The Tibetan Book of the Dead: The Great Book of Natural Liberation Through Understanding In The Between. Translated by Robert A.F. Thurman. Bantam Books. 1994.

Treading the Mill: Practical Craft Working in Modern Traditional Witchcraft. Nigel G. Pearson. Capall Bann Publishing. 2007.

Understanding In The Between. Translated by Robert A.F. Thurman. Bantam Books. 1994.

The Underworld Initiation: A Journey Towards Psychic Transformation. R. J. Stewart. Mercury Publishing Inc. 1990.

Walking The Twilight Path: A Gothic Book of the Dead. Michelle Belanger. Llewellyn Publications. 2008.

Wightridden: Paths of Northern-Tradition Shamanism. Raven Kaldera. Asphodel Press. 2007.

Wyrdwalkers: Techniques of Norther-Traditions Shamanism. Raven Kaldera. Asphodel Press. 2006.

Index